KU-146-868

AMERICA
BEFORE THE
EUROPEAN INVASIONS

Alice Beck Kehoe

Longman

An imprint of **Pearson Education**

London · New York · Toronto · Sydney · Tokyo · Singapore · Hong Kong · Cape Town
New Delhi · Madrid · Paris · Amsterdam · Munich · Milan · Stockholm

KING ALFRED'S COLLEGE
LIBRARY

PEARSON EDUCATION LIMITED

Head Office:
Edinburgh Gate
Harlow CM20 2JE
Tel: +44 (0)1279 623623
Fax: +44 (0) 1279 431059

London Office:
128 Long Acre
London WC2E 9AN
Tel: +44 (0)20 7447 2000
Fax: +44 (0)20 7240 5771
Website: www.history-minds.com

KING ALFRED'S COLLEGE
WINCHESTER

0277998 973.1
KEH

First published in Great Britain in 2002

© Alice Beck Kehoe, 2002

The right of Alice Beck Kehoe to be identified as Author
of this Work has been asserted by her in accordance
with the Copyright, Designs and Patents Act 1988.

ISBN 0 582 41486 5

British Library Cataloguing in Publication Data
A CIP catalogue record for this book can be obtained from the British Library

Library of Congress Cataloguing in Publication Data
A CIP catalogue record for this book can be obtained from the Library of
Congress

All rights reserved; no part of this publication may be reproduced, stored
in a retrieval system, or transmitted in any form or by any means, electronic,
mechanical, photocopying, recording, or otherwise without either the prior
written permission of the Publishers or a licence permitting restricted copying
in the United Kingdom issued by the Copyright Licensing Agency Ltd,
90 Tottenham Court Road, London W1P 0LP. This book may not be lent,
resold, hired out or otherwise disposed of by way of trade in any form
of binding or cover other than that in which it is published, without the
prior consent of the Publishers.

10 9 8 7 6 5 4 3 2 1

Typeset in 10.5/12.5pt Baskerville by Graphicraft Limited, Hong Kong
Produced by Pearson Education Asia Pte Ltd.
Printed in Malaysia

The Publishers' policy is to use paper manufactured from sustainable forests.

CONTENTS

LIST OF ILLUSTRATIONS

Illustrations

Maps

ACKNOWLEDGMENTS

Reginald Horsman, my neighbor and colleague, persuaded Series Editor Mark White that American history did not begin in 1492, and suggested he commission me to write the volume on America before the European invasions. It is a privilege and pleasure to merge archaeology and history in this manner, adding another dimension to the "New History" Professor White brings to this series.

Anglo-American connections in the writing of pre-Columbian American history go back a century and a half, to Scottish immigrant Daniel Wilson whose 1862 *Prehistoric Man* drew substantially on American archaeology to lay out, for the first time in a general work, a science of prehistory. Wilson quoted from Thomas Carlyle's comment on the novelist Walter Scott, that he would

> teach all men this truth, which looks like a truism, and yet was as good as unknown to writers of history and others, till so taught – that the bygone ages of the world were actually filled by living men (quoted in Kehoe 1998: 4*).

This book endeavors to follow in the path Daniel Wilson blazed.

The assistance of Longman editor Heather McCallum and her staff, the helpful review of the manuscript by Guy Gibbon, and the illustrations by Anne Chojnacki are gratefully acknowledged.

Alice Kehoe
Milwaukee, Wisconsin, 2002

---

*Kehoe, Alice Beck (1998), *The Land of Prehistory: A Critical History of American Archaeology*. New York: Routledge.

The publishers would like to thank the following for permission to reproduce copyright material:

Extract from Bahr, Donald, Juan Smith, William Smith Allison, Julian Hayden (1994) *The Short Swift Time of Gods on Earth: The Hohokam Chronicles*. Berkeley: University of California Press; extract from *Life Lived Like a Story: Life Stories of Three Yukon Native Elders* by Julie Cruikshank in collaboration with Angela Sidney, Kitty Smith, and Annie Ned by permission of the University of Nebraska Press. Copyright © 1990 by the University of Nebraska Press; extract from Sandstrom, Alan R. (1991) *Corn Is Our Blood: Culture and Ethnic Identity in a Contemporary Aztec Indian Village*. Norman: University of Oklahoma Press. Used by permission; extract from *'In vain I tried to tell you' Essays in Native American Ethnopoetics* by Dell Hymes. Copyright © 1981 by Dell Hymes. Reprinted with permission of the University of Pennsylvania Press; extract from *Cultures in Contact* edited by William W. Fitzhugh; copyright © 1985 by the Smithsonian Institution. Used by permission of the publisher.

INTRODUCTION: HISTORY WITHOUT DOCUMENTS

It has been conventional to treat American history as if it were identical with United States history. Such a myopic view cuts students off from the context in which the United States developed, a larger history that will not go away. America's history begins some fourteen thousand years ago with evidence of human activities discovered through archaeology. Even the early humans affected the American scene. Invading Europeans met no wilderness, but landscapes and resources rendered through millennia of human actions.

Conventional histories of Europeans and their overseas descendants depend upon written documents, some the primary texts of eyewitness accounts and business instruments, some descriptions and reflections written later. Participants' names, statuses, calendar or dynastic dates, and place names frequently anchor the documents in time, space, and event. Archaeological evidence, in contrast, seldom provides participants' names, may only hint at social statuses, indicates only general time periods rather than calendar dates, and locates its human actions only to the site itself, without clear signs to their makers' political and economic affiliations. On the face of it, documentary evidence would seem to tell much more than archaeological data; on the other hand, mute archaeological data don't deliberately mislead readers. Ideally, documentary historians and archaeologists work together, written texts fleshing out the archaeological ruins and remnants and the archaeology providing checks upon the text claims, for example on whether a household was wealthy or poor. For America before the European invasions of the sixteenth and subsequent centuries, only the Maya kingdoms of eastern Mexico and Central America provide written texts to complement archaeological data. This book, limited to United States territory, must draw upon archaeological data alone.

Evidence from archaeology is the material residue from human actions. Human behavior that leaves no permanent physical effect, such as speech and gestures, vanishes out of history. The archaeological record therefore is biased toward material culture, the structures and objects made by people. Material culture is winnowed by decay, soft organic materials generally disappearing soon after discard with only hard inorganic materials remaining. For this reason, archaeologists spend inordinate amounts of time studying stone and fired clay objects, simply because not much else of material culture will be left in the ground. Kitchens, with their hard inorganic knives and choppers, pots, and hearths, are over-represented in archaeological records, while places of song, dance, laughter and love under-indicated. This history of America before the European invasions has almost no politics, but then the other volumes in this series don't tell you much about kitchens, or even what most people were usually eating. An archaeological history may seem unconventional, yet the human actions it records were quite literally absolutely vital.

The Data of Archaeology

American archaeologists do not, as a rule, work with standing ruins. (The dry Southwest is an exception.) A project begins with a survey of the locale, walking over it looking at the ground for bits of artifacts (any human-made object) and signs that the landscape had been disturbed by human activity. The archaeologist will be at the locale because a local resident or construction workers reported artifacts, or because examination is mandated by laws requiring cultural heritage to be searched for and preserved before construction destroys a locale, or – least often – because the locale promises to yield data that may solve a question of history. "Problem-oriented," "pure science" projects are what archaeologists wish for but have difficulty raising funds for, while cultural–resource–management projects mandated by heritage protection laws have funds built in the budgets of commercial and public-sector construction. These projects thus greatly outnumber "pure science" problem-orientated archaeology, and also another type of project, the public-participation projects run by Department of Interior agencies and non-profit research groups. Before the 1960s, the picture was reversed, as up until then, heritage-protection laws were weak and limited. This means that earlier archaeology tended to work at relatively more spectacular sites that intrigued rich philanthropists, while post-1960s archaeology produces numbing thousands of reports on little campsites and sections of commonplace villages. Put the two eras together and we get a more balanced picture of the past, but still full of gaps – it often seems that the more we know, the more we know we don't know about the past.

Having noted evidence of human activities at the locale, the archaeologist next prepares a contour map of it, keyed in to its US Geological Survey topographic map and satellite geographic positioning. Once this is drawn, a surveyors' transit is used to mark out a grid of lines a meter apart over the area to be excavated. (Many cultural–resource–management mandated projects can only work within the area to be affected by the construction that provides the funds, even if it is obvious that interesting activity areas lie outside the overall project limits.) The archaeologist today often uses magnetic resonance or a similar device to sound below the earth surface, indicating "anomalies" below that are likely to be buried walls, hearths, or graves. Excavation itself proceeds by stripping off the surface sod or perhaps the plowed soil already churned up; a backhoe may be hired to remove this layer efficiently, the archaeological crew following the machine closely to warn the operator if an ancient feature is indicated. The crew, possibly college students, possibly laborers, then settles in to dig. Each crew person gets a one-meter square, marked off with string between pins or stakes set at the intersections of the grid, and does most of the digging with a sharpened mason's trowel, supplemented with brushes, a dulled grapefruit knife and a dental pick for fine work. The reason such small tools are used is to expose artifacts and activity features without moving them out of their meaningful context.

Every bit of object uncovered is saved in bags labeled with the exact find spot keyed into the overall grid and contour map, and every observable difference in soil color and texture is photographed, drawn to scale on graph paper, and written up in fieldnotes. Often a hearth, storage pit, or hut floor is no more than a slight discoloration or soil texture difference from the undisturbed natural soil. Excavated soil is screened through metal mesh to catch small objects and fragments, and much of it is also dumped into buckets of water so that seeds, tiny animal bones and shells, and pollen will float up to be skimmed out and analyzed in the lab. Bits of charcoal are saved in foil to be run through machines that count the emissions from the radioactive isotope of atmosphere carbon,[14] giving an estimate of the time elapsed since the wood was last living and thereby a date for when it was burned by people.

All this meticulous uncovering and recording of buried evidence yields solid data on the imperishable residue of activities. Interpretation of the social context of those activities is another matter. Although these terms are not in general use among archaeologists, it may help to distinguish between *syntagm*, the actual material and its pattern laying in the ground, and *paradigm*, the interpretive model encompassing these data. One solidly recorded syntagm – the brute data – may be interpreted through more than one paradigm, for example a woman's skeleton with her skull resting on a sharp stone blade (an actual 11,000-year-old find near Buhl, Idaho) could be interpreted as a woman buried with the kitchen knife she used to prepare food, or it could be hypothesized that her people laid her upon the knife so that the spirit of the knife would protect her soul on its final journey. One interpretation is cautious, close to the syntagm itself, the second draws upon religious concepts reported for some of the indigenous First Nations in Idaho; however, historic Idaho First Nations are not known to have put knives under corpses' heads for soul protection, and 11,000 years separate the Buhl woman from historic First Nations. This *ethnographic analogy* (interpretation made on analogy with ethnographic descriptions of historic peoples) is plausible but not verifiable. The cautious interpretation, that the woman was given her own daily-use tool, is no more verifiable although less romantic. Ambiguities abound in archaeology.

Paradigms that mold interpretation of archaeological data change as new methods and technology produce previously unavailable kinds of data, and also through clashes between ideological positions (in America, whether the First Nations were primitive savages destined to vanish, or creators of diverse sophisticated societies), and the efforts of ambitious individuals to advance their careers by trumpeting a supposedly brilliant new theory. Some archaeologists trudge along identifying new data by classifying them a standard way learned in graduate school, others are thoughtful or skeptical, so that, as with historians, conclusions do not automatically follow examination of data and may differ radically even when opposing interpretations are each linked carefully to primary data. There are Marxist archaeologists alert to indications of ancient class conflict, feminist archaeologists sensitive to subtle signs of women's statuses, Whig archaeologists telling the story of how we progressed to our present happy state, "cultural materialists" claiming that technology strongly molds culture, "ecological determinists" convinced that climate changes explain cultural changes, postmodern archaeologists sure that knowledge is so tentative we may as well give up seeking "facts," quantifiers and humanists. These are the reputable varieties. There are also psychics who don't bother excavating, they can channel or see all the past via soul journeys; Goddess worshippers who recognize Her image on rocks everywhere; discoverers of lost prophecies telling us Lord Pacal of Palenque was an extraterrestial (pay no attention to the Maya hieroglyphic inscriptions that give his earthbound history); and a few persons who know the hidden cave tombs of the exiled kings of a legendary land, and will readily sell you dozens of their genuine gold tablets.

Ethnographic Analogy

The crux of archaeological interpretation lies at the juncture where the material data – artifacts and soil features – are related to social behavior, that is, where the syntagm is fitted into a paradigm. In the heyday of National Science Foundation generous funding of problem-orientated "pure science" projects, during the 1960s and 1970s, some American archaeologists wanted to discard ethnographic analogies, hoping they could discover historically unknown forms of human behavior by manipulating quantified data statistically. Logically, there probably were ancient societies different from any described historically; the problem is that we may be able to see *variance* but to *vary* is to vary *from something*. An ancient society may differ considerably from any known historical group, yet we identify the differences *by comparison* with more familiar societies. Furthermore, every archaeologist has been socialized to recognize certain familiar human behavior, standards that can't be erased from the scientist's brain. Thus, ethnographic analogies are inevitable: the prehistoric past does not speak directly to us and we see its residue through brains already holding images of how humans live. What is important for sound interpretation is to be conscious and explicit about the models that are used as paradigms.

American prehistory is customarily divided into epochs that reflect ethnographic paradigms. The Paleoindian period is the terminal millennium of the last major glacial era, when climate, fauna and flora even far south of the massive continental glaciers were different from historical conditions. Ethnographic parallels for this period are taken from descriptions of far northern and Plains hunting societies. More or less modern climate and ecology followed, with several millennia of the Archaic period, as archaeologists term it, during which descendants of the Paleoindians discovered how to exploit a diversity of regional habitats. Models for the Archaic are taken from descriptions of societies dependent on wild foods, including the Shoshone of western Nevada, California Indians, and Ojibwe (Anishinabe) in Canada. Experiments with increasing harvests of wild foods culminated in the domestication of a number of plants, notably maize (corn). Agricultural populations are reflected in towns and villages of the Late Prehistoric period, approximately the past two thousand years; models for these are taken from descriptions of the historic Eastern and Midwestern villages encountered by European colonists. Interpreting archaeological remains from these ethnographic examples must make allowance for the effects of these invasions and colonizations disrupting native economic and political patterns, in part by introducing terrible epidemics that decimated indigenous populations.

Because the historical sciences (geology, paleontology, archaeology) explain data from the past through matching them to effects of processes observed in the present, interpretations inevitably resemble historically known situations. Flights of fancy are unscientific, however lively and insightful they may be. In effect, archaeological data constitute *research puzzles*. Evidence from a particular occupation layer in a site may be laid out, like a jigsaw puzzle, to make a scene of life in the settlement. Data are also entered like a crossword puzzle, as it were, "DOWN" and "ACROSS" on charts to link a series of occupations through time and across geographical locations. The following chapters endeavor to chronicle the pre-European history of North America, particularly the United States area, through weighing the archaeological data against ethnographic and historical descriptions of descendants of the fifteenth-century societies, cognizant of the gaps between pre-invasion life and European documentation, and of our bias to see these societies through the lens of European cultures. Each chapter presents research puzzles and possible outcomes.

Bibliographical Note

Of the several introductory archaeology textbooks available, the most suitable for readers of this book may be Colin Renfrew and Paul Bahn, *Archaeology: Theories, Methods, and Practices* (London, 3rd edn, 2000). Brian Fagan is a prolific and reliable author of books about archaeology; his *Ancient North America: The Archaeology of a Continent* (New York, 3rd edn, 2000) is a readable textbook on North American prehistory. *Archaeology of Prehistoric Native America: An Encyclopedia* (New York, 1998) is authoritative without being too technical, and facilitates looking up information by name or term. From a perspective traditionally neglected, Karen Olsen Bruhns and Karen E. Stothert present *Women in Ancient America* (Norman, OK, 1999).

Both Bahn and Fagan have published illustrated general histories of archaeology, respectively for Cambridge and Oxford University Presses. The standard history of American archaeology is Gordon R. Willey and Jeremy A. Sabloff, *A History of American Archaeology* (New York, 3rd edn, 1993), while Alice B. Kehoe's *The Land of Prehistory: A Critical History of American Archaeology* (New York, 1998), as its subtitle declares, discusses ideological factors including Manifest Destiny beliefs that subtly influenced practice and interpretation in North American archaeology.

Reference

Bruhns, Karen Olsen and Karen E. Stothert (1999), *Women in Ancient America.* Norman, OK: University of Oklahoma Press.

Map 1 North America, showing Paleoindian sites (Chapter 1) and sites in Alaska (Chapter 7)

1

FIRST AMERICANS

The Americas were initially populated during the Pleistocene Ice Age, at least fifteen thousand years ago. Many descendants of America's First Nations consider their religious traditions, that they originated in a spiritual realm connected to this world, to be sufficient knowledge for the question of earliest population. A scientific worldview, by definition of science limited to empirically demonstrable data, cannot admit spiritually revealed knowledge. Thus there may appear to be strong differences between a First Nation's accounts of its earliest history, and the narratives prepared by professional archaeologists and paleoanthropologists. Unhappily, some Indian champions feel challenged by European-derived science, and some archaeologists defend narrowly scientific explanations against any other beliefs. It is important to understand that theology and science need not conflict: an account of spiritual origins conveys religious knowledge and generally can accommodate the more limited empirically based interpretations developed by scientists.

Physical and genetic data link American Indians to Asian populations, supporting the obvious probability that humans entered North America from the nearest continental mass, Asia. From the early nineteenth century, geographers pointed to the Bering Strait, between northeastern Siberia and Alaska, as the likely route. A north polar projection map (not the common Mercator equatorial projection) or a globe will show that the Spitzbergen Peninsula from northwestern Norway ends close to Baffin Land in northeastern Canada, and zoologists note that reindeer moved along routes between Norway and northeasternmost Canada, but this region was heavily glaciated during Pleistocene ice advances and has always been less hospitable to humans than the North Pacific, warmed by the Japanese

Current flowing north along the American coast and hosting a rich bounty of fish, sea mammals, and birds. Therefore, the North Pacific–Bering Strait region remains the most likely link between Eurasia, where modern humans gradually spread over more than a hundred thousand years, and the Americas where no earlier forms of humans, and no apes, have been discovered. Archaeological, biological, and linguistic similarities between northeastern Asian and northwestern American sites and populations support the picture of a series of movements of small human groups from Asia into America through the Bering region.

Asia has had human populations for over a million years, and in the Late Pleistocene, 40,000–10,000 years ago, it was home to a diversity of regional groups anatomically modern in all essential characteristics (such as brain size, upright posture) but differing like contemporary populations in facial features, coloring, and average size. What we now think of as "typical Asians," the Chinese–Japanese–Mongolian populations with high projecting cheekbones and a fold over the nose side of the eyelid, spread over eastern Asia quite late, after some immigration into America had already taken place. Before the domination by "Mongoloids," eastern Asia had more widespread populations resembling the historic Ainu of Japan, perhaps best described as "generalized Eurasian" – relatively light-skinned, dark hair, brown eyes, neither very tall nor very short, a range from which descendants could develop into Indo-Chinese, Polynesians, Siberians, and American Indians as well as the stereotyped "Mongoloids." The few skeletons found in North America dating from the end of the Pleistocene, such as Kennewick Man buried along the Columbia River, are "generalized" like this rather than showing exclusively distinctive American Indian physical characteristics.

Evidence for Early Settlement

It has been conventionally held that during much of the Late Pleistocene epoch, what is now the sea channel Bering Strait was a broad land mostly covered with tundra. The Aleutian Islands would be the remnants of the southern coast of this land, called Beringia by geologists. Russian geologist Mikhail Grosswald[1] counters the conventional picture with evidence he interprets to indicate massive glacial ice lay over Beringia during the last major glaciation of the Pleistocene. According to Grosswald, only the few centuries 12,500–

12,000 BCE (geologists' Bølling-Allerød interstadial warm phase) would have opened a land bridge unencumbered by impassable ice. Whichever picture of Beringia is correct, its southern margins would teem with fish and sea mammals feeding on plants and microorganisms nourished by the rich flow of nutrients from glaciers' melting edges.

For the past five thousand years, most of Beringia has been under water. The presently existing sea channel, only a hundred miles wide, is broken by two islands (the Diomedes) in the middle, and can freeze over in the winter, so it has not been much of a barrier to human movements – historically, Alaskan Yuit and Siberian Chukchi traded and raided back and forth, with some people born on one side marrying into communities on the other. Pleistocene Beringia may have bridged the present continents, but its submergence did not cut off travel between them.

For years, archaeologists searched for evidence of the earliest humans in the Americas in the interior valleys of Alaska, the Yukon, and Alberta. It was assumed that mountain glaciers like those in Alaska today covered the Pacific coast during the glacial advances of the Late Pleistocene, and that an "ice-free corridor" existed along the western High Plains between the huge continental glacier centered in eastern Canada, and the mountain glaciers of the Rockies and Coast Ranges. Searches found nothing older than terminal Pleistocene, 9000 BCE, for example the Sibbald Creek campsite in Alberta on the edge of Banff National Park. Further research by geologists failed to establish any significant ice-free corridor east of the Rockies during the last Pleistocene glacial maximum. A counter-hypothesis was advanced by British Columbia archaeologist Knut Fladmark, arguing that the post-Pleistocene rise in sea level that flooded much of Beringia also flooded the ancient Pacific coast, leaving late-Pleistocene (indeed, up to 3000 BCE) sites on the coastal plains now under water on the continental shelf. Fladmark of course could not produce site features or artifacts from these possible locations now covered by sea-floor muck and water.

The most controversial claims come from South America, so concern this book only peripherally. Pedra Furada, against a cliff face in interior northeast Brazil, has crude fractured stones and lenses of charcoal said to date 33,000 years ago, but this material looks like it eroded from the plateau edge down into a chimney-shaped cleft in the cliff. At the base of the cliff, excavations revealed a panel of little figures painted in red on the rock; these have been dated at 12,000 BCE by association with apparent occupation material below the panel, more feasible evidence for terminal Pleistocene habitation in northern South America. Other sites, in Ecuador, Venezuela, and Peru, are dated later, to 9000 BCE, filling out evidence for populating the Americas.

In the 1990s, discoveries including Kennewick Man in the Columbia River Valley and particularly Monte Verde in Chile turned scholarly attention back to Fladmark's hypothesis, for the idea that the earliest Americans had utilized Pacific coastal resources led to postulating southward migrations from Beringia all the way to Chile. We know Asians used watercraft at least 40,000 years ago, because humans could not have reached Australia, as they did by that time, without means of crossing the water gap between Melanesia and Australia. Fishing and hunting sea mammals from boats would have produced a strong economic base for coastal northern Asians, who could have advanced eastward along Beringia and the Aleutians, or wherever the southern Arctic coast was in the Late Pleistocene, into Pacific Alaska without encountering any radical challenges. If their descendants continued exploiting coastal resources ever southward, some could have ended up in Chile within a couple of thousand years even if none were deliberately exploring long distances (and who is to say none of them were actively seeking out new lands?).

The Monte Verde site in Chile was excavated by the American archaeologist Tom Dillehay. Situated in a pleasant creek valley, the site evidenced wooden slabs possibly from huts, and simple but serviceable bone and stone artifacts, dated to 10,500 BCE. (The dating was based on radiocarbon, here calibrated with other measures of terminal Pleistocene age.[2]) A delegation of prominent archaeologists examined the site in 1997 with Dillehay after his report on the work was completed and, although some had been skeptical, they agreed after the visit and laboratory inspection that Dillehay's work seemed scientifically sound. Subsequently, close examination of the published report fomented renewed debate over dating of the few diagnostic artifacts and Dillehay's interpretation of the wood as hut planks. Such intense protracted debate typifies reports of humans in the Americas earlier than the 9000 BCE "Clovis horizon," the oldest thoroughly documented archaeological evidence in the continent.

The most practical route from Asia to Chile would have been along the Pacific coast. Postulating sailing during the Pleistocene from Australia across the immense South Pacific to Chile would be a wild card. Unlike protohistoric Polynesians who used highly sophisticated navigational skills and watercraft to sail across the Pacific,[3] Pleistocene humans probably lacked sails on their rafts and canoes. That no evidence has been found of settlements on the mid-Pacific Polynesian islands before Polynesian colonizations beginning in the second millennium BCE, argues against any likelihood of earlier crossings of the vast ocean. With the general consensus that Dillehay's Monte Verde was the oldest professionally excavated, definitely human occupation site in the Americas, Fladmark's Pacific route gained credence.

Accepting Monte Verde as an authentic human settlement more than twelve thousand years ago in southernmost South America upset conventional archaeology on two counts, that humans had come into the Americas earlier than the dates for the Clovis finds, 9000 BCE, and that these earlier people made artifacts less distinctive than the Clovis stone blades. In effect, Monte Verde opened the door to a raggle-taggle crowd of contenders for first-come: it had been simple to declare that the first-comers were virtuoso flintknappers ("knap," "to break with a snap," as in chipping flint) leaving signature masterfully chipped stone blades at their sites; now archaeologists had to consider sites with nondescript artifacts like those at Monte Verde. The geological context and chronometry (methods of dating) would be more critical than ever in evaluating possibly early sites, and these can be tricky. For example, a child's skeleton found in a Pleistocene layer in a cliff face in southern Alberta turned out to have been buried by pushing it into a cleft in the cliff which then filled up with soil, practically obliterating the cleft. Radiocarbon dating indicated the child is a few thousand years old, closer to us than to the Pleistocene. Radiocarbon dating itself runs into odd effects just at the end of the Pleistocene, due to strong and relatively rapid fluctuations in global climate when the glaciers released incredible floods of their meltwater, changing evaporation rates and thereby the amounts of radioactive carbon rising into the air. Increased cosmic ray penetration of the atmosphere at this time of extraordinary global changes may also have added unusual amounts of radioactive carbon to the air. Organisms at this time probably breathed in more of the carbon isotope, leaving a greater amount in their bodies when they died and so more when the amount was measured millennia later. Paleoindian material can be as much as two thousand years older than the radiocarbon count calculates and, to further confuse researchers, materials from each side of the climate flip-flops can measure the same although they may have existed a thousand years apart.

Clovis and Other Mammoth Hunters

Finding butchered mammoth remains securely identifies a Paleoindian site – the animals became extinct in North America about 11,000 BCE (by Stuart Fiedel's revised calibrations of radiocarbon dates). The type site at Clovis, New Mexico, Blackwater Draw in northwestern Texas at Lubbock, and the Murray Springs, Naco, and Lehner sites in Arizona were among the first excavated to establish the association of Clovis stone blades with slaughtered mammoths. Butchered mammoths with nondescript stone tools, such as two in southeastern Wisconsin, clearly belong in the Paleoindian period, confirmed by radiocarbon dates and geological context. Archaeologists cannot tell whether the butchers' artifact tradition did not favor the Clovis style, or instead it merely happened that the butchers' Clovis blades were taken along to the next camp, or not fallen in the excavated sections of the sites.

Clovis style is remarkable for its beautiful stone blades, frequently made on pleasingly colored, fine crystalline material quarried in blocks that often were carried hundreds of kilometers to ensure the quality of Clovis artifacts. To manufacture the blades, artisans first struck large flakes off the blocks, using the sharp flakes for everyday cutting and scraping tasks, then with exquisite control struck long ribbon-like flakes across the faces of the formed blade to thin it evenly. Finally, the hallmark of the Clovis style was produced, an oval channel running up the face of the blade from its base: the "fluting." Fluted bases uniquely mark Clovis and the similar but later and shorter Folsom style blades, Clovis associated with mammoths and Folsom with large extinct species of bison. The fluting channel was expedient for hafting the blade to its shaft, in tongue-and-groove manner. Unfluted but still exquisitely ribbon-flaked stone blades continued the Fluted Tradition technique into the early Holocene, to around 8000 BCE.

All known Paleoindian habitation sites seem to have been camps, generally on ridges where people could watch for game animals coming to streams or marsh edges; besides mammoths, mastodons, musk-oxen, horses, camels, bears, antelopes, deer, and small game were killed. Paleoindians could live surprisingly close to the margins of the great glaciers, because nutriment-rich meltwaters supported rich grazing for mammoths and other prey for hunters. Archaeology indicates communities were composed of a few families, moving at least several times a year. Small campfires with broken or worn-out stone and bone tools indicate household activity areas, probably in or beside tents or wigwam-type dwellings. Stacks of butchered game bones suggest storage caches of meat; other cache clusters contain complete or partially finished stone artifacts and sometimes red ochre. There is one grave known, in a small rockshelter in Montana, with a Clovis artifact cache beside it.

Essentially, Paleoindians were, in global terms, Late Paleolithic people, fully modern anatomically but without agriculture and permanent villages. They lived by hunting, exhibiting high skill in manufacturing weapons and in strategies for moving into range to use their spears, either propelled by hand throw or with the added leverage of the atlatl (spear-thrower board), or thrust directly into the animal. Changing camps to follow game movements and harvest plant foods in season, their habitation sites look meager. Their nomadic life was well adapted not only to surviving on the abundant game of the Late Pleistocene, but also to adjusting to the tremendous shifts in climate and environments of the terminal Pleistocene. Clovis blades are found throughout the United States, proving the makers' remarkable capacity to enter and exploit new habitat zones, filling the continent with human families.

The Early People

Skeletons from early Holocene times are few, with none so far definitely dated to the Pleistocene. The most complete skeleton is known as Kennewick Man, from the discovery locality on the lower Columbia River (near Richland, Washington).[4] From Kennewick Man's nearly entire skeleton, found eroding out of the riverbank, and his physical characteristics differing from some common among contemporary American Indians of the region, it was initially concluded that he was a historic Euro-American immigrant. Then the archaeologist noticed a stone spearpoint embedded in his hip! Radiocarbon dating revealed he lived about 7500 BCE. He was taller than general for Plateau Indians, with a long rather than broad face, altogether somewhat resembling in build the Ainu of northern Japan. Since Ainu are believed to represent an Asian population pushed into their northern island refuge by expanding more typical Mongoloid Asians, quite possibly as late as the historic era, it is hardly surprising that a northwest American man resembles people directly across the North Pacific. Ainu, incidentally, were accustomed from ancient times to using boats and fishing, consistent with the Pacific coastal route for movements into America from Asia. What is important to realize about Kennewick Man is that given the nine thousand years between him and historic American Indians, he and his relatives could have been among the ancestors of American Indians, their genes eventually mixed with those of Arctic Mongoloids (like the Siberian Chukchi) more directly ancestral to Aleuts, Dené, and Inuit.

Biological anthropologists have analyzed genes and skeletal traits for a number of American Indian populations, confirming the Arctic Mongoloid ancestry of the northwestern (Aleut, Inuit and Alaskan Indian) indigenous American populations. Other American Indians are genetically more distant, if still closer to Asians than to other major populations. The oldest (naturally dried) mummified corpse in North America, that of a man wrapped in a fabric shroud and placed in a dry cave in Nevada, is radiocarbon dated to the same age as Kennewick Man and, like him, differs from historic Nevada Indians. Spirit Cave Man, as he is named, like Kennewick has a face more narrow than characteristic of later American Indians, and a longer head. Whether the genetic and skeletal traits that distinguish historic American Indian populations from Asians and others evolved here in America through the generations, or in part derive from immigrations earlier than terminal Pleistocene, cannot be decided yet. Genetics suggest the northwesternmost (and Arctic Inuit) indigenous Americans represent movements into America later than those of the ancestors of all other American Indians, but genetics cannot say whether these two principal American populations had already separated in northeastern Asia, whether the major American population came here many or a few millennia before the Holocene, or whether they spread throughout the Americas quickly or slowly in the late Pleistocene.

Language is another line of inquiry into population histories. Linguists agree that the indigenous languages of the Americas are substantially distinct from languages of the other continents. Some linguists have recognized certain similarities between the Dené, Tlingit and Haida languages (termed Na-Dené) of northwestern America and Sino-Tibetan (Chinese and Tibetan) in eastern Asia – for one thing, they are tonal languages – and that Inuktitut, the Inuit (Eskimo) language, seems distantly related to northern Eurasian languages (Caucasian, Indo-European). The majority of linguists simply don't want to discuss what may be extremely ancient origins for which the data are, in the opinion of some, occasional coincidences or were selected contrary to accepted methodologies. Proponents of postulating three major language families or stocks in the

Americas, "Amerind," Na-Dené, and Eskimo-Aleut, emphasize the congruence between their three stocks and groupings derived from genetic or skeletal traits, with the minor exception that the Aleuts are biologically somewhat closer to Na-Dené speakers than to Inuit. Where the real controversy lies is in the hypothesis that three language stocks and three clusters of biological traits must indicate three ancestral populations and three migrations into America. Any number of biologically distinguishable populations or of languages could have become extinct or assimilated, in Asia or in America, over twelve thousand or more years. A sensible conclusion is that after the principal migration(s) into America had led to humans throughout the continent and South America, the northwesternmost historic peoples speaking Na-Dené languages moved in from northeastern Asia, and more or less about that time, several millennia ago, Eskimo-Aleut communities adapted to the high Arctic coasts spread eastward from northeasternmost Siberia. Present methodology either in biology or linguistics cannot determine definitively whether "Amerind" is primarily an amalgamation of many migrations, or diversification from one or a few movements in the late Pleistocene.

Controversial Scenarios

Cautious anthropologists accept Clovis mammoth hunters as the first humans to inhabit North America, and make no guesses on what language the hunters spoke. Clovis is interpreted to have been highly skilled hunters whose nomadic way of life rapidly dispersed their families over the landscape, wherever mammoths roamed. The extinction of their prime prey forced Clovis people to modify their economy, restricting family movements to seasonal rounds within a region where they had learned to exploit a variety of game and plants. From this, archaeologists see the late Paleoindians, of the early Holocene era, manufacturing different styles of spearpoints according to region and changing over time, to about 7000 BCE. Because logically Clovis people could often have carried their distinctive Clovis blades away with them to the next camp instead of leaving some as a sign for archaeologists, archaeologists must admit some sites may be Paleoindian without the Clovis insignia. Chesrow sites in southeastern Wisconsin, for example, contain butchered mammoths and only nondescript stone tools. Radiocarbon dates put Chesrow at 11,500–10,500 BCE, when the sites would have been close to the glacial ice front. Chesrow artifacts are made of poorer quality stone unsuited for virtuoso knapping; central Wisconsin stone quarries prized by later peoples would have been still buried under tons of ice. Clovis blades found in Wisconsin are generally manufactured from high-quality stone from these quarries, indirectly supporting an earlier dating for Chesrow people than Clovis. They were intrepid pioneers indeed, cutting up woolly mammoths within a few days' walk of ice fields stretching north beyond the horizon.

Some archaeologists advance claims for Paleoindians much older than Clovis. These include Meadowcroft Rockshelter in northwestern Pennsylvania, where radiocarbon dates may reflect contamination from coal dust eroding out of a coal seam in the rockshelter bluff and no extinct Pleistocene animals nor distinctive fluted blades have been found. Pendejo Cave in New Mexico is alleged to have human occupations possibly as long as 50,000 years ago, with nondescript stone tools, possible human fingerprints on hardened bits of clay, and human hairs said to have been preserved from Pleistocene times. In the Yukon and also in Plains sites, chunks of mammoth bone have been noticed that look as if they were knapped like flint into rough tools such as sharp-edged flake knives and scrapers. The localities from which these mammoth-bone artifacts come, if indeed they are not the result of natural breakage, are dated to the Pleistocene and believed to be earlier than Clovis. None of the flaked mammoth bone locations are clearly human habitation or kill-butchering sites.

In the 1930s, claims were made that artifacts, mostly stone slab metates and manos (grinding stones), lay in some geological strata perhaps 100,000 years old exposed around San Diego, California; the localities are now covered with urban development and have not been re-evaluated. On Santa Rosa Island off Santa Barbara, California, dwarf mammoths were discovered apparently butchered and near hearths. Decades later, paleontologists on Wrangel Island in the Bering Strait found probably the latest mammoths to survive, up to 1700 BCE. These, too, were smaller than the immense Late Pleistocene beasts, and it is likely that the California mammoths similarly survived into the Holocene on their island protected by ocean currents. Holocene dwarf mammoths on islands and serviceable but undistinguished stone tools with Pleistocene mammoths make archaeologists chary of simple scenarios picturing Clovis hunters marching southeastward from Beringia.

Are all American Indians descended from Asians? Was America totally cut off from Europe before the Norse landed in CE 1000?

From time to time, a scholar sees evidence for prehistoric contacts, even migrations, between northwestern Europe and northeastern America. The hypothesis for a Late Pleistocene migration is now framed around similarities between the virtuoso flintknapping of Clovis and of European Upper Paleolithic Solutreans, dated to 18,000–14,000 BCE. In favor of this hypothesis is not only the difficult flintkapping techniques so skillfully exhibited on Clovis and Solutrean stone blades, but also that both were used by nomadic hunters of Late Pleistocene northern big game, and finds of Clovis throughout eastern North America. There seems to be some gap in time between Solutrean and Clovis, a gap that may be narrowed if more deeply buried Clovis occupations are excavated in eastern North America. Proponents of the Solutrean–Clovis connection propose that Clovis progenitors crossed westward along the ice margins of the North Atlantic during the Late Pleistocene glaciation; they might have crossed over in canoes, island-hopping, their coastal sites now disappeared in the flooded continental shelf.

An interesting observation by a Pleistocene specialist[5] correlated Late Pleistocene geographical regions with American Indian language groups. Algonkian, historically primarily in the northern half of eastern North America, might have occupied glacial margins some fourteen thousand years ago, moving northward with coniferous forests, moose and caribou as glaciers melted. To the west, open grasslands carried American camels, lions, and antelopes; the extent of this Late Pleistocene geographical zone corresponds to the historic locations of Aztec-Tanoan languages (among them Ute, Kiowa, Hopi, and the languages of northwestern and central Mexico including Nahuatl, the language of the Aztecs). To the southeast, a mixed deciduous forest with deer as principal game could have harbored humans speaking Siouan and Caddoan languages, expanding northward with their mixed forest in the early Holocene. South of these along the Gulf of Mexico, which then had a wide continental shelf now under water, Muskogean languages (including Creek and Choctaw) may have occupied the semi-tropical forests with ground sloths, armadillos, and capybaras. California is the center of Penutian languages, of which ancestral speakers may have been adapted to living in the coniferous forests of the Sierra Nevada. Na-Dené speakers would have hunted along the westernmost ice margins, expanding into Alaska as that land opened in the Holocene. The implication of this reconstruction is that speakers of these ancestral languages, possibly excluding Na-Dené and Penutian, were in North America south of the continental ice sheets long enough, in the Late

Pleistocene, to have developed adaptations to quite different habitats, the Western grasslands, southeastern broadleaf forests, and semi-tropical Gulf, as well as the northern coniferous forests. Correlations such as these are only suggestions for further research, possibly stemming from persisting ecological factors to which linguistically related groups developed economic adaptations.

Among controversial theories, we should recognize the insistence of many First Nations that they originated in their homelands, in the dawn of time or through acts of a superhuman creator. The reconstruction of Late Pleistocene geographical zones correlated with major language groups would be compatible with this view. Some legal experts are bemused by Indians' denial of having migrated to America, since Anglo law holds that land belongs to its first discoverer: shouldn't the theory of Late-Pleistocene immigrations be useful to Indians arguing in Anglo courts that their nations still legally hold priority rights to North America? Opposition by some Indians to explaining their origins by migrations into America seems to rest on general distrust of appeals to science, based on centuries of European and Euro-American scientific theories denying American Indians' civilizations and intelligence – only, in this instance, science may seem to uphold Indians' interests. Readers should realize that such distrust of science is far from prevalent among members of contemporary First Nations, among whom are a number of respected scientists including archaeologists. There are "fundamentalists" among American Indians as among adherents of Western and Asian religions and, as among these others, a fundamentalist position may serve a political agenda.

Research Puzzle

The first humans coming into America were few, and the continent vast. Their campsites were small and apt to be either deeply buried by later soil or destroyed by erosion or historic constructions. The likelihood of a professional archaeologist finding and excavating one of their campsites is extremely small. A cautious scientist looks for unequivocal data such as Clovis fluted blades, of which hundreds have been consistently dated by association with radiocarbon-assayed organic material to around 9000 BCE. The "Clovis horizon" is well established with data, yet logically such an abundance of distinctively styled stone blades across the continent cannot represent the very first, few migrants.

Another logical quandary lies with the hypothesis that much of the early migration moved along the Pleistocene coastal plains now covered by the sea. Settlement sites and artifacts, in this case, would be not only under water but under deep muck, impossible to excavate. Ethnographic and historic analogies suggest coastal plains attract human habitation and facilitate travel. Can a scientist argue for a hypothesis resting on unobtainable data? Perhaps we will eventually have enough carefully excavated and dated Late Pleistocene sites in the Americas that a distribution appears of earlier sites on the margins of the continents and somewhat later sites in the interiors; that would imply coastal routes even though the sites are beyond recovery. We do not see such a distribution now. In the absence of any clear distribution pattern, for which we need hundreds of well-dated sites, coastal routes remain a viable hypothesis awaiting testing by more data. Initial peopling of the Americas poses a research puzzle that continues to challenge archaeologists.

Bibliographical Note

The Center for the Study of the First Americans, at Oregon State University, Corvallis, publishes a quarterly newsletter, *Mammoth Trumpet*, an annual scholarly journal *Current Research in the Pleistocene*, and occasional edited volumes from its conferences. These include Robson Bonnichsen and Karen L. Turnmire (eds), *Ice Age People of North America* (Corvallis OR, 1999), and Bonnichsen and D. Gentry Steele (eds), *Method and Theory for Investigating the Peopling of the Americas* (Corvallis, 1994). Tom Dillehay and David Meltzer (eds), *The First Americans: Search and Research* (Boca Raton, FL, 1991) is more explicitly theoretical than the Bonnichsen volumes. E. James Dixon's *Quest for the Origins of the First Americans* (Albuquerque, NM, 1993), focusing on Alaskan sites, is written in popular style but, like Fagan's books, by an experienced archaeologist. Two early syntheses of Paleoindian finds in North America, still useful for their detailed descriptions of sites, are H. Marie Wormington's *Ancient Man in North America* (Denver, CO, 1949) and E. H. Sellards's *Early Man in America* (Austin, TX, 1952).

Notes

1. Grosswald, Mikhail G., "Ice Age Environments of Northern Eurasia with Special Reference to the Beringian Margin of Siberia," in Robson Bonnichsen and Karen L. Turnmire (eds), *Ice Age People of North America* (Corvallis, OR, 1999), p. 37.

2. Fiedel, Stuart J., "Older Than We Thought: Implications of Corrected Dates for Paleoindians," *American Antiquity* 64 (1999), p. 106.

3. Goodenough, Ward H. (ed.), *Prehistoric Settlement of the Pacific* (Philadelphia, 1996).

4. Chatters, James C., "The Recovery and First Analysis of an Early Holocene Human Skeleton from Kennewick, Washington," *American Antiquity* 65(2) (2000): 291–316.

5. Rogers, R. A., L. D. Martin, and T. D. Nicklas, "Geography and Languages," *Journal of Biogeography* 17 (1990): 117–30.

References

Bonnichsen, Robson and D. Gentry Steele (eds) (1994), *Method and Theory for Investigating the Peopling of the Americas.* Corvallis, OR: Center for the Study of the First Americans.

Bonnichsen, Robson and Karen L. Turnmire (eds) (1999), *Ice Age People of North America: Environments, Origins, and Adaptations.* Corvallis, OR: Center for the Study of the First Americans.

Chatters, James C. (2000), "The Recovery and First Analysis of an Early Holocene Human Skeleton from Kennewick, Washington," *American Antiquity* 65(2): 291–316.

Dillehay, Tom D. and David J. Meltzer (eds) (1991), *The First Americans: Search and Research.* Boca Raton, FL: CRC Press.

Dixon, E. James (1993), *Quest for the Origins of the First Americans.* Albuquerque, NM: University of New Mexico Press.

Fiedel, Stuart J. (1999), "Older Than We Thought: Implications of Corrected Dates for Paleoindians," *American Antiquity* 64(1): 95–115, 106.

Grosswald, Mikhail G. (1999), "Ice Age Environments of Northern Eurasia with Special Reference to the Beringian Margin of Siberia," in Robson Bonnichsen and Karen L. Turnmire (eds), *Ice Age People of North America.* Corvallis, OR: Oregon State University Press, pp. 27–41.

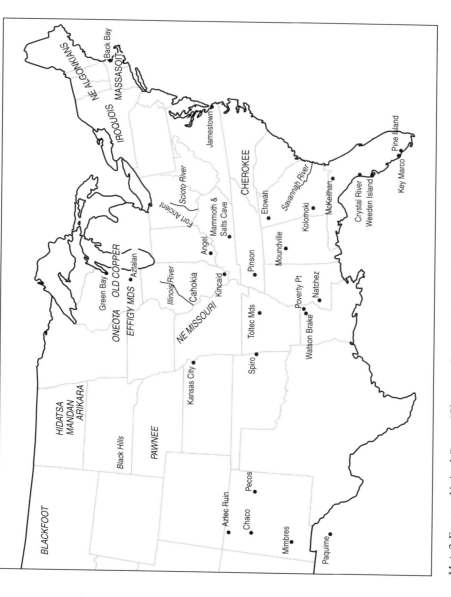

Map 2 Eastern United States (Chapters 2, 4, 5, 10, 11, 12)

2

THE ARCHAIC PERIOD: 7000–1000 BCE

About 9600 BCE, the climate warming trend that had been halted for a millennium resumed, to reach its maximum between 7000 and 3000 BCE. Geologists term the present epoch, beginning with the final melting of continental glaciers, the Holocene. Compared with the preceding Pleistocene epoch, the "Ice Age," our Holocene has had no extreme global shifts: geographic conditions have been more or less familiar for the past ten thousand years. "More or less" – local and regional conditions have indeed changed, necessitating human adaptations again and again. Archaeologists' Archaic period is the era of slowly stabilizing regional cultural patterns, culminating in economies based on techniques of intensified food production. The American landscape still exhibits constructed monuments from the later Archaic, round and also flat-topped mounds and embankments that rival anything constructed in Europe in those times.

From Pleistocene to Holocene: Extinctions and Ecological Shifts

Americans' first great challenge in the early Holocene was adjusting to the extinction of many Pleistocene game animals. Mammoths and then mastodons went completely extinct, musk-oxen retreated far north, horses, camels, and sloths disappeared from North America, and bison[1] were reduced to one species half the size of the Pleistocene species. "Megafauna" – giant beasts – and several mid-sized game animals were no longer to be had in America. Did human hunters cause their extinction? The question has been debated for years.

A couple of short temperature aberrations occurred in the terminal Pleistocene, a cold episode in the Allerød warming phase followed, 9000 BCE, by a brief two centuries of warmer climate abruptly aborted by the final (geologists' "Younger Dryas") glacial advances. For temperate-latitude America, these couple of centuries seem to have suffered drier conditions that would have reduced water available for animals' drinking and for the plants on which they depended for food. Huge beasts such as bull mammoths, eating hundreds of pounds of forage daily, would have moved out of much of their former range. Refuge populations would have been smaller than previous range-wide numbers, breeding partners fewer and their groups isolated from others. Malnourishment threatened, with its consequences of less resistance to disease and to predators. It may be that human hunters took advantage of stressed mammoth herds and hunters' slaughter brought the breeding groups below survival numbers. The coincidence of Clovis blades and mammoth kills, then no Clovis and no mammoths, might mean humans literally dealt the final death blows to America's mammoths – as Eurasian hunters would then have been doing to their mammoths.

On the other hand, mammoths were adapted to a kind of steppe environment that ceased to exist early in the Holocene. Pleistocene northern steppes had a greater variety of plants than Holocene tundras, farther north (therefore with less sunlight) than those earlier cold steppes, or than Holocene temperate grasslands. Very likely, neither the Holocene tundras with their long dark winters, nor the temperate grasslands produced enough forage for viable herds of mammoths. The crucial factor of amount of forage is indicated by the survival until 1700 BCE, on Wrangel Island in the Bering Sea, of dwarfed mammoths adjusted to Holocene resources by natural selection for much smaller body size. Very similar reduction in species' body size occurred to bison at the beginning of the Holocene. Bison, however, were able to stay healthy on Holocene grasslands forage, and the disappearance of mammoths left bison without competition for forage in that huge area. Bison, in other words, did not go extinct, only evolved into a smaller race adapted for Holocene grasslands grazing. When, eventually, First Nations humans began managing the grasslands through regular burning, bison flourished into the uncountable millions that awed early European explorers.

Geographers are particularly impressed with what paleontologists report as a shift in the early Holocene from a "mosaic" of plants across the continent to "stripe" zones with more limited plant resources. More varied plant resources had meant more variety of animals in late-Pleistocene North America, less variety in the Holocene reduced the numbers of species. Thus it wasn't just that horses disappeared; there had been at least three kinds of horses, each with its particular landform adaptation. Bison compete directly with horses for forage and water (a major factor in the nineteenth-century CE extinction of wild bison herds; wild bison survived only in northern Alberta woodlands, present Wood Buffalo Park). Rapidly evolving into the Holocene smaller form, bison may have prospered while horses and camels were stressed, not because they needed so very much food as that they were stressed by the herds of bison dominating their ranges. The opposite happened in Eurasia, horses and camels segregating into two Holocene zones and horses doing well in the temperate steppe grasslands while European bison re-treated into woodlands, surviving today only in one protected herd in a Polish forest.

Human Adaptations in Holocene America

Evidence for Paleoindians' plant foods is scanty, in part because most Paleoindian sites are chance exposures on present, windblown, land surfaces, and excavated sites have been, for the greater part, kill and butchering sites. We can be confident Paleoindians collected plant foods because humans need the nutrients in greens and fruits, and seeds and fruits are calorie-rich. More Holocene camp sites have been excavated (the less ancient, the more likely to be preserved and discovered) and both bits of food plants and apparatus for processing them have been studied. Students reading archaeology get the impression that use of plant foods begins in the Holocene, not realizing preservation factors have biased our picture.

It does seem true that Holocene humans in the temperate latitudes paid closer attention to plant resources than their Pleistocene ancestors did. One argument for this interpretation is that agriculture was developed in the Holocene. That development can be traced through several millennia during which native plants suitable for food begin to show up in sites, with seeds larger than those of strictly wild specimens: people had been cultivating them, perhaps also sowing and watering to maximize harvests. By the Late Archaic, a few unusual plants – notably maize (corn) – passed beyond their natural habitats to be widely grown as domesticates. The view can be taken that with the disappearance of the Pleistocene "mosaic" pattern of varied plant-animal ecologies, humans modified the

Holocene "stripe" zones by experiments to manage natural resources, including importing alien plants into habitats.

Few American animals were domesticated. Dogs presumably came over from Asia with human migrants, perhaps deliberately taken along and perhaps hanging out as scavengers at camps. Historically, First Nations bred several kinds of dogs, pack dogs to carry or pull loads and smaller dogs to be fattened and eaten ("like chicken"). Turkeys were domesticated, just when is difficult to determine because wild turkeys were abundant in eastern North America and butchered bones in sites could come from either wild or penned birds. Macaws and other parrots were bred in Mexico for their gorgeous feathers, as far northwest as the Pueblos in the US Southwest. Although guinea pigs (hamster-like rodents) were domesticated in South America where they are still kept for food in peasant homes, and were introduced into some Caribbean islands by CE 900, they were not taken up by United States First Nations.

European colonists observed First Nations actively managing wild game populations by burning pastures and forest edges to keep out trees and shrubs and rejuvenate grass. Firing broadened the margins of natural grasslands, in some areas adding thousands of square kilometers of grazing for bison or deer.[2] First Nations thus maintained favored game populations higher than natural environments would have provided. In this sense, these animals were livestock, integral elements in the nations' economies produced by human management. Labor expenditure for this type of livestock management was less than Eurasians put into controlling stock, and generally kept stock healthier. Technically, meat animals (other than dogs) were not domesticated in North America – they were not bred by human selection – but in terms of cost effectiveness, First Nations management of resources was efficient. In terms of sophisticated knowledge of the qualities of plants and animals, First Nations were inferior to none of their contemporaries in other continents: they allocated labor somewhat differently.

The first two-thirds of the Holocene, around 7000 BCE to the first millennium BCE, is termed the Archaic period in America. By its close, North America could be divided into two principal areas on the basis of economic bases. What I call the Continental Core stretched from Mexico to the St Lawrence Valley in the Northeast, southern Michigan, Wisconsin and Minnesota in the Midwest, and the Colorado Plateau in the southwest. Throughout the Continental Core, maize was known; in the ensuing Woodland and Southwestern Hohokam and Anasazi cultures, maize would be intensively farmed.

The northern limits of maize agriculture were the boundaries of the Continental Core. West of the Continental Core was the Pacific Drainage, from the Rockies westward, from Baja California north through British Columbia. First Nations in this area cultivated indigenous plants such as camas bulbs, wapato, acorn oaks, and seed-bearing grasses. Like livestock management, these techniques of producing food with less labor expenditure than Eurasian or Continental Core agriculture were seldom recognized by European observers. Instead, the nations were described as "hunter-gatherers" or "foragers" living off wild foods. There is a third ecological–economic area in North America, the High Latitudes of Alaska and Canada where plant productivity is low and people must subsist on fish, game animals, and birds. Since the High Latitudes are outside the United States' Lower Forty-eight, their prehistory will receive less attention here.

Early Archaic, 7000–6000 BCE

Archaeologists noticed that fluted stone blades – Clovis and Folsom types – seemed not to have been made in the Holocene. It may be that tongue-in-groove hafting of spear blade to shaft (the "fluting" channel running up the blade) was needed only for megafauna, and once mammoths and giant bison were gone, it was enough to secure blades in spear shafts by binding thinned or narrowed bases into slots in the shafts. Thinning the lower edge of a stone blade, or chipping the lower corners to make a tang or stem, is easier than delivering the precise force that slivers off a long oval flake vertically up the face of the blade. Early Archaic stone knife and spear blades include many types that continue the flintknapping skill demonstrated in narrow ribbon-like flakes running across the blade faces for final finishing; only the method of preparing the base for hafting was changed.

Different regions of North America exhibit differing varieties of stone blades, some such as the Agate Basin type, on the Plains, much like Clovis, some such as the Dalton type, in the Midwest, with serrated blade edges, some such as Windust in the Northwest with stem bases. Clearly, North America after 10,000 BCE has many human populations, all experimenting with means to live better in their widely differing regional environments. Without preservation of art (other than beautifully knapped blades of attractively colored or banded cherts and chalcedonies), written texts, or perishable crafts such as fabrics, we cannot judge whether distinctively styled stone blades indicate cultural distinctions the people themselves recognized, or are merely technological items shared across language and societal boundaries. Common geographical conditions, and being neighbors, produce "culture areas" of ecological adaptations and material goods, without necessarily involving common speech, religion, or social values.

Studies of Early Archaic sites in the Southeast indicate the need for stone especially suited to knapping blades and scrapers influenced settlement. Within a few miles of quarries are fairly large sites resulting from many centuries of camps where people reduced the weight of quarried pieces by roughly chipping them into "blanks" that could be finished elsewhere as required. Instead of camping beside craggy rock outcrops, sites were placed overlooking rivers or lakes, convenient for gathering food, firewood, and tent or wigwam materials. Artifacts made from a particular outcrop are common within irregular areas of about one hundred miles diameter, and occur less frequently for as much as several hundred miles farther, especially if the stone is unusually pretty. These studies show Early Archaic bands mapped out across the Eastern Woodlands linked to high-quality knapping stone quarries, creating territories each encompassing several days' travel to the optimum quarry. The territories in the Southeast covered both Piedmont uplands and Coastal Plain valleys, so that a band could exploit a wide variety of food and other resource materials. Large sites at the Fall Line where the upland streams cascade into the coastal plains tend to be approximately equidistant from two favored quarries and contain stone artifacts from each, either because at these points a band could as easily travel to one or the other, or because bands met here and exchanged materials or artifacts.[3]

Slabs of stone with hollowed-out basins or cups mark Archaic sites contrasted with Paleoindian camps. The stones, coarser-grained than rock used for sharp-edged blades and scrapers, were used to grind seeds or nuts into flour that could be mixed with water into a paste, formed into flattened cakes, and baked among the warm ashes of a hearth, or the flour could be dried and stored for winter use. In the Eastern Woodlands (including the Midwest), nut flours from acorns, walnuts, hickory nuts, and hazelnuts seem to have been used for the staple daily bread; this is evidenced both by stone mortars (cup-shaped depressions) for crushing nuts and the presence of nutshells in occupation debris in sites. In the West during the Early Archaic, basin-shaped grinding slabs similar to Pueblos' corn-grinding metates indicate use of seeds, and locations of sites adjacent to water meadows and flats where edible roots grow suggest harvesting of bulbs and roots such as historically were processed into nutritious flour. (Bulbs and roots would have decayed rapidly in trash debris, where nutshells may be preserved.)

Along with nut, seed, and root flour, Early Archaic subsistence looked to deer, rabbits, other small game (squirrels, raccoons, beaver), and fish and some shellfish, the latter two not generally directly evidenced in Early Archaic sites as they are, abundantly, in later millennia of the Archaic. On the Plains and Plateau (interior) Northwest, bison were a major food, with antelope and elk also frequently taken. Camps were located on upland flats, river terraces, and in rockshelters. We lack direct evidence of structures, so infer that Early Archaic people lived in tents, light wigwams (dome-shaped, bent-over-sapling structures covered with bark slabs, mats, or hides), or wickiups (thatch structures, with or without light pole frames). Very likely, Early Archaic people had canoes – dugouts and bark-covered boats in the Woodlands, reed-bundle boats in the West, dugouts in the Northwest, possibly already sea-mammal hide-covered frame boats in Alaska – not preserved for archaeological inspection.

Clothing is known only from exceptionally dry rockshelters in the Desert West (eastern Oregon and Nevada). Needles made from thin polished slivers of bone have been preserved in a few sites elsewhere, and awls made from sharpened deer leg bones that could have been used for sewing leather or making mats, baskets, or fabrics. Astonishing proof of Early Archaic fabrics comes from Spirit Cave, Nevada, where about 7000 BCE, a man's corpse was interred wrapped in a twined fabric shroud and then in a large diamond-patterned mat, and two cremations were placed in fabric bags. The corpse's shroud is made of narrow twisted strips of fur intertwined with fine split bulrush stems, its outer mat of the finely split bulrush through which were woven fine cords. One of the woven bags is decorated with spaced, interwoven strips of leather and of dark-colored tule stems, the other has dark bands of juniper or sage, and both have brown and white bird feathers inserted and fastened into the fabric as further decoration, and were finished with fringes. The skill of these weavers, more than nine thousand years ago, astounded today's experts: the split reeds and fur so narrow and even, the cord threads so well spun, the weaving itself close, tight, and even, and the variety of techniques and decoration. These fabrics preserved in the dry American desert cave are the oldest complete fabrics known in the world.

The Spirit Cave corpse, naturally mummified by the dry air, was a man in his forties, not especially robust. He suffered from abscesses in three teeth, an infection that probably spread and caused his death. Once he had been hit on the forehead, an injury that had healed, and years earlier he had broken a finger. On his feet were well-worn leather moccasins sewn out of three sections, a sole extending over the toes, side vamp, and ankle wrap; tule strips woven into moccasin liners served him as socks. (Other dry rockshelters have equally old yucca-fiber sandals.) His last meals had included fish – chub, suckers, and minnow-like dace – and bulrush seeds; Spirit Cave overlooked an extensive marsh. In the cave near, although not directly with, the burials were a couple of broken weapon points made out of obsidian (volcanic glass), both with ribbon flaking typical of the Early Holocene, and two wood foreshafts that would hold stone points and socket into a spear shaft, allowing the shaft to be retrieved from a hit; a stone metate and two round "rubbing stones" that were used to pulverize something, possibly seeds; two flaked stone scraper blades and a slotted wooden knife handle; and a simple pendant made from the end of a bighorn mountain sheep horn. Archaeologists studying these artifacts mention that bighorn rams roam the rough high country, a challenge to human hunters.[4]

Middle Archaic, 6000–3000 BCE

Throughout the United States, Early Archaic sites indicate small communities exploiting lakeside and marsh resources and game similar to historic species. People knew of sources of stone superior for knapping sharp-edged artifacts or for grinding seeds, and would procure valued stone over considerable distances. Such sophisticated knowledge of raw materials counters any impression, from the small campsites, that Early Archaic people were timid, tied to familiar localities.

Sites dating to the Middle Archaic, around 6000–3000 BCE, suggest considerably more complicated human habitation over the continent. Regional differences in artifact styles are more distinct, site distributions imply territorial claims and boundaries including no man's lands between more densely occupied zones, and the number of skeletons with embedded weapon points or fractures likely caused in attacks (for example, lower arms broken in the middle as if warding off blows) have rather surprised archaeologists. Long-distance procurement of valued stone continues, balancing the evidence for warfare with that for alliances and/or safe transit to prized quarries. Middle Archaic is the period of rising climate temperature climax, drying out some desert basins and contributing to the spread of pine woods in the Southeast – less productive for humans than the hardwood forests the pines replaced – but overall, climate did not adversely affect humans in America in this period.

Middle Archaic people seem to have become more interested in riverine and marsh habitats, collecting a diversity of plants and smaller animals, down to shellfish. The largest game would be bison and deer, plus antelope and mountain sheep in the West. Rock art in the Black Hills shows small groups of people cooperating in chasing or trapping these animals. A loop design probably depicts use of large nets to get them positioned for clubbing or spearing, the way historic Great Basin Indian people formed large circles holding a net and then closed in within a valley or pass, driving game into the shrinking middle to be slaughtered. On the rock art panels, one human may be represented apparently standing on the back of an animal, possibly the "antelope boss" or "rabbit boss" who directed the hunting operation. Many of the Black Hills hunting scenes are at rock defiles or box canyons that would facilitate game drives; the pictures may be signs marking such suitable locations, or records of success.[5] In the forested Eastern Woodlands, riverine and coastal sites exhibit another kind of success, immense heaps of emptied shellfish. Increasing populations would have been fed by establishing seasonal settlements at mussel shoals or oyster banks, older people and women caring for young children collecting the shellfish while younger men hunted deer. The ties people felt toward these settlements is seen by their placing burials in the shellheaps.

Back Bay in Boston revealed weirs – fish traps – that in this case radiocarbon-dated 3000–1000 BCE, the span of the Late Archaic, but probably had been invented somewhat earlier. Back Bay during these two millennia was a shallow tidal backwater. People cut saplings, drove them as stakes in long rows parallel to shore at the line of low tide, and filled spaces between the stakes with bunches of brush. High tide flooded over the wooden fences, and, as the tide receded, twice a day, the water level dropped below the fence top, trapping small fish. Twice a day, people could scoop up fish with nets or baskets; furthermore, the fences provided ideal habitat for oysters, one might say an oyster farm. Eventually, Back Bay silted up, burying the weirs. Construction of a subway line and office buildings at Boylston Street exposed thousands of stakes, patiently sorted out by archaeologists into hundreds of weirs superimposed over many centuries. An intriguing sight against Boston's most prestigious office buildings, the ingenious fish traps demonstrate how Middle and Late Archaic Americans effectively increased food supplies.

New forms of art appear in the Middle Archaic. Virtuoso flint-knapping, that producing the narrow ribbon-like flakes across the faces of blades, has disappeared – Archaic stone blades are quite competently made but the craftsmanship is not so extraordinary as with Paleoindian and Early Archaic blades. Finishing blades for hafting varies more regionally in the Archaic, giving archaeologists stylistic clues to social groupings. Midwestern artisans made handsome bone pins, some with holes in the top so they could be used as pendants or tied to a belt, all well polished and many with attractive finely incised patterns of sets of lines. These distinctive pins are dispersed throughout the central Midwest, demonstrating contacts across regions counteracting the trend toward greater exploitation of local resources. In Windover Pond near Cape Canaveral, Florida, interment in waterlogged peat preserved sixth-millennium BCE bodies wrapped in fabric shrouds, like the Spirit Cave, Nevada, corpses, and like them furnished also with fine and coarse cloth, twined bags, and mats, in Florida made with fibers processed from palms as well as weedy plants. Carved stone atlatl (spearthrower) weights appear in the Middle Archaic, to become hallmarks later of the Late Archaic. Often termed "bannerstones," atlatl weights were manufactured by grinding rather than chipping rock, producing sleek smooth surfaces enhancing the beauty of the colored and banded stone chosen. Shapes may be geometric or highly stylized birds or butterflies; they can be mistaken for modern abstract small sculptures.

Late Archaic, 3000–1000 BCE

After around 3000 BCE, sea level stabilized at its historic global level and climate, vegetation, and fauna were essentially as we know them ("stabilized" isn't quite the word considering recurrent fluctuations such as the El Niño storm pattern shifts). Population growth was reaching critical mass if dependent only on wild foods. A cultural breakthrough was occurring: in the Late Archaic, cultivation of plants became common. Human communities increasingly labored in fields to produce more and more food, leading to what can properly be termed civilization, living in "civitas" ("civilization's" Latin root, "city" or state).

Agriculture was no light-bulb flash in one brain. Our earliest evidence in the Americas is nearly as old as in Eurasia. Experimentation with increasing food harvests probably began in the late Pleistocene. During the early Holocene in Mexico, people in Oaxaca (pronounced Wah-ha-ka) in southwestern Mexico were planting and cultivating maize (Indian corn) and squash that were not native to that region, proving human efforts to amplify resources. Changes in pollen deposits in the Valley of Oaxaca indicate fields were cleared near the river. Neither maize nor squash was basic to diet at that time; squash may have been grown for its shell, like gourds, or its seeds, and maize kernels grown and roasted for snacks. Curiously, no wild maize existed: the plant is a mutant from a wild grass called teosinte, and entirely dependent on human manipulation for its propagation.

Millennia went by before Mexicans became sufficiently concerned over food supplies that they selected conscientiously for the largest maize kernels and cobs, breeding varieties suitable for grinding into flour in addition to the older popping corn. (Ground seed flour was cooked into porridge as well as baked as flatbread.) Maize appears in the US Southwest in the second millennium BCE, on cobs much smaller than present-day cobs, and takes another millennium to become a significant crop to Southwesterners. In the Midwest, maize pollen has been detected in village sites equally early, and again, minor in the diet – unless the few kernels in kitchen areas and storage pits reflect consumption of most of the corn while tender and still green, rather than processed mature and dry into ground meal or hominy. Actual kernels of maize have not been recovered from Late Archaic sites, only from Middle Woodland and later. Midwesterners of the Late Archaic cultivated indigenous temperate-zone seed crops – chenopods (such as goosefoot), sumpweed, marshelder – that now are considered weeds. These plants have abundant tiny seeds high in vegetable protein but not easy to grind, hence nuts were important as another abundant source of carbohydrates and protein. Squash was widely cultivated, as far north as southern Maine in the Archaic, presumably originally obtained from Midwesterners who seem to have domesticated a species native to the Ozarks. A dry rockshelter in northern Arkansas preserved a 3000-year-old stored set of cultivated seeds: a gallon of mixed seeds, three bags of chenopod seeds, and one of squash and sunflower seeds; antlers and perforated mussel shells with the seeds probably were the hoes used to work the seed plots.

One definitive source of information on Late Archaic diet is desiccated human feces preserved in the labyrinthine Mammoth cave system in Kentucky. Late Archaic people penetrated half a mile into twisting precipitous totally dark cave tunnels, illuminating their path with wood torches, and sometimes they stopped to relieve themselves in corners of the tunnels. The dry remains can be radiocarbon dated and analyzed for components. This research hints that the intrepid explorers fortified themselves with a fermented beer-type beverage brewed from maygrass, a plant no longer used in historic America.[6] Other components of the feces confirmed eating the indigenous seeds so common in Late Archaic and Early Woodland sites. Apparently the goal of these early cavers was to procure pieces of pure white gypsum outcropping deep in the tunnels; why they would go to such risk to get the gypsum, no one knows.

A highly significant innovation of the Eastern Woodlands Late Archaic is construction of earth mounds over burials. Communities wanted highly visible reminders of their deceased, memorials still to be noticed on the landscape four or five thousand years later! The earliest known burial mound, radiocarbon-dated at 5300 BCE, lies on the Canadian Maritimes coast at the Quebec–Labrador boundary, across the Strait of Belle Isle from Newfoundland. An adolescent (whether boy or girl could not be determined) was laid face down in a sandy pit, between a pair of fires. The youth had around its neck a bone pendant and a whistle with three stops, and beside the body were a walrus tusk, a harpoon, three stone knives, a cluster of stone and bone weapon points, and red-ochre and graphite pebbles with an antler tine that could be used to crush the minerals for use as paint. A rock slab covered the body and two short rows of upright slabs were set in sand above it before being buried under sand and stream boulders. In the pit was a used caribou-antler shovel. It's a puzzle why this youth was given such attention, so far unique for the Middle Archaic that far north.

More typical, Late Archaic in date and common in the temperate Woodlands, are earthen mounds built near bluff edges overlooking river valleys with settlements. One in northeast Missouri, for example, contained a total of 109 persons, of which 28 had been corpses laid at what would be the base of the mound and five had been decomposed before interment and the bones bundled. Near three infants were pieces of galena (lead) and hematite (iron ore), a broken pendant, bone awls, a bird bone and a raccoon lower jaw, antler tines used for flaking stone blades, and a ten-inch-long narrow, beautifully flaked (almost ribbon-flaked) stone blade. Near an adolescent were more galena and hematite, bone and antler tools, stone drills, two beaver incisor teeth probably used as knives, stone blades, and a

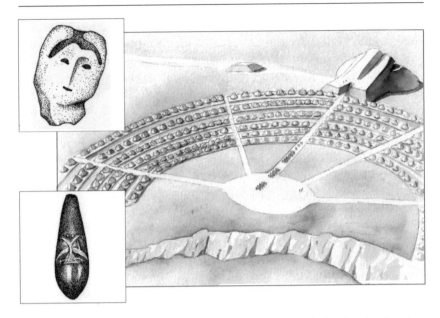

Figure 1 Poverty Point (Louisiana), 1000 BC. *Insets*: Small clay figurine head, polished stone pendant with nestling bird engraved. Drawn by Anne Chojnacki

small mano (grinding stone). It looks as if a community's dead were placed here over a period of time before all were covered with a layer of earth. Subsequently, more layers of earth and limestone rocks were piled on, with cremated human remains buried in these layers. Three thousand years later, Late Woodland people took advantage of this monument to add on top a few of their own dead, with a final layer of earth.

The heartland of Late Archaic moundbuilding was the Lower Mississippi River Valley. The custom began in the mid-fourth millennium BCE in northeast Louisiana, where the site of Watson Brake has a circle formed by eleven mounds, the tallest 25 feet high, connected by a low embankment. Evidence for cooking suggests activities were carried out on the mounds, although since they seem to have been rounded they would not have been designed for house structures. Quantities of mussel shells, snail shells, and bones of fish, deer, small mammals and turkeys indicate diet rich in meat; plants must have been gathered, too. Pottery wasn't yet known, yet the people made little cubes of clay and fired them, for what purpose we can't guess.

Watson Brake's little clay cubes, as well as its mounds and embankment, are clues to cultural continuity between these earliest

Late Archaic earth-builders and the spectacular site of Poverty Point, in the same northeastern corner of Louisiana. Long an enormous – literally – puzzle to archaeologists, Poverty Point covers a square mile along a bayou waterway. Six concentric arcs of six-foot-high earth embankments, the outer diameter three-quarters of a mile, apparently served to raise residential structures. Inside the six half-circles of homes was a thirty-five-acre plaza constructed by filling in a gully and preparing a level surface. Five narrow streets broach the residential arcs, leading out from the waterfront plaza. At the head of one street is a massive mound eighty-two feet at the flat summit of its highest platform; a broad ramp leads up from street level. From the air, this mound, with its pair of side lobes, seems to have a bird shape. A conical mound twenty-one feet high and a low flat mound were built near the great mound; a fifty-two-foot mound a mile and a half north and a smaller mound the same distance south complete these earthworks created between 1500 and 1000 BCE.

Like Watson Brake and the other known late Middle and Late Archaic mound sites in the Lower Mississippi Valley, Poverty Point lacks evidence of agriculture other than squash, even of cultivation of indigenous seed plants such as were important to Indian nations in the central Midwest at the time. Nuts were commonly gathered and processed in quantities, and fish and deer were mainstays. How the houses on the embankments looked, or the structures on top of the mounds, is unknown; shelters would have been light and airy in the warm, humid climate. Artifacts are the array usual in the Late Archaic Eastern Woodlands, with the exception of a number of small figurines artistically carved from attractive stones such as jasper; these may have been amulets or jewelry. Distinctive at Poverty Point, and found throughout the Coastal Lowlands province from Missouri through the Gulf of Mexico coast and Florida, are what are termed Poverty Point Objects (PPOs), uncountable thousands at Poverty Point itself. The objects were molded in the hand of local clay, placed by dozens into earth-oven pits, a fire burned on top of them, and then food laid to bake on the hot PPOs. Rocks suitable for retaining heat in earth ovens are scarce in the Gulf Coastal Lowlands, so these quickly made clay objects were substituted. PPOs ceased to be made about 700 BCE, when Lower Mississippi Valley people learned to manufacture clay cooking pots.

Earth constructions reaching, at Poverty Point, stupendous scale are one impressive development of the Late Archaic. The other still-visible product of the period, this time more in the northern Eastern Woodlands, is copper manufactures. Whether it is correct to call them "metallurgy" is debated, because the metal came from ore so pure it didn't require smelting to extract the copper. The point here is that smelting involves furnaces in which temperatures much hotter than open fires can be achieved, that is to say, heat technology in addition to techniques for working the metal itself. This technology was developed in Peru, to a high degree, in the second millennium BCE and spread as far north as Mexico by CE 1200, but not into the United States. Techniques for copper used in the Late Archaic sufficed there until European invasions – copper was greatly valued for its sun-like gleam, the sound of bits of copper tinkling (precursors of today's powwow Jingle Dance for girls) was delightful, copper awls and daggers and harpoon points were useful, yet stone continued to be satisfactory for most cutting and pounding instruments. Archaeological research in Eurasia shows that iron smelting and forging is not a simple transfer from copper working: iron melts at a higher temperature, also necessary for melting out its ore impurities (slag), and its superiority over other tool metals comes from the process of carbonizing it into steel. America's iron deposits near Lake Superior were unexplored while, for five millennia, Lake Superior copper deposits were extensively worked.

Radiocarbon dates as early as 6000 BCE have been obtained on material associated with copper implements in the Upper Midwest. The bulk of copper artifacts are dated between 4000 and 1000 BCE, Late Archaic.[7] "Bulk" here means not only the greater number of known copper artifacts, but also the heaviest ones, adzes, socketed axes, harpoons, tanged or socketed weapon points secured to hafts with rivets, and smaller tools such as awls. Three "Old Copper" cemeteries have been excavated in Wisconsin (excavated, incidentally, because severe erosion or commercial quarrying were rapidly destroying the sites; in none of the cases was human remains disturbed in order to get research data). The oldest dates to the fourth millennium BCE. Among its graves was one in which a year-old child lay with a flat copper crescent, probably an ornament, bits of birchbark and string adhering to the copper. An older child had been given a flute made from a swan's wing bone. A young woman with a newborn infant wore a copper bracelet and another of strung perforated pond snail shells, plus a broken ocean whelk shell and two local mussel shells lay with her. Adult men included one with a copper fishhook, another with a copper spatula, copper crescent-shaped knife blades, and a couple with stone dart points. Tanged copper dart points were salvaged from near the excavated burials. An estimated 200 people had been buried in this Late Archaic cemetery, about three-quarters lost before qualified archaeologists reached the damaged site.

"Old Copper" artifacts have been found throughout the Great Lakes region and its western peripheries, most often by farmers. Makers of these copper implements apparently lived in small camps, moving in a seasonal round to their harvests and, when necessary, to the band's cemetery. Some copper artifacts were traded south to the Central Midwestern communities cultivating indigenous seed plants, squash, and a little maize. Old Copper manufacturers lived in a more northern habitat where these plants would not flourish. East of the Old Copper Great Lakes region, in the St Lawrence Valley and adjacent Ontario and New York, implements shaped exactly like many Old Copper ones were made by grinding slate. Slate is abundant in the northern Appalachians, copper is less common; Late Archaic people in the Northeast apparently found it more economical to make popular types of tools out of slate. Since a cache of Old Copper artifacts has been discovered as far east as Quebec, we know there were connections between the Old Copper and slate provinces.

The Archaic period, the first six millennia of the Holocene, saw the continent's vegetation and fauna shifting into patterns familiar to us yet. Human populations increased inexorably, gradually investing more labor in plant cultivation and processing while continuing hunting and fishing. By the Late Archaic, ground stone artifacts and, in the northern Midwest, copper diversified material culture; in the Lower Mississippi Valley, social organization literally moved the earth into permanent signs of humans' power to transcend what nature may provide. The following Early Woodland period expanded these trends.

Bibliographical Note

Brian Fagan's *Ancient North America: The Archaeology of a Continent* (New York, 2nd edn, 1995) and my own *North American Indians: A Comprehensive Account* (Englewood Cliffs, NJ, 2nd edn, 1992) cover the Archaic period in chapters organized by geographical areas. *Archaeology of Prehistoric Native America: An Encyclopedia* (New York, 1998) has entries for the Archaic period and many sites and artifacts associated with it. *Imperfect Balance: Landscape Transformations in the Precolumbian Americas* (New York, 2000) provides descriptive summaries of human use and modification of plants and landscapes throughout the agricultural regions of the Americas.

KING ALFRED'S COLLEGE
LIBRARY

Notes

1. "Bison" is the proper term for the American bovids commonly called buffalo. True buffalo are found only in Asia and Africa.

2. Shepard Krech III, *The Ecological Indian* (New York, 1999).

3. I. Randolph Daniel Jr, *Hardaway Revisited: Early Archaic Settlement in the Southeast* (Tuscaloosa, AL, 1998).

4. *Nevada Historical Society Quarterly* 40(1) (1997), is a set of papers on the Spirit Cave burials and artifacts, organized and edited by researchers Donald R. Tuohy and Amy Dansie. Windover Pond fabrics are mentioned by the excavators, Doran and Dickel, in their chapter in Barbara A. Purdy (ed.), *Wet Site Archaeology* (Caldwell, NJ, 1988), pp. 263–89.

5. Alice M. Tratebras, "Reexamining the Plains Archaic McKean Culture," in Mark G. Plew (ed.), *Explorations in American Archaeology: Essays in Honor of Wesley R. Hurt* (Lanham, MD, 1998), pp. 259–309.

6. James Schoenwetter, "Ethnobotanical Expressions of Prehistoric Ritual: An Early Woodland Case," in Penelope B. Drooker (ed.), *Fleeting Identities* (Carbondale, IL, 2001).

7. Thomas Cary Pleger, "Social Complexity, Trade, and Subsistence During the Archaic/Woodland Transition in the Western Great Lakes (4000–400 BC): A Diachronic Study of Copper-Using Cultures at the Oconto and Riverside Cemeteries," unpublished dissertation submitted to the Department of Anthropology, University of Wisconsin-Madison, 1998.

References

Daniel, I. Randolph, Jr (1998), *Hardaway Revisited: Early Archaic Settlement in the Southeast.* Tuscaloosa, AL: University of Alabama Press.

Doran, Glen H. and David M. Dickel (1988), "Multidisciplinary Investigations at the Windover Sit," in Barbara A. Purdy (ed.), *Wet Site Archaeology.* Caldwell, NJ: Telford, pp. 263–89.

Fagan, Brian M. (1995), *Ancient North America: The Archaeology of a Continent.* 2nd edn. New York: Thames & Hudson.

Gibbon, Guy (ed.) (1998), *Archaeology of Prehistoric Native America: An Encyclopedia.* New York: Garland.

Green, Wiliam (ed.) (1994), "Agricultural Origins and Development in the Midcontinent," Report 19, Office of the State Archaeologist, University of Iowa, Iowa City.

Kehoe, Alice Beck (1992), *North American Indians: A Comprehensive Account.* 2nd edn. Upper Saddle River NJ: Prentice-Hall.

Krech, Shepard, III (1999), *The Ecological Indian: Myth and History.* New York: W. W. Norton.

Lentz, David L. (ed.) (2000), *Imperfect Balance: Landscape Transformations in the Precolumbian Americas.* New York: Columbia University Press.

Pleger, Thomas Cary (1998), "Social Complexity, Trade, and Subsistence During the Archaic/Woodland Transition in the Western Great Lakes (4000–400 BC): A Diachronic Study of Copper-Using Cultures at the Oconto and Riverside Cemeteries," unpublished dissertation submitted to the Department of Anthropology, University of Wisconsin-Madison.

Schoenwetter, James (2001), "Ethnobotanical Expressions of Prehistoric Ritual: An Early Woodland Case," in Penelope B. Drooker (ed.), *Fleeting Identities.* Carbondale, IL: Center for Archaeological Investigations.

Sellards, E. H. (1952), *Early Man in America.* Austin: University of Texas Press.

Tratebras, Alice M. (1998), "Reexamining the Plains Archaic McKean Culture," in Mark G. Plew (ed.), *Explorations in American Archaeology: Essays in Honor of Wesley R. Hurt.* Lanham, MD: University Press of America, pp. 259–309.

Tuohy, Donald R. and Amy Dansie (eds.) (1997), *Nevada Historical Society Quarterly* 40(1).

Wormington, H. Marie (1949), *Ancient Man in North America.* Denver: Denver Museum of Natural History.

3

NUCLEAR AMERICA

It had seemed obvious to American archaeologists that nations of the Eastern Woodlands and Southwest had contacts with those of Mexico. If nothing else, planting maize proved it: maize was domesticated in Mexico and the mutation that makes it profitable for farmers prevents it from reproducing in the wild. Early twentieth-century archaeologists accepted the concept of "Nuclear America," a zone from Mexico south through Peru, where the major crops of maize, beans, and squashes were domesticated, pottery was invented, monumental architecture developed, and the most elaborate arts and political empires created. Outreach from these expanding populations fueled by agriculture would have affected hunter-gatherer nations, whether from pressuring them for land, seeking their products and resources in trade, or eventually, seizing them for slaves. Hunter-gatherers, in response, would have added crops to their subsistence and imitated practices observed in the glamorous metropolises.

Indisputable as is the spread of maize from Mexico into temperate North America, in the 1960s American archaeologists became loath to discuss the concept of a Nuclear America cradle of innovations. Instead, they emphasized adaptations to geographic regions. One reason for the shift in research questions was a shift in funding sources, from museums and universities accustomed to humanities perspectives to the National Science Foundation, a Cold War entity dispensing millions of dollars for physical and natural science. Projects allying archaeologists with zoologists, botanists, chemists, and physical geologists attracted NSF grants, so that it became more feasible to study ancient procurement and processing of wild game and plants in collaboration with faunal or floral laboratory specialists than the question of how maize was obtained by temperate-zone societies – a historical question. Another factor was the increasing number of archaeologists and their employment in local cultural resource management; up through mid-century, the relatively few archaeologists were likely to be experienced in several quite different regions, while CRM jobs call for local expertise.

"Nuclear America" nevertheless remains a useful concept. The history of Mexico is as relevant to United States indigenous histories as that of Rome is to the histories of European nations beyond Italy. No one believes temperate-zone First Nations were pale clones of Mexico, but neither were they fenced off from the discoveries and events of the realms to the south. An overview of Mexican history provides background to that in the United States before the European invasions.

Development of Agriculture

The earliest direct evidence for agriculture in the Americas is fragments of squash left in a rockshelter overlooking the Oaxaca Valley in southwest Mexico, 8000 BCE. No wild varieties of this squash grow in Oaxaca; it was probably taken to Oaxaca from farther north in Mexico, presumably to eat its seeds, possibly to use the shell as container. At the same time, the banks of the river in the valley seem to have been cleared of their thickets to make open plots for cultivated plants. Pollen from maize was recovered in the same rockshelter, but without cobs or kernels; whether it was already domesticated cannot be determined. Maize mutated from a wild seed grass, teosinte, native to western and south-central Mexico. Some time before about 3500 BCE, alert and knowledgable Mexican cultivators noticed the mutation with multiple "naked" kernels (no hard shell around each kernel as in teosinte) on cob spikes. Only planting and cultivation by humans could have perpetuated this mutation – no natural agency can disperse the kernel seeds in the manner necessary for this large-stalk plant. Excavations in the Valley of Mexico produced bits of teosinte, amaranth, and tomatillos from Archaic hunter-gatherer sites earlier than those with maize, showing that Archaic people were collecting and perhaps cultivating not-yet-domesticated forebears of these valued crops.

In another valley of central Mexico, Tehuacán (not to be confused with Teotihuacán northeast of Mexico City), Archaic people left a variety of plant remains when they camped in dry rockshelters. Earlier

Holocene occupations had the small but numerous and nutritious seeds from foxtail millet and amaranth, prickly pear cactus with its sweet fruit and thick leaves edible if young, avocados, and mesquite, with bean-like fruit in pods. Later in the mid-Holocene, people were definitely planting and cultivating peppers, squash, cotton, and agave, in addition to foxtail millet. Occupations dated 3500 BCE have the first maize in the Tehuacán Valley, small cobs with kernels that were probably prepared by popping. (Many native grains were parched – lightly roasted – for example by shaking in a tray with hot coals, similar to popping corn.) Mexicans continued selectively breeding maize, developing varieties for diverse conditions and increasing the size of both cobs and kernels.

Toward the end of the first millennium BCE, Mexicans had a domesticated bean, apparently from a Mexican wild form, although beans had been domesticated in Peru as early as maize appeared in Tehuacán. If the Mexicans planted their beans together with maize, they would have seen that the maize benefited from the newer domesticate's nitrogen-fixing ability, making that necessary element available to neighboring plants. Beans also furnish high-quality vegetable protein to humans. We don't know when Mexicans began soaking maize kernels in lime, softening them for hominy or then drying the softened kernels in order to grind them into meal. Lime-soaked maize gains calcium from the lime; eating maize thus processed with beans yields a diet sound in basic nutrients. Add a chile-pepper salsa and some greens to round out the vitamins, occasional deer, fowl, or fish for more protein and necessary fat, or oil-rich seeds such as sunflower, and you have the healthy cuisine characteristic of America from Mexico through eastern and southern North America.

This Nuclear American food base is the famous "Three Sisters," maize, beans, and squash interplanted to maintain nitrogen and phosphorus through bacteria and fungi in their roots. Interplanting makes all three plants stronger and increases yield, a lesson farmers today could profitably learn from prehistoric forerunners. Millennia of experimentation in the Americas taught that the best growing conditions for the Three Sisters are raised tilled beds; if the water table is high, raised beds allow drainage down into the adjacent ditches, preventing waterlogged roots, and, if the water table is low or the climate arid, water can be run into the ditches from rivers or lakes, irrigating the plants. Raised beds may be long parallel rows that look like plowed fields, or rectangles, or small mounds – corn hills – or, in arid zones, the reverse, sunken plots that hold water. There are even "rock mulch" plots in the desert Southwest (and, incidentally, on Easter Island), ordinary cobbles piled in small mounds or lines including some along contours to impede slopewash. The rock cover keeps soil underneath softer, absorbing rain better than sunbaked hardpan, and slows evaporation. Hohokam in the Southwest grew agave under the rock mulch and baked the tough plant for a couple of days in nearby large pits until it became sweet and edible.[1]

Water management is a component in any agricultural regime. Not only are conservation techniques such as contour terracing and check-dams, and water provision through irrigation essential in the semi-arid lands comprising so much of Mexico and the American West, drainage management is needed in humid zones, and rainfall patterns everywhere are crucial to successful planting and harvests. Villages in the Tehuacán Valley built an earth dam in an arroyo in 700 BCE, then enlarged it in the next century to impound a reservoir holding a million and a half cubic meters of water. Using this year-round source of water to feed irrigation canals, the farmers raised quantities of tropical crops including cotton and palm nuts to market at higher, colder settlements. Because irrigation systems are later in the American Southwest than in Mexico and appear in conjunction with pottery and structures similar to western Mexican types, it is likely that Hohokam were migrants from, or learned from, Mexican agriculturists to extend fields beyond what Nature would water. These First Nations agricultural engineers avoided the modern problem of salt accumulation in irrigated fields by diverting storm runoff carrying fertile soil particles on to their farmlands as well as layering on rich muck cleaned out of irrigation channels. Techniques of water management seem to have been widely shared in the Americas, each region fine-tuning and further inventing practices called for by its particular circumstances.

Diversity, "don't put all your eggs in one basket," has been a principle of indigenous American agriculture. Both in Mexico and in temperate North America, seed-bearing weeds were tolerated or even cultivated. Chenopods (goosefoot), amaranth, and foxtail millet flourish on open disturbed soil such as would have been created by hunting-gathering camps. After maize was domesticated, these and other plants such as mesquite with seeds higher in protein than maize were retained between or in addition to maize fields. The Aztecs grew amaranth in quantities second only to maize and required loads of amaranth in tribute from vassals raising it. First Nations people maintained knowledge of wild food and medicinal plants through botanical specialists and by families regularly going out berry-picking, for greens and herbs, tree fruits and nuts, and the wild seeds. European colonists disdained what they considered distractions from the labor of farming, at the same time marveling at Indians' encyclopedic knowledge of flora and fauna, not seeing that a diversified resource base is intelligent risk management. Lean seasons and famines could occur, there is evidence in slowed-growth lines in human bones that children had suffered nutritional setbacks, but no archaeological signs of widespread starvation even during protracted droughts. Instead, people left hopeless fields to live in small bands collecting wild foods inured to dry conditions, utilizing information passed down through millennia from hunter-gatherer ancestors.

Religious Concepts

The concept of Nuclear America includes a set of religious ideas expressed through symbols that persist for millennia, indeed into today on the Mexican flag's eagle grasping a serpent. Mexican artist Miguel Covarrubias called these ideas the Mother Culture for Mesoamerica, identifying them as earliest in Olmec, Mexico's earliest major civilization, later second millennium BCE. The ideas support state societies dependent on agriculture.

The Nuclear American cosmos is divided into heavens, earth, and underworld, symbolized respectively by bird, jaguar, and serpent. A World Tree may rise, linking the three sectors, pictured with a large bird on its top branches and an underworld monster at its roots. The famous sarcophagus in the tomb of Lord Pacal of Palenque, a Maya king of the seventh century AD, depicts the deceased king rising up from the massive head of the underworld monster, the World Tree carved with hieroglyphs behind him and an elaborately feathered bird looking down at him from its perch at the top. The Aztecs had two orders of knights, the Eagle Knights and the Jaguars, representing the fierce predatory powers of heavens and earth fronting their armies. Serpents, specifically deadly rattlesnakes, represented cosmic power, often carved or painted with feathers and horns to indicate it encompasses more than the realm of the underworld. In Nahuatl, language of the Aztecs, this was Quetzalcoatl, "quetzal" the prized gorgeously plumed tropical bird and "coatl," "snake." Quetzalcoatl was Lord of the Winds, bringer of wisdom, and the deity who danced our present world into being out of the ashes of cataclysmic destruction, hence founder of dynastic rule. Conch shells, blown as trumpets, were his symbol, especially the conch's pearly spiral columella resembling a vortex.

Back in the second millennium BCE, the Olmec who built Mexico's first large pyramidal mounds, cities, stone sculptures, and large-scale maize farming conceived of earthly power born of the Jaguar Lord of the Earth. The earth itself they pictured as a huge serpent, caves as its gaping jaws. We don't know their religious texts, since they were just developing writing and their glyphs, in short inscriptions, are not deciphered, but a number of statues and figurines show an infant with a fearsome jaguar face, carried in the arms of a fully human man, as if the founder of their dynasty claimed descent from a jaguar consorting with a human. Three stone statues in a row in an Olmec city are a seated jaguar facing two men kneeling to it. Olmec also carved giant portrait heads of their rulers, apparently using the stone block thrones on which the kings had seated themselves, turning the blocks into memorials after their deaths. It is a curious fact noticed by the great British archaeologist V. Gordon Childe that realistic portraiture appears only when large populations organize into states.

Mexican nations revered the maize sustaining their people. It was shown either as a maiden paired with a male hunter, or a beautiful young man. Maiden or youth, maize shyly looks out from its protective green husk. It needs water, so sculptured panels and paintings may add a watery world beneath it, with shells and fishes and crocodiles, the last of course masters of the watery domain – bull crocodiles do a roaring thrashing dance in the water that is said to be unforgettable! Deer are the free-ranging food complementing maize, and may be pictured with flowering plants as in a lush meadow. Butterflies were said to be souls of men and women who had died sacrificing their lives for their country, men in battle and women in childbirth. Aztecs thought of flowers and birdsongs worshipping the gods, nature's altars and hymns, and metaphorically referred to their own religious ceremonies as "flower and song."

Many Mexican religious symbols are shared with North American First Nations, translated into familiar forms. Hawks and eagles are generally classed as varieties of raptors, more or less interchangeable, with hawks and peregrine falcons favored in the Eastern Woodlands. Bears substituted for jaguars north of the feline's range. Quetzalcoatl serpents are clearly reproduced on Mississippian artifacts in the Late Prehistoric period of the Eastern Woodlands, and also dancing men with conch columella spiral necklace pendants, like the Mexican Postclassic (Late Prehistoric) Quetzalcoatl as dynasty founders.

Master of the waters is described as a great serpent-tailed, horned creature that roils up the waves in storms and devours unlucky people who fall into its realm. One name for it is Underwater Panther, giving it a feline body with serpent tail; sometimes it isn't directly named lest it be aroused, called Great Brown One, or metaphorically in comparison with bison, Underwater Bull. Adventures of miraculously conceived "Hero twins" are recounted in Mexican and many North American religious texts, one being more good and his twin more wild or dangerous. Another very widespread concept is that Venus the Morning Star is a young warrior, impregnating Evening Star or a human woman he takes to wife, and beseeched to lead one's soldiers successfully into battle as he leads the sun to its full brilliance in the day.

Southwestern religions, both Puebloan and Hohokam/'O'odham, evidence Late Prehistoric contacts with Mexico, similar to those in the Southeast in the same period: Quetzalcoatl, Hero Twins, Jaguar (Mountain Lion) Lord of the Earth and Beasts (hunting), Maize Deity, and more than the Southeast, rain spirits coming from the mountains. The fact that maize was brought into the Southwest and planted by the middle of the second millennium BCE, northwestern Mexico style pottery more than a thousand years later in the early first millennium AD, and Mexican-made copper bells and tropical macaws centuries after that, indicates series of contacts mediated through existing settlements in northwestern Mexico and the Southwest. Intensification of contacts beginning in the tenth century AD was in part stimulated by a growing Mexican fashion valuing turquoise for ornaments: substantial quantities of turquoise were imported from the American Southwest, and copper bells and macaws may have been exchanged for it. Because live macaws had to be constantly tended and new owners in the Southwest instructed on their care and feeding, the hundreds of macaw remains in Southwestern pueblos are clear proof of direct relationships between Southwesterners and Mexicans, in the context of transferring animals used in religious displays in both regions. That religious ideas accompanied the transfers is hardly to be doubted.

Architecture

Olmec, second half of the second millennium BCE, began Mexican architectural styles as well as sculpture and full-scale maize agriculture. Their farmers lived in households of home and small outbuildings around a patio or courtyard, dooryard garden adjacent and cornfields beyond it. Households were dispersed, often in hamlets, out from towns where the aristocracy resided. That higher class lived on a higher level, on acropolis hills or, where swampy lowlands predominated, on earth platforms. Earth pyramid platform mounds were erected in the towns around plazas with large stone sculptures. North of the Olmec kingdoms around the Isthmus of Tehuantepec (south-central Mexico), other kingdoms used natural landmark hills, building plazas, temples, and aristocrats' residences on lower slopes or at the base, with commoners' households and fields spreading out from the elite center. This basic idea of urban design, a "green city" integrated with its suburbs, contrasts with "stone-girt cities" such as were common in Europe, densely packed within strong defensive walls, their supporting farmers in villages distinct from the urban center. "Green cities," not unique to America, were a usual form in much of southern and eastern Asia and Africa. There might be a walled Forbidden City in the center, secluding the divinely descended king, his concubines and servants, and high priests.

Each Mexican city had its particular layout of plazas and platform mounds topped with temples and palaces. Many had similar orientations for major mounds and buildings, determined by astronomical sightlines. Spanish invaders saw aqueducts bringing clean water into cities, and in the Aztec capital underlying present Mexico City, beautiful gardens with exotic plants and animals. Chaco, in New Mexico, and Cahokia at present St Louis, both flourishing in the eleventh and twelfth centuries AD, were the largest cities in prehistoric America north of Mexico. Chaco built in stone slabs, Cahokia in timber now long decayed away. Cahokia reproduced the basic Mexican urban plan of grids of rectangular plazas bordered by platform mounds, its suburbs and farmsteads stretching over its floodplain setting. Chaco lies in a small river valley ("wash") bordered by steep bluffs, its buildings strung along the wash; perhaps because of their arid plateau surroundings, it and other Southwestern pueblos don't reflect the basic Mexican plan the way Cahokia does. Lesser Mississippian towns in the Mississippi Valley and Southeast have earth platform mounds and plazas without the replication of these units that makes Cahokia so extensive a built landscape.

On a more mundane level, Mexico, the Southeast and Midwest Plains shared the custom of cleansing in a sauna-like sweat house. These structures are small, even ephemeral north of Mexico, therefore seldom identified by archaeologists, although some postulate that small round constructions near Mississippian houses may have been sweatlodges; alternately, they may have been enclosures for smoking tanned hides to make them resistant to stiffening. Pole-wattle-and-daub houses (wattle is pliable branches interwoven around upright poles, daub is plastered mud or clay) were another common construction, but such houses are found worldwide in warmer climates. Mississippian houses and Puebloan rooms are rectangular, a change from earlier round or oval houses, possibly copied from dwellings typical of Mexico, but again, hardly distinctive of Mexico.

American Originals

In reaction to the earlier emphasis on Nuclear America as the Mother Culture, archaeologists in the later twentieth century emphasized differences between American First Nations and Mexico. Nowhere north of Mexico are there pyramid mounds faced with finely dressed stone veneers, or fine stone masonry buildings – Puebloan stone slab masonry does not reach the artistically proportioned, carved and stuccoed noble edifices of the great Mexican cities. Nowhere were there bureaucratically supervised large daily urban markets comparable to those of the Mexican kingdoms. So far as archaeologists can deduce, there were no armies of thousands such as the Spanish invaders contended with, pictured too in Maya murals centuries earlier. Cahokia's Monks Mound compares in awesome size to the principal pyramids of Teotihuacán and Cholula, built some centuries earlier, yet Cahokia had none of the sophisticated splendour of its Maya contemporary Chichén Itzá. Nuclear America fostered artists to a degree not seen north of Mexico, except on the Northwest Coast on the Pacific Rim.

Religious differences abound between regions of North America, reflecting persisting traditions interacting with ideas carried from other regions. Variations in the Hero Twins legends are good examples of the many guises of common motifs. A chilling area of study is that of human sacrifices, notorious in Aztec Mexico where frequent offerings of beating human hearts were believed to be required to nourish the Sun. Human sacrifice was carried out by at least one division of the Pawnee, who tied a young captive to an upright scaffold over a pit and shot her, or him, with arrows. The victim's blood dripping into the pit was held to fertilize the earth, as the maiden Evening Star's did when Morning Star entered her garden and penetrated her sexually. Abhorrent as this observance is to us, and was to many Pawnee in the 1830s when a young man dramatically rescued the last captive to be offered, this one Aztec-like ritual is radically less than the Aztecs believed obligatory. Other Mexican nations held many fewer human sacrifices than the Aztecs, still these amounted to many more than the Pawnee, the Natchez, or other nations north of Mexico. Instead of killing captives or slaves, Lakota and some others north of Mexico believed they should offer their own blood, by cutting bits of flesh, to draw the benevolent pity of the Almighty. This said, it remains reminiscent of the Aztecs that Iroquois and some of their neighbors subjected hundreds of captured enemies to frightful tortures before crowds (like public hangings in the historic US and Europe).

Skeptical archaeologists reiterate the lack of Mexican artifacts in sites or historic First Nations north of Mexico. Southwest copper bells, pyrites mirrors, macaws, and a miniscule number of ceramic sherds sum it up for that region, nothing so unequivocal for the Southeast. Mounds are actually earlier in the Southeast (Watson Brake, mid-fourth millennium BCE, a circle of eleven mounds) than in Mexico, although no one seems to infer that Olmec learned mound-building from Louisianans. For the Southeast, it comes down to maize, a certain import from Mexico during the Late Archaic, at the end of the fourth millennium BCE. Some information on its cultivation must have accompanied the seeds. At that time, the American Southeast and Mexico were similar in that plant cultivation was generally practiced, on several seed crops, by villagers politically independent yet connected to inter-regional trade. Nuclear America was then a broad tropical to warm temperate zone arcing from the central Midwest down through Mexico and Guatemala (excluding the desert Southwest). Numerous rivers facilitated travel, and since the islands of the Caribbean had been colonized, people were traversing the Gulf of Mexico. Pottery-making apparently crossed north out of northernmost South America.

Greater divergence developed toward the end of the second millennium BCE, Olmec and subsequently the Classic civilizations of the Maya and Teotihuacán achieving world-class architecture, art, and large populations governed through bureaucratic officials, while Southeasterners sustained smaller populations in more dispersed settlements, leaders who seem more warlords than monarchs, and a limited repertoire of art compared to Mexico. Politics intruded, complicating contacts. Hopewell, contemporary with transitions in Mexico to Early Classic kingdoms, had neither urban societies nor fully agricultural economies. Elements of designs on some tomb pottery resemble some, earlier, in Mexico; otherwise, these temperate-latitude societies are quite distinct from those far to the south.

Cahokia and, after its collapse, other Mississippian societies swing the balance back. Increased contacts with Postclassic Mexico, indisputably evidenced in the contemporary Southwest, are implied by Mississippian iconography. These contacts between major kingdoms such as Cortés met in 1519 and the smaller ones De Soto ravished twenty years later would have been on a quite different order, carried on by professional merchants and diplomats, than contacts between villagers four thousand years earlier.

Conclusion

Nuclear America domesticated maize, thereby laying the economic foundation for all the American urban civilizations. This cultigen, its symbiotic beans and squash "sisters," its raised-bed cultivation method, and its symbolic power personified as a beautiful youth or young woman, flower of life, underlies American cultures throughout the Eastern Woodlands and Southwest. Over the millennia during which maize cultivation gradually improved through countless experiments, colonizations of new areas and continued contacts, waning and waxing as populations changed and political forms interposed, reinforced some similarities and from time to time introduced new ones. First Nations of the southern half of the United States cannot be understood without reference to developments in Mexico and the Gulf of Mexico. That global perspective cannot overshadow the variety of First Nations, their largely independent histories and dynamic relationships. The following chapters describe these, by geographic regions.

Research Puzzles

It would seem obvious – it did to archaeologists a century ago – that American First Nations raising maize shared more than the seed corn itself. People had been in contact to observe, or be told, how to plant and cultivate corn and prepare it for eating. Tracing the spread of maize cultivation in detail turned out to be an ongoing research puzzle. Botanists debated for decades whether maize had a wild ancestor, or was a mutant or hybrid of the wild Mexican grass teosinte. Maize was grown in small quantities for a thousand or more years in Mexico and the United States, before becoming the intensively farmed staple food seen by European invaders. For what purpose small quantities of maize were grown is not known (a snack food?).

If growing maize was not the simple spread of a basic foodstuff, it could not have been part of a simple movement of related religious and architectural ideas. We now know that sets of mounds go back earlier in the Lower Mississippi Valley than the Olmec; that pottery-making seems to have crossed the Gulf of Mexico from northern South America to Florida and Georgia, independently of maize cultivation; that the Aztec conception of a maize goddess was not general in Mesoamerica, nor in the American Southwest and Southeast. In other words, maize proves contacts, but these were multiple and there was no package of "Nuclear American culture."

Research on contacts between the major regions of North America, including Mexico, took a back seat to establishing through archaeology the culture histories of the regions. Finding contacts looks like chasing will-o'-the-wisps, compared to the solid building-up, through field surveys and excavation, of sequences of settlements and artifacts in a locality. It's sobering to realize that even the journey of Hernando de Soto and his army of men, horses and pigs, through the Southeast, 1539–41, is difficult to trace archaeologically, in spite of several accounts written afterward by participants or through interviews with them. We can distinguish between the few definite and specific data of inter-American contact such as tropical macaws in the Southwest and Southwestern turquoise in Mexico, and similarities that seem too detailed to have arisen by chance: for example, figures engraved on conch-shell cups in Late Prehistoric eastern Mexico and the American Southeast, where the conch shells must have come from the Gulf of Mexico or Florida. Given the abundant evidence for pre-conquest long-distance trade and travel in the Americas, the puzzle is to disentangle and document contacts through foreign objects (like macaws and conch shells) or close matches in art such as the katcina figures in the Southwest and Mississippian engravings of costumed dancers and symbols in the Southeast, both fitting contemporary Postclassic Mexican images. "Nuclear America" is not one but several jigsaw puzzles.

Bibliographical Note

David L. Lentz (ed.), *Imperfect Balance: Landscape Transformations in the Precolumbian Americas* (New York, 2000) discusses pre-conquest plant domestication and agricultural systems throughout the Americas. Cobb, Maymon and McGuire's chapter, in Jill E. Neitzel (ed.), *Great Towns and Regional Polities in the Prehistoric American Southwest and Southeast* (Albuquerque, NM, 1999), pp. 165–81 summarizes debates over Mexican influences on the Southwest and Southeast; other essays in this volume compare the two American regions.

Note

1. Suzanne K. Fish, "Hohokam Impacts on Sonoran Desert Environment," David L. Lentz (ed.), *Imperfect Balance: Landscape Transformations in the Precolumbian Americas* (New York, 2000), pp. 251–80.

References

Cobb, Charles R., Jeffrey Maymon, and Randall H. McGuire (1999), "Feathered, Horned, and Antlered Serpents: Mesoamerican Connections with the Southwest and Southeast," in Jill E. Neitzel (ed.), *Great Towns and Regional Polities in the Prehistoric American Southwest and Southeast.* Albuquerque, NM: University of New Mexico Press, pp. 165–81.

Lentz, David L (ed.) (2000), *Imperfect Balance: Landscape Transformations in the Precolumbian Americas.* New York: Columbia University Press. Chapters in this volume that I have drawn upon directly include Suzanne K. Fish, "Hohokam Impacts on Sonoran Desert Environment," pp. 251–80; David L. Lentz, "Anthropocentric Food Webs in the Precolumbian Americas," pp. 89–121; Emily McClung de Tapia, "Prehispanic Agricultural Systems in the Basin of Mexico," pp. 121–46; and Charles S. Spencer, "Prehispanic Water Management and Agricultural Intensification in Mexico and Venezuela: Implications for Contemporary Ecological Planning," pp. 147–78.

Alan R. Sandstrom, *Corn Is Our Blood*, pp. 239–40

Where does the corn come from, where does it emerge? It comes out of the earth. All things of value come out of the earth, even money. And yet here we are disturbing the earth, occupying it and planting on it all through our lives. Well, the earth can get annoyed because we disturb it. We plant beans, corn…and camotes. Whatever it is, we plant it in the earth. We go back and forth to the market on it, and we get drunk on it but we don't give the earth any beer. We don't give her bread…and we don't give her joy.

We don't give her what she wants and that is the reason that she forsakes us and doesn't want to produce. And people say, "Let's go call the father." But you can't speak to the father. The ancient lord made her [the earth] here and the father over there. The earth asks, "When are they going to remember me, when will it be my turn, when will they light a candle? I give them all the things to eat. You are big and healthy because I give you people strength." We are living here and we are born here. We sprout like young corn. It is born and sprouts here, and for us it is likewise. You already ate, you're full and you have been so all of your life. You've been drunk. Well, likewise the earth also wants its offering. Corn is extremely delicate. Corn is our blood. How can we grab from the earth when it is our own blood that we are eating?

Recorded in Nahuatl from Aurelio of Amatlán, Mexico, in the 1970s.

Sandstrom, Alan R. (1991), *Corn Is Our Blood: Culture and Ethnic Identity in a Contemporary Aztec Indian Village*. Norman, OK: University of Oklahoma Press.

4

EARLY WOODLAND, 1000–100 BC

Early Woodland sites are distinguished by somewhat crude pottery, the earliest in central and northeastern America. Why is the presence of ceramics so meaningful here? Archaeologists put a lot of weight on pottery sherds because, unlike most artifacts, they are practically imperishable, usually abundant in a site, and can vary stylistically to a greater degree than stone or bone artifacts. Pottery clays may be mixed with pulverized stone, shell, or sherds, or with fibrous plants, they can be shaped into plates, jars, cups, large or small, globular or with elegant curves, left plain, burnished, decorated with incised lines, stamps, patterned fabric, colored slips or washes, paints, decorated on the body and on the rim with different designs, fired to blacken or to lighten. Clay sources may be determined by laboratory analysis, to answer the question of whether a pot was made locally or traded in. Sites with ceramics offer more, and more distinctive, data to archaeologists than Paleoindian or Archaic sites. So much for archaeologists' procedures: should a few crude sherds be reason to designate a new cultural "stage"?

The question hinges on how ceramics came to be made in America. An archaeologist working in the northern American Southwest thought he saw a sequence from baskets, in the Late Archaic, to clay-lined baskets, to shaped ceramics around AD 300, implying the invention of pottery there. Straightforward as the story appeared, it was soon invalidated by discoveries of earlier, very competent ceramics in the southern part of the Southwest and much earlier ceramics in Mexico, these sufficiently similar in technology and design to indicate cultural contacts across centuries. A parallel story came out of the Southeast, where archaeology seemed to show a sequence from pots carved out of soft soapstone, then ceramics of similar shape. More fine-grained archaeological research, in terms of strati-graphic cuts through series of occupations and of radiocarbon dating, revealed the ceramics to precede and the soapstone vessels to be back-woods copies of clay pots made by people on the Georgia–South Carolina coastal lowlands and inland along the Savannah River. Com-plicating the newer story, from the early fourth millennium BCE, Savannah River valley people cut soapstone into perforated slabs that they heated and lowered into water-filled cooking containers of per-ishable material. These soapstone pieces were the equivalent of con-temporary clay "Poverty Point Objects," only more durable in use than the rather friable PPOs or the pebbles generally used for stone-boiling (heated stones in a pot would raise the temperature of water to simmering). Around 2000 BCE, ceramics began to be made in the Savannah River valley, while for several centuries the people con-tinued using their soapstone heating pieces as well. Farther north in the Atlantic states, soapstone vessels and ceramic ones both come in at the beginning of the first millennium BCE.[1]

In the Southeast and in the Midwest around Kansas City, the earliest ceramics – from mid-third millennium BCE in the Southeast and late second millennium BCE around the Missouri–Kansas border – look rather crude because chopped grass and reed stems were mixed into the clay, along with more conventional temper of crushed potsherds. Experiments indicate that the fibers, which burn out during firing, leaving tubular channels in the clay, reduce the pro-blem of the pot walls sagging as the potter works, and also reduce cracking when the pot is in use. Fiber tempering went out, replaced by sand and pulverized rock, in the mid-first millennium BCE. These pots were thick, simply shaped like straight-walled or slightly flaring flower-pots, the outside impressed with coarse fabric (either wrapped around the potter's paddle, or the pot may have been molded inside a coarse bag that would separate from the pot as it dried). First-millennium BCE pots in the Northeast are less thick, conical in shape, but similarly marked over the outside by coarse fabric; the uneven surface of slight ridges and furrows impressed by the fabric weave lessens the tendency of the pot to crack while drying.

Pottery appearing in the first millennium BCE reflects steadily increasing populations and entrepreneurship through the Archaic period, stimulating innovations. Ceramics appeared late (AD 300) in the Southwest where desert or semi-arid conditions limited popula-tions until irrigation technology, like ceramics originating in Mexico, enabled agriculture. Pottery was relatively late, at the beginning of the Common Era, in the Northern Plains where bison hunting from shifting campsites was the only reliable economic base. In the East and Midwest, Late Archaic cultivation of indigenous seed plants, such as chenopods and of squash and perhaps small plots of maize, demonstrated potential for supporting larger populations. Looking at the earliest ceramics in the Southeast and Northeast, as in the southern Southwest, the earliest ceramics are technically competent. Those in the Northeast resemble ceramics from the European North Sea region, those in the Southeast resemble ceramics from northeastern South America. Earliest Southeastern and Northeastern ceramics do not resemble each other. Do these innovations indicate immigrants from across the Caribbean into the Southeast, and occasional trips across the North Atlantic by Scandinavian fishermen? or by American boatmen voyaging eastward on the Gulf Stream after they paddled out for deep-sea fishing? Most American archaeologists, unfamiliar with pre-modern boat-building and navigation, are uncomfortable thinking about such distant possibilities.

Accompanying the early ceramics in the Southeast, as later in the Southwest, were innovations in residence plans. In the Savannah River valley, where the earliest pottery is, at mid-third millennium BCE (still Late Archaic), discarded shellfish shells encircle round, level villages. Alternately in the region, large heaps or mounds of discarded shells mark riverside settlements. Meanwhile, in the uplands, camps were small, and in one instance archaeologists have found a modest pithouse (perishable walls and roof constructed up from a round dugout). Deer were a major source of food and their antlers and bones raw material for tools; turtles, fish, and hickory nuts also occur in quantities, if not in such heaps as shellfish, in these Savannah River/coastal lowlands sites. Evidence of trade between the Southeastern Atlantic lowlands and Poverty Point in Louisiana at its heyday, second millennium BCE, followed by an apparent decline in big settlements in both regions at the beginning of the first millennium BCE, suggest changes in lowland Southeast Late Archaic societies at that time.

The Northeast and Midwest seem to add ceramics to their craft repertoires around 1000 BCE without other notable innovations. However, a Wisconsin Early Woodland cemetery was, quite literally, richer than an Archaic Old Copper cemetery nearby three thousand years older.[2] The Early Woodland cemetery is on a sandy knoll overlooking a bend in a river flowing to Green Bay, a sheltered arm of Lake Michigan. Later, the knoll was favored for villages. A single man's grave at the Early Woodland cemetery contained more copper (by weight, 238 grams) than the combined copper from all the recovered

Archaic Old Copper graves. The Early Woodland man was interred with nine copper and three stone weapon points, a whetstone, sixteen stone scraper blades, nine beaver incisor teeth (probably hafted and used as knives), two dog skulls, a perforated lynx scapula, and a broad section of caribou antler. Powdered red ocher had been liberally sprinkled over the body. Lynx and, especially, caribou live far north of Green Bay, Wisconsin; these bones and two of the stone scrapers, made from a fine chert also found far from Green Bay, suggest the man may have traveled hundreds of miles before dying. Even more exotic is a substantial block of obsidian (volcanic glass) quarried from Obsidian Cliff in Yellowstone Park, Montana! Strikingly black and shiny, the obsidian and a chain of 102 copper beads, small ones at the ends and larger, heavy beads in the center, had been individually wrapped in bark and laid together on top of the cremated remains of a young woman and her infant and, as with the man, the burial was generously sprinkled with red ocher. A newborn infant had received similar burial in the cemetery, a string of 92 copper beads and a copper axe placed with the tiny corpse, while a young child had been laid on 110 leaf-shaped stone blades of cherts from southwestern Wisconsin, arranged in a triskelion design (three curving branches). Another cremated young woman had been dressed with 330 thin tubular copper beads apparently sewn in rows on her clothing, while a young woman buried without cremation wore a necklace with beads from marine shell and had a long copper awl wrapped in hide, and eight handsomely flaked but not yet sharpened blades of southern Indiana chert. Several graves contained copper crescent blades, one of which retained traces of its Y-shaped wooden handle, the ends of the crescent fastened to the forks of the handle. An older woman wearing hundreds of copper beads wrapped around her lower arms had a copper axe, a dozen of the handsome Indiana chert blades, and grapes, hazelnuts, and a bit of deer. One woman had four stone weapon points in her grave but not as offerings: they had caused her mortal wounds. Taken together, these graves in a single cemetery demonstrate the Early Woodland community procured exotic items from sources over a thousand miles away, east and west, honoring some of its members, even infants, by burying these as well as copper valuables in their graves. Not everyone was so honored, or perhaps loved – the murdered woman had no offerings – and women outnumbered men in receiving offerings.

Throughout the Eastern Woodlands in the Early Woodland period, communities responded to death as never before. Cemeteries were customarily located on knolls or terraces overlooking streams and, in addition to ornaments, the dead were often interred with large, distinctive, well-made but unused, stone blades or pendants. One archaeologist wonders whether these objects might have been whirled on the end of a thong, producing a bull-roarer sound.[3] Copious sprinkling of red ocher on burials and the precious, perhaps ritual, objects demonstrate a widespread symbolic practice.

In the Lower Mississippi Valley, relatively small round earth mounds (up to around sixteen feet high) were constructed to cover a community's dead, partially decomposed (probably on wooden platforms inside fenced areas, as historically in the Southeast) so the bones could be compactly interred. In this region, artifacts were not laid with the dead. Following, as it does in time, the Poverty Point mounds and embankments, Early Woodland in the Lower Mississippi Valley seems a rejection of those elaborate and labor-costly constructions. We must not infer degeneration because artifacts are diverse and functional, if not spectacular, and ceramics include pots with legs and designs made with stamps, incising, or punching circles. These ceramics occur at Poverty Point in its late occupations, demonstrating continuity between that extraordinary Late Archaic culture and the region's Early Woodland. That period in the Lower Mississippi Valley exhibits broad exploitation of marshes and floodplains, people living on low islands that in some cases sank slowly beneath the weight of discarded shells and other refuse, the surface of the small island kept above water level by the build-up of midden! Alligators were among the game taken by the people, who did plant squash and bottle gourds as well as harvest wild plants, fish, and hunt deer on higher ground.

Settlements in the more temperate Eastern Woodlands were sited both in river floodplains and on uplands, and it seems probable that, in both types of locale, agriculture was gaining importance. The most definitive information comes direct from human guts, dried feces in corners of the Salts and Mammoth cave system in Kentucky. Late Archaic and Early Woodland people sheltered in the mouths of these caves and rockshelters in the region, and some remarkably intrepid people penetrated as deeply as half a mile into Salts' pitch-dark maze, relying on wood torches for light. They secured a pure-white gypsum from a vein deep in the cave, for what purpose we can only guess (one archaeologist remarked that gypsum is a laxative, to which a colleague replied, "There are plenty of plant laxatives easily picked outside that frightening black hole!"). Whatever the goal of the cave explorers, they and the people at the cave mouths regularly ate seeds of cultivated chenopods (goosefoot), knotweed, a small-seeded barley, and maygrass for carbohydrates, and the oily seeds of sumpweed, squash and sunflower. Sunflowers were native farther west, brought into the Eastern Woodlands as a cultigen. The spread of pottery and the spread of cultivated grains – these several seed plants – very likely were linked, the pots needed to cook families' daily porridge. Nuts and fruits such as wild plums were still significant in the diet, as well as game and fish, but the feces prove how the cultivated seeds had become common staples.

Tobacco was a different kind of cultigen. Two species were grown in the United States at the time of the first European invasions, a strong type native to South America, and a milder type native to western America. Tobacco seeds have been identified in Middle Woodland sites in the Midwest; which species is represented is difficult to determine from the seeds, so it isn't known whether the tobacco came from west of the Rockies or from Latin America. Smoking pipes date from Early Woodland sites in the Midwest, tubular in shape with the tobacco end flaring and the mouth end narrowed. Carbonized residue in these pipes prove they were used for smoking, but whether for tobacco or for other herbs (like the kinnikinnick mixtures also smoked by American Indians) couldn't be resolved.

There is no doubt that the introduction of smoking was for ritual, not personal indulgence – even in the twentieth century, many conservative First Nations members would not casually smoke commercial cigarettes. Everyone has heard about "peace pipes," long-stemmed pipes carved of soft stone (that hardens upon exposure to air) or wood with stone bowls. These are properly termed "calumet pipes," from a French word for reed, reeds sometimes being used for pipestems. The pipe was an incense burner: instead of burning incense in a pot that could be swung as in Christian churches, or set on a stand, American Indians generally placed their tobacco incense in a small bowl attached to a tube through which air could be blown to keep the incense alight, and invoked the attention of the Almighty by waving this incense-burner toward the four cardinal directions, Above, and Below. Rituals marking alliances between nations sought the blessing of the Almighty with this invocation through incense, hence the European observers' term "peace pipe." Consecrated pipes may be brought out from their wrappings to quell quarrels, because no breaches of morality can be condoned in the presence of the sanctified instrument. Archaeologist Robert Hall[4] notes a resemblance between calumet pipes, courting flutes, and atlatls (spearthrowers, a narrow wooden board with a hook at the thrower's end). All three are related to war, the atlatl as a weapon component, the flute used – historically, at least – to draw men to join the player for a war expedition, and the calumet to solemnize alliances. True, the flute was played to attract young women for amorous expeditions, to Hall an extension of its connotation of manly virtue. The introduction of pipe smoking, so very probably as a means of incense burning, and tobacco in Early Woodland times does not imply that warfare, or even the rituals for invoking blessing on a war expedition or its cessation, were unknown in America before the Early Woodland. Pipes and tobacco seeds are the preserved material available to the archaeologist, allowing us to say we have *evidence* for a ceremony that in its general form may well have been much older than Early Woodland, and that probably was associated with war that, likewise, had been occurring earlier than that period.

Early Woodland was a time of substantive shifts in American societies. Agriculture was established alongside harvesting naturally growing foods, game, fish, and shellfish. Pottery was introduced, presumably for its superior capacity to cook the cultivated starchy seeds. Indirectly, pottery signals greater commitment to producing food rather than relying on naturally occurring sources. Related to selecting and maintaining fields, a stronger sense of territoriality appears in the development of cemeteries on knolls overlooking defendable territory, and more ritual attention to communities' dead, placing specially prepared ornaments and symbolic objects with corpses and showering them with red ocher. By the end of the first millennium BCE, these trends had climaxed in the spectacular Hopewell kingdoms of the Middle Woodland period.

Research Puzzles

A perennial problem in archaeology is to distinguish between local inventions and those imported from other societies – "independent invention" versus "diffusion." How pottery came to be made in the several regions of America is an example of the issue. Anthropologists who favor "independent invention" consider that if something was invented once, somewhere, it obviously could be invented again. Anthropologists who favor contacts between societies as the source of innovations point to historians' studies documenting the spread of such inventions as gunpowder and printing, analogies for the spread of more ancient technologies. Finds of natural objects such as obsidian or maize far from their natural occurrence demonstrate prehistoric people's long-distance travels and trade, indirectly supporting the explanation of inter-societal contacts for the innovation of pottery in at least some regions. Differences in technology and style might indicate independent invention, or, equally, might indicate local variation on an innovation taken from another society. Gaps of centuries as well as miles between similar technologies or styles might indicate independent invention, or that archaeologists have yet to discover sites bridging the apparent gap. Just to complicate matters, there are cases of craftspeople reviving much older styles, not only for today's tourist markets, but prehistorically.

Debates over independent invention versus "diffusion" (inter-societal contacts) unfortunately sometimes degenerate into charges of racism, the notion being that independent invention demonstrates the intelligence of people in a community, whereas taking an innovation from another society doesn't require brains. If that were so, Americans would be the dumbest people ever, for most of our artifacts were invented elsewhere (including gunpowder and printing, and pizza and the automobile). History and historical geography tell us that truly independent invention is rare, while taking ideas from other societies and creating variation on them very common. It's not "diffusion" *versus* independent invention, it's "diffusion" stimulating invention. Historic examples are American Indians taking horses from Spanish ranches in New Mexico and, in a little more than a century, spreading horse-riding and packing over most of America and creating distinctive breeds and styles of horse gear. Another example is Indians' use of European glass beads for embroidery, creating new techniques for ornamental beading. Curiosity and inventiveness are as characteristic of American Indians as of other humans, with results tantalizing archaeologists trying to figure out whether new types of artifacts were uniquely invented or, more likely, stimulated by contacts with other nations.

Notes

1. Kenneth E. Sassaman, "A Southeastern Perspective on Soapstone Vessel Technology in the Northeast," in Mary Ann Levine, Kenneth E. Sassaman and Michael S. Nassaney (eds), *The Archaeological Northeast* (Westport, CT, 1999), pp. 75–95.

2. Thomas Cary Pleger, "Social Complexity, Trade, and Subsistence During the Archaic/Woodland Transition in the Western Great Lakes (4000–400 BC): A Diachronic Study of Copper-Using Cultures at the Oconto and Riverside Cemeteries," unpublished dissertation submitted to the Department of Anthropology, University of Wisconsin-Madison, 1998.

KING ALFRED'S COLLEGE
LIBRARY

3.   Robert L. Hall, "A Pan-Continental Perspective on Red Ocher and Glacial Kame Ceremonialism," in Robert C. Dunnell and Donald K. Grayson (eds), *Lulu Linear Punctated: Essays in Honor of George Irving Quimby* (Ann Arbor, MI, 1983), pp. 74–107.

4.   Robert L. Hall, *An Archaeology of the Soul* (Urbana Il, 1997), pp. 109–23.

References

Hall, Robert L. (1983), "A Pan-Continental Perspective on Red Ocher and Glacial Kame Ceremonialism," in Robert C. Dunnell and Donald K. Grayson (eds), *Lulu Linear Punctated: Essays in Honor of George Irving Quimby*. Ann Arbor, MI: Anthropological Papers of the Museum of Anthropology of the University of Michigan no. 72, pp. 74–107.

Hall, Robert L. (1997), *An Archaeology of the Soul*. Urbana, IL: University of Illinois Press.

Pleger, Thomas Cary (1998), "Social Complexity, Trade, and Subsistence During the Archaic/Woodland Transition in the Western Great Lakes (4000–400 BC): A Diachronic Study of Copper-Using Cultures at the Oconto and Riverside Cemeteries," unpublished dissertation submitted to the Department of Anthropology, University of Wisconsin-Madison.

Sassaman, Kenneth E. (1999), "A Southeastern Perspective on Soapstone Vessel Technology in the Northeast," in Mary Ann Levine, Kenneth E. Sassaman and Michael S. Nassaney (eds), *The Archaeological Northeast*. Westport, CT: Bergin & Garvey, pp. 75–95.

Figure 2 Hopewell Earthworks, Marietta, Ohio (After Squier and Davis, 1848)

5

MIDDLE WOODLAND,
100 BC–AD 400

Around two thousand years ago,[1] extraordinary constructions appeared on the landscapes of the Ohio Valley. Precisely engineered geometric figures so immense that one encloses a full-size golf course, four-square-mile sets of huge geometric embankments, figures linked by orientation and sight-lines over thirty miles – the scale of Ohio Valley Middle Woodland building is truly stupendous. Nowhere else in the world are there so many, such exact and cosmically huge geometric constructions of no apparent practical use. There's no mystery about the Egyptian pharaohs' pyramid tombs, little mystery about Stonehenge's solstice-aligned temple enclosure, yet of America's Hopewell earthworks we know only that they had sophisticated builders and, one must suppose, symbolic significance.

Today, most of the Ohio Middle Woodland earthworks have been obliterated or greatly reduced by plowing, urban and suburban construction. In 1838 the Circleville Squaring Company began destruction of that pioneer Ohio town's namesake embankment.[2] Ten years later, the Smithsonian Institution's first scientific publication, *Ancient Monuments of the Mississippi Valley*, incorporated professionally surveyed maps of the Middle Woodland earthworks, knowledge saved in defiance of the colonists' determination to square the circles. Edwin Davis, a medical doctor in Chillicothe, Ohio, had collaborated with the young journalist Ephraim Squier, happily trained in civil engineering, to record accurately the astounding ancient monuments around their town. ("The Mississippi Valley" was broadly interpreted by Squier and Davis to include its tributaries such as the Ohio.) Were it not for Squier's indefatigable surveying, the majority of these mind-boggling works would be now quite lost; thanks to

Squier's maps, some of them can be located and researched through archaeological techniques.

For archaeologists, Hopewell presents two challenges: first, interpreting the massive and precise earthworks, and, second, reconciling such huge enterprises with the data indicating the builders lived in small farmsteads and hamlets strung along stream valleys. No one lived permanently within the geometric embankments. Hopewell was a unique civilization without cities. Its economy maximized resources by holding lands along the edges of the final glacial fronts of the Late Pleistocene, where glacier-molded uplands overlook outwash floodplains.

Ecological diversity and abundant water buffered the population's demands for food and wood, their reliance on indigenous plants and game giving them a reasonably secure subsistence base. Maize continued to be a minor component of the farm crops, the major crops those cultivated since the Late Archaic: chenopods (goosefoot), knotweed and maygrass for grain carbohydrates, sumpweed, squash, and sunflower for oil-rich seeds. Raspberries, elderberries, and sumac berries were fruits that flourished, along with hazelnut bushes, along the edges of cleared fields and when the fields were left fallow; these also were components of Middle Woodland farmers' cultivation plans. Hickory nuts, acorns, and black walnuts were gathered from trees, which like the berries would have benefited from the farmers' extensive clearings opening up river-valley forests. Timber so felled went into building tombs and gathering halls at the great embankment enclosures, as well as into the more lightly constructed domestic dwellings. By Late Woodland times, centuries of farming had markedly reduced the virgin forests in Ohio, allowing second-growth types of trees such as locust and pine to take over many localities.

Hopewell settlement pattern, farmsteads and hamlets within hailing distance of one another, continuously along floodplains and terraces or loosely clustered on uplands, is a pattern persisting to the present among descendants of Midwestern First Nations (much to the frustration of US government bureaucrats demanding conformity to efficient water- and sewer-line layouts). Middle Woodland relatively greater population made the pattern more visible to archaeologists than it had been earlier, when farming was less important and seasonal movements to wild harvests probably more common. Historically, farmsteads and hamlets dispersed but visible to one another ("We want to be able to yell for help but not hear our neighbors' family arguments," said one Lakota arguing against a Bureau of Indian Affairs tight grid housing scheme) embodied an ethos balancing personal autonomy with high social value on assisting community members. To maintain the settlement pattern embodying their social ethos, Midwestern First Nations moved again and again in the nineteenth century AD, just ahead of the colonizing frontier displacing them.[3]

Command of the land through keen observation of ecology, selecting those particular locations where good soil, rainfall and overall humidity, orientation to sunlight, low frost vulnerability, all combined to optimize crop success, may be reflected in the Hopewell grand geometrics imposed on the land. Or perhaps the shrewd understanding of the farmers sustained an elite wrapped up in cosmography, taking for granted the farmers' competence. We can appreciate the farmers' science; we cannot detect to what degree landlords were involved in the business of daily life, whether they lived adjacent to the great embanked enclosures or in modest houses, similar to commoners', in the countryside. There are deposits of domestic artifacts and debris just outside many enclosures, but these could result from barracks of construction workers for the enclosures.

If the homes of Hopewell nobility are not obvious, their tombs dramatically mark their status. Near present Chillicothe and the Scioto River, a tributary of the Ohio in southern Ohio, is a complex of five sites each with linked geometric embankments consisting of a large circle, a smaller circle, and a square.[4] Squier and Davis recorded each large circle having a diameter of 1700 feet, each smaller circle of 800 feet, and each square measured 1080 feet per side (that is to say, each side of a square measured *one-fifth of a mile!*); these precise measurements were duplicated in every one of the five sites miles apart. Recent measurements take a few feet off these long measurements, but Squier and Davis may have been correct for what was better preserved in the 1840s. They noted that the large circles and the squares had gateway openings, sometimes with small mounds adjacent, in their embankment walls, while the smaller circles were unbroken. Within two of the larger circles were imposing mounds covering two-thirds of an acre, not quite identical in measurements but each close to 160 feet long or wide, fifteen to thirty feet high (in the 1840s), and the larger of the two 240 feet long. Field studies begun in 1965 by civil engineer James Marshall revealed that Hopewell draftsmen began with 3–4–5 right triangles and measured in units that are either multiples or fractions of 132 feet (40.2 meters) or 187 feet (57 meters).[5] Numerous smaller mounds, composed of selected colored soils and clays, lay within or outside the embankments of these sites.

Figure 3 Newark site (Hopewell) geometric embankments, aerial photo. National Anthropological Archives, Smithsonian Institution, #196, Dache Reeves Collection.

Excavations early in the twentieth century revealed tombs in some of the mounds, and more recent excavations revealed timber buildings 35 feet long, divided into rooms with antechambers. Absence of household debris on the floors of these buildings indicate they were not residences, although whether they served as temples or council chambers cannot be told. Tombs of the principal leaders were also timber structures subsequently buried under carefully layered earth and clay. These leaders' tombs typically have a man's corpse in the center, with men and women – wives, concubines, servants or guards, we suppose – placed on earth benches around their leader. The majority of the burials in the mounds had been cremated, including sometimes those apparently accompanying a leader in death. The principal corpse in one of the tombs seems to have lain under a canopy. Rare and valuable artifacts graced the burials: spool-shaped ear ornaments covered with beaten copper, copper rectangles, some with embossed designs, and cut-out figures; sheet mica including cut-out figures; reed panpipes covered with copper; conch shells, shark teeth, barracuda jaws, and ocean turtle shell from the Atlantic; grizzly-bear canine teeth sometimes inlaid with pearls; freshwater pearl, shell, copper, and galena beads; nodules of meteoric iron; chlorite disks; platform-style smoking pipes, many with the bowls carved into animal or human shapes; figurines of men and women; knives with blades of fine flint, North Dakota translucent brown chalcedony ("Knife River flint"), and even black obsidian from Yellowstone Park; silver and a few small gold nuggets; carved bone and shell ornaments; copper celts (axes or adzes); and handsomely decorated, wellmade ceramic vessels. Deposits of valuables separate from any burials suggest temple offerings. Overall, Hopewell is the earliest American civilization to impress Euroamerican archaeologists with displays of wealth objects reminiscent of European concepts of wealth and status display.

Conspicuous consumption of rare imported materials may lend a familiar feel to Ohio Hopewell mound contents, yet relationships between the major sites are unclear. Because giant geometric enclosures are linked over miles of valley by orientation, sets of figures, and measurements, we could suppose a Hopewell lord ruled at least a watershed region; but then, why duplicate sets of enclosure figures? If each enclosure site was the ritual center of a tiny kingdom, why were they linked at such a scale? Not only are sets of figures replicated, leading out of the large octagon-shaped enclosure in the Newark, Ohio, set is a straight road built between low parallel embankments. Nineteenth-century colonists noticed many such ancient roads in southern Ohio, leading from one set of enclosures to others.[6] Hopewell art, on the stone pipes, copper plates, mica cut-outs, and no doubt in wood and on textiles (fragments of finely woven cloth from local plant fibers such as nettle have been found preserved as wrappings of copper objects), mostly shows fierce birds, pumas, bird and bear claws, warlike themes. Hopewell extensive and substantial long-distance trade needed some sort of safe-conduct for purveyors of such fragile goods as sheet mica from the southern Appalachians. Historically, descendants of Hopewell conducted formal ceremonies using the flat-stemmed calumet pipe ("peace pipe") to link nations symbolically, the leader of the visiting delegation adopted into the host group as embodiment of the spirit of a deceased host leader.[7] Valor and power such as seen in raptor birds and beasts would have been attributed to these renowned leaders, even as they extended hands in alliance.

Middle Woodland outside Ohio

Beyond southern Ohio, Hopewell flavors Middle Woodland societies from the Southeast to Kansas on the west and Ontario on the north. Mounds are common but the great geometric embankments are restricted to the Ohio heartland. Closest to Ohio Hopewell culture was that of Middle Woodland southern Illinois, where the lower Illinois River meets the Mississippi. This land holds a multitude of sloughs, lakes and marshes in broad floodplains, for this reason forming the major mid-continental flyway for migrating birds. Food was abundant, whether harvested from the wild or from cultivated chenopods, knotweed and maygrass. Topography, with bluffs far apart across the shifting floodplains, would not have favored construction of permanent sets of huge geometrics, although we don't know whether that, alone, explains their absence. Another contrast to Ohio Hopewell is that people appear to have resided in villages a day's walk (twenty kilometers, twelve miles) apart along the rivers, rather than in the more or less continuous farmsteads and hamlets found in the narrower southern Ohio valleys. Analysis of skeletons indicated family continuity within villages, less marriage between villages.

Southern Illinois Middle Woodland merits the label Hopewell through its burial mounds and associated artifacts. Like those in Ohio, Illinois Hopewell burial mounds tend to have a central male accompanied by expensive goods and retainers. These central males were usually somewhat taller than the average man in common graves, suggesting aristocratic families whose boys were better nourished than ordinary boys. (The same distinction is seen between men in aristocrats' tombs and commoner cemeteries in Europe, beginning in the Bronze Age.) Illinois Hopewell made handsome, dark burnished ceramic vessels engraved with highly stylized raptorial birds or with comb-like short lines of dots in sections alternating with burnished smooth portions. Other artifacts in the tombs are much like those in Ohio, but fewer. Small ceramic human figurines were made in both areas, with several from one village in Illinois: most depict women wearing a simple skirt and armbands, hair down their backs to the waist, one suckling a baby, another holding her child straddling her back, others standing holding a pair of objects, or sitting with legs tucked sideways beneath her, just as historic Indian women have been accustomed to sit. A male figurine wears a breechcloth, his hair in a bun, and kneels, holding a club-like object upright in front of him.

Outside the Ohio heartland, the most impressive Middle Woodland site is Pinson Mounds in southwestern Tennessee. With a geometric embankment, five rectangular platform mounds and at least seven additional mounds lying on a plateau overlooking a river floodplain, Pinson might be the southernmost truly Hopewell center, compared to thousands of other Middle Woodland sites evidencing Hopewell contact but not its full panoply of ritual. One Pinson mound covered four log tombs holding sixteen bodies, some of them wearing necklaces of freshwater pearls and headdresses of copper ornaments sewn to fiber frames. Thanks to meticulous recent excavation, this mound is known to have been constructed as a series of different-colored soils over a clay cap protecting the tombs. Distinctively decorated ceramic vessels clustered in one locality of the site indicate trade, or perhaps pilgrims, from far to the south, southern Georgia, Mobile, Alabama, and Louisiana.

In the valleys of the Missouri River and the lower Kansas River flowing into it on the Kansas–Missouri border, Kansas City Hopewell people lived like those in southern Illinois in villages at the edge of the floodplain, above the expected annual inundation level, with camps on the uplands above. Their crops, stored in many lined pits dug near the houses included marsh elder, sunflowers, squash and a little maize, along with chenopods, amaranth, and nuts that may have grown independently of cultivation. Deer, turkeys, raccoons, fish, and turtles were staples supplemented with bison and elk, prairie game available to these villages on the western border of the Hopewell cultural outreach. Kansas City Hopewell tombs in earth mounds were built on the bluffs overlooking their villages, and the graves inside were lined with dry-laid stones, differentiating the culture of these communities from Hopewell to the east. As one would expect, the expensive imported items in the tombs were meager compared to the wealth in Ohio, or even Illinois, Hopewell: a flake of obsidian, fragments of mica, a piece of galena, one Caribbean shell, a few copper tools, plain platform pipes, and some rather crude ceramic figurines.

Looking north, Hopewell mounds and artifacts occur as far as southern Wisconsin, mostly along the Mississippi Valley. Burial mounds overlay log crypts covered with bark sheets (like historic wigwams in the region), with up to several dozen corpses interred apparently over some lapse of time – i.e., natural deaths rather than sacrifices of retainers seem likely. Grave offerings include a few fine Hopewell ceramic vessels resembling those made in Illinois and equally few obsidian artifacts, freshwater pearls, plain platform pipes, silver beads, and a relative abundance of copper objects – sheets, plaques, earspools, and beads – appropriate to a region that had been an early center of copper manufactures. Fading out in central Wisconsin nearing northern colder climates, Hopewell flourished only where agriculture flourished; although its societies' economies included game, fish, and wild plants, cultivation of the indigenous crops was necessary to their way of life.

Toward the northeast, Hopewell is visible in small burial mounds with contents like those in southern Wisconsin and Michigan. Archaeologists working in the Northeast, including southern Ontario, hotly debate whether Middle Woodland people there spoke Algonkian or Iroquoian languages. Population seems to have increased considerably during the Middle Woodland – is that because people immigrated into the region; or because agriculture fueled population growth; or both, immigrants moving in alongside natives because agriculture supported greater population density? One group of archaeologists notes that the separation of Cherokee, spoken historically in the southern Appalachians, and Iroquoian languages, in the Northeast, is dated by linguists to around two thousand years ago. Prior to that divergence, Iroquoian/Cherokee ancestors were related to Proto-Siouan speakers, historically in the Midwest and Southeast. Was the homeland of these ancestors, during the Late Archaic/Early Woodland, the Midwest? or the Southeast? Did Hopewellians speak Proto-Siouan/Iroquoian? Alternately, some archaeologists see Algonkian speakers moving into the Northeast in Middle Woodland, from the Great Lakes region. Historically, Algonkian languages covered much of the Middle Atlantic and Northeast United States as well as the northern Midwest and Canada east of the Rockies. It is plausible that both Iroquoians and Algonkians moved into the North-east, absorbing people whose languages disappeared well before European contacts. Yet another possibility, to be discussed in the next chapter, is that the Algonkians were Middle Woodland immi-grants and Iroquoians invaded centuries later in the Late Woodland period.

In the South, historically the dominant indigenous language group has been Muskogean, comprising Creek, Seminole, Miccosukkee, Alabama, and Choctaw-Chickasaw. Muskogean languages were found exclusively in the Southeast, along with languages such as Natchez, Tunica, and Calusa that died out before linguists could study their relationships, and Catawba (in the Carolinas) and Yuchi (in eastern Tennessee), Catawba definitely and Yuchi probably related to Midwestern Siouan languages. Significantly, in the Southeast as in the Northeast, languages apparently diverged from parent proto-Muskogean and also Siouan-Catawba around two thousand years ago. Hopewell connected all of the eastern half of America from the Rockies to the Atlantic, Great Lakes and St Lawrence to the Gulf of Mexico, and at the same time, during its heyday a number of societies split, with branches settling into what became historic homelands in many cases hundreds of miles apart. The linguistic and political map of America toward the decline of Hopewell was quite different from what it had been a millennium earlier at the beginning of Early Woodland.

Middle Woodland in the lower Mississippi Valley and the Gulf lowlands opens with ceramics displaying the distinctive Hopewell raptor bird motif and decoration contrasting plain burnished with infilled stippled zones. Relatively small conical burial mounds were built, covering a number of corpses probably representing the natural deaths of residents of nearby villages with wooden houses and storage pits. In the highlands of northern Alabama, Middle Woodland villages buried many of their dead in wooden boat-like coffins placed in caves; whether in caves or in burial mounds, the deceased were given the usual Hopewell artifacts – copper pendants, earspools and celts, freshwater pearls, galena, elbow (rather than platform) pipes, and cups and beads made from marine shells. One cave is so dry that the trough-like coffins, cane mat shrouds, and wooden bowls and plates were preserved. Oddly, northern Alabamans manufactured ceramics and decorated some with Hopewell-style zoned designs but did not leave pots with their dead. Southern Alabamans took advantage of the Gulf coast to procure teeth of sharks, alligators, and barracuda that could be traded north, as well as minerals – salt from saline springs, ocher for paint, and fine quartzite and chalcedony for stone tools and weapon points.

The most southeasterly sector, Florida and adjacent southern Georgia and Alabama, contributed its subtropical products to the Hopewell world and incorporated style concepts in its ceramic decoration, while ultimately resisting whatever led central Hopewellians to give up great geometric embankments and sumptuous tombs under mounds. Never as spectacular as Ohio Hopewell, the far southeasterners maintained their somewhat more modest art and the practice of wealth-laden burials under mounds generations longer than classic Hopewell in the central Eastern Woodlands. On the broad Gulf coastal plain, about AD 300 – i.e., at the close of classic Hopewell to the north – villages exploiting marine fish and shellfish created embankments in the shape of rings, horseshoes, or rectangles, not (it seems) purely as constructions but to dispose of refuse in an orderly manner outside the residential area. The region's semi-tropical climate called for lightly built, airy shelters like the present-day Seminole *chickees* that leave virtually no structural traces archaeologically. Open plazas in the middle of the midden-ringed villages served for community gatherings, and both burial and platform mounds were constructed within the ring. Deposited within the east sides of burial mounds were groups of fine painted ceramics, many modeled as human, animal, or plant effigies, or more conventionally shaped bowls decorated with stylized carved-stamp impressions, Hopewell-like stippling, or incised designs. At the largest of these southeastern towns of the first millennium AD, Kolomoki in Georgia, a mound with four tombs built of logs and stone included bodies that may have been sacrificed to accompany the deceased noble, although alternately it could be that they had died earlier, or in war, and had been interred in the ritual entombment.

Crystal River in northwest Florida is the Middle Woodland site most provocatively interpreted.[8] Two limestone boulders with incised lines, set up on the central plaza near two of its four mounds, might be provincial attempts to copy Maya cities with their hieroglyphic stelae on plazas. Limestone is a soft stone, especially in a humid climate, and the Crystal River boulders are difficult to decipher; in any case, no one thinks they were inscribed with actual Maya glyphs. Across the Gulf of Mexico from the populous Maya kingdoms with their regular water routes for trade, Crystal River nobles may well have visited those gleaming cities and imitated their layouts. Early in the twentieth century, a wealthy archaeologist working from his private houseboat-laboratory hired laborers to dig out some of the Crystal River mounds, as he did hundreds of other mounds throughout the Southeast and, altogether, about 600 individuals were disinterred, ranging from complete skeletons through bundles of disarticulated bones to lone skulls. Pipes and quantities of copper artifacts give a Hopewellian look to grave offerings, amplified with unusually valuable ornaments such as earspools covered with silver or meteoric iron, in one example with pearl insets. Crystal River was certainly not a Maya colony, and its two upright boulders in the plaza perhaps were not intended to look like Maya stelae. It was a busy town for about a thousand years, manufacturing its own fine wares and importing and exporting throughout the Southeast, into the Midwest, and quite possibly across the Gulf.

The Middle Woodland period climaxed trends in population growth and increasing societal complexity. Trans-America routes brought beautiful manufactures, sophisticated decorative styles, and exotic materials to an aristocratic class symbolized (as in Europe) by feared predatory animals – hawks (as in Europe, eagles), pumas/lions, bears. As in Europe during its Bronze and Iron Ages, up to Roman conquests, nobles were interred in log tombs covered with earth as high as two- or three-storey buildings, accompanied by ceramic serving vessels, jewelry, expensive metal ornaments, and sometimes sacrificed retainers or slaves. In Europe one would have heard trumpets, in America, the music of panpipes. Similar marks of social ranking could be seen in Latin America, Asia, Africa, and Pacific islands, raised to a stupendous scale around the Mediterranean, in southern Asia and China, Mexico, and Peru. Hopewell geometric embankments remain unique, embodying mathematical knowledge as no other civilization envisaged.

Research Puzzles

The dominant question in Middle Woodland studies is, for what purpose were the huge Ohio geometric earthworks built? A related question is, what social purpose did they serve? (Their builders' purpose may have involved ideas of cosmology and supernatural power, while the actual effect of the constructions, in human social terms, may have been to ally and integrate communities.) It is curious to note that in Iron Age Europe, first millennium BCE, similar log tombs under earth mounds were built for aristocrats, similarly accoutered with fine ceramic vessels and valuable ornaments evidencing long-distance trade. In Classical Greece, at this time, geometry was a major intellectual interest, with Pythagoras and his followers investing mystical meanings to geometric figures – but no one in Europe built huge earth embankments of precise geometric forms. Most archaeologists assume that the parallels between Iron Age Europe and eastern North America represent a tendency for societies of similar population densities in subsistence-agricultural economies to mark aristocrats' status with prominent tombs and expensive grave offerings, and in similar temperate forested regions, to build the tombs of logs covered with earth. It doesn't seem possible to *prove* that this is a universal human tendency (we would need many more cases to indicate it happened regularly), nor is there any brute evidence that Europeans or Americans visited one another across the Atlantic in the first millennium BCE. The possibility of trans-Atlantic visits cannot be denied, neither can the premise that societies comparable in density, economics, and environment would be likely to build similar tombs for aristocrats. Either way, the Ohio Hopewell geometric earthworks remain unique, the conscious purpose of their builders and their societal effect unknown.

Notes

1. The conventional notations "BC" and "AD" impose an inappropriate Christian chronology upon histories. "BCE" means "Before the Common Era," accepting that the last two millennia have been so involved with Romano-Christian societies that they constitute a Common Era. "CE" then becomes the notation for the past two millennia. Good intentions notwithstanding, these notations still impose an ethnocentric Western standpoint upon all histories. For this book, I have chosen to use BCE for times prior to 2000 years ago, retaining the familiar "BC" without imposing "Christ" upon societies remote from that personage. To maintain maximum clarity for students, I use AD for the most recent two millennia, because "CE" may be confusing for students unaccustomed to academic fine-tuning. Most readers will be comfortable with the notion that we live in "years of our Lord [or Creator]," *Anni Domini.*

2. Roger G. Kennedy, *Hidden Cities* (New York, 1994), p. 241. Kennedy's lively book describes the history of antiquarian researches into Hopewell and Mississippian sites, emphasizing the policy of Thomas Jefferson and his advisor, Albert Gallatin, to record indigenous history and antiquities. Jefferson's policy was ignored under mid-nineteenth-century Manifest Destiny propaganda, to the degree that even an eminent US historian such

as Kennedy (Director of the American History Museum of the Smithsonian Institution, then Director of the National Park Service) was until late in his career, ignorant of these pre-Columbian civilizations.

3. Joseph B. Herring, *The Enduring Indians of Kansas* (Lawrence, KS, 1990).

4. Ephraim G. Squier and Edwin H. Davis, *Ancient Monuments of the Mississippi Valley* (Washington DC, 1848; reprinted 1998), plates 20, 21, pp. 56–60.

5. James A. Marshall, "Astronomical Alignments Claimed to Exist on the Eastern North American Prehistoric Earthworks and the Evidence and Arguments Against Them," *Ohio Archaeologist* 45(1) (1995): 4–16.

6. Kennedy, *Hidden Cities*, pp. 52–60.

7. Robert L. Hall, *An Archaeology of the Soul* (Urbana, IL, 1997), pp. 156–7. Hall, who is himself Mohican from the emigrant Stockbridge–Mohican community in Wisconsin, sees the calumet pipestem as a symbolic form of the atlatl, retained in ritual after its use as weapon armature became obsolete with the importation of bows and arrows. Hall is aware, too, of the phallic form of the atlatl-calumet, significant in begetting the new person (the adoptee).

8. Ripley P. Bullen, "Stela at the Crystal River Site, Florida," *American Antiquity* 31(4) (1966): 861–5.

References

Bullen, Ripley P. (1966), "Stela at the Crystal River Site, Florida," *American Antiquity* 31(4): 861–5.

Hall, Robert L. (1997), *An Archaeology of the Soul.* Urbana, IL, University of Illinois Press.

Herring, Joseph B. (1990), *The Enduring Indians of Kansas.* Lawrence, KS: University Press of Kansas.

Kennedy, Roger G. (1994), *Hidden Cities.* New York: Free Press and Penguin.

Marshall, James A. (1995), "Astronomical Alignments Claimed to Exist on the Eastern North American Prehistoric Earthworks and the Evidence and Arguments Against Them," *Ohio Archaeologist* 45(1): 4–16.

Marshall, James A. (2000), "The Prehistoric Earthworks of Eastern North America, Their Mathematics, and Implications for the Study of Culture," paper presented April 22, 2000, Central States Anthropological Society annual meeting, Bloomington, IN.

Squier, Ephraim G. and Edwin H. Davis (1848), *Ancient Monuments of the Mississippi Valley.* Washington DC: Smithsonian Institution. Reprinted by the Smithsonian, 1998.

Map 3 Western United States (Chapters 6, 8, 9)

6

THE WEST COAST

The west coast of North America is a segment of the Pacific Rim. Its history reflects its connections to Asia, connections not yet well charted but evidenced by such items as iron knives used for many centuries before European contacts. United States territory here is broken by Canada's British Columbia, the classic Northwest Coast cultures primarily in that province but extending into southeast Alaska and the state of Washington. Most of coastal Alaska, and the Aleutians, have been occupied by communities hunting sea mammals and fishing with sophisticated technology, while interior Alaskan nations depend on land hunting and stream fishing in an environment that can support only very low population densities. In contrast, California had one of the highest population densities in aboriginal America, supported by rich marine resources coupled with land game, nut orchards, and fields of sown indigenous seed grasses. Great as the differences are, trade linked region to region, and the coastal and Western Cordillera mountain chains limited contacts or movements eastward into the heart of the continent.

Chapter 1 discussed the argument for migrations into North America from northeastern Asia along the coastal plains of the Late Pleistocene. This scenario replaces a simpler picture of people trekking eastward across Beringia and then fanning out into North America: the mountain chains are older than any humans in America and would have channeled people southward, especially when continental glaciers covered most of Canada. California has representatives of all the principal language families of North America, presumably indicating some families stayed in bountiful California when others in their communities moved on. (Alternatively, people could have been moving westward once America was populated, and found the ocean blocked further migration, inducing them to settle.) Alaska, on the other hand, seems to have received later migrations out of northeast Asia, both the coast-adapted Inuit whose eastward expansion through the Arctic eventually brought them into Greenland about the same time Norse from Scandinavia were colonizing there, and the Dené who now fill inland Alaska and western Canada.

This chapter describes these contrasting regions, looking first at California, then at the United States' northwestern corner and its outlier in southeastern Alaska. The chapter will follow interpretations of these histories at odds with a position that dominated anthropology textbooks, claiming West Coast societies were small, egalitarian groups living from wild resources. The anomaly that West Coast population densities were among the highest on the continent, whereas wild resources normally support only relatively low human densities, was explained away by assuming the resources were exceptionally bountiful.

It may sound facetious, but the evaluation of West Coast societies seems to have been based on a nineteenth-century scale that degree of civilization is gauged by amount of clothing – nineteenth-century European modes with multiple layers leaving only face and hands exposed were equated with the apex of evolution, "naked savages" were the lowest. Californians enjoyed a climate encouraging wearing next to nothing, the equivalent of today's bikinis, and Northwest Coast people generally coped with their mild drizzle by wearing raincapes but not much else. Ergo, West Coast peoples were "naked savages." Alaskans, of course, were well covered with carefully tailored clothing, but since most of it was made from animal skins, it could be ranked lower than woven-fabric clothes. Biblical accounts starting history with a naked Adam and Eve, then a skin-clad Esau too stupid to understand his more sophisticated brother wearing woven fabric, were taken as the revealed model for human development.

By the 1980s, ethnohistorians had compiled observations by Europeans, including Russians extending their empire along the Pacific Rim, and oral histories from First Nations, and archaeologists were discovering remains that were testimony to societies with class structure, professional artists and traders, organized warfare, and other traits associated with civilizations. French anthropologist Claude Lévi-Strauss, who had studied Northwest Coast societies through the massive ethnographies compiled by Franz Boas and his Kwakiutl-affiliated collaborator George Hunt, broke through the nineteenth-century model of savages by comparing these societies to the medieval

French. Lévi-Strauss was struck by the use of the term "house" in both cultures to designate a noble family, its manor and lands, and its serfs or tenant families.[1] He realized the physical house, the French manor or the Northwest Coast huge timber lineage house, was the metaphor for class-structured, resource-controlling social groups. This view of aristocrat-managed feudal societies fit the data for technologies for producing quantities of food and goods similar to commercial fishing and resource management.

Canadian courts have been confronted with territorial claims by British Columbia First Nations arguing against the nineteenth-century imperial model picturing them as naked savages. The tenacity of that pernicious model is worth pondering. In *Delgamuukw v. The Queen*, 1991, Chief Justice Allan McEachern, presiding, declared that the Gitksan and Wet'suwet'en nations petitioning the court for restoration of homeland territories should not be granted these lands because they were no longer

> living off the land in pristine wilderness…a remote and
> virtually inaccessible territory…being of a culture…where
> everyone looked after himself or perished….The plaintiffs'
> ancestors had no written language, no horses or wheeled
> vehicles, slavery and starvation was not uncommon, and there
> is no doubt, to quote Hobbs [*sic*], that aboriginal life in the
> territory was, at best, "nasty, brutish and short."[2]

Quite literally Eurocentric – the Gitksan and Wet'suwet'en never considered their territories to be "remote" or "inaccessible" – McEachern wrote that "Nearly every word of testimony, given by expert and lay witnesses, has both a factual and cultural perspective,"[3] then dismissed statements on the plaintiffs' territorial and societal organization as "cultural," not "factual." He stated that "in the absence of any written history, wheeled vehicles, or beasts of burden," the Gitksan and Wet'suwet'en "fall within a much lower, even primitive order."[4]

Such was the opinion of nineteenth-century United States immigrants to California, some of whom enjoyed a Sunday sport of shooting Indians. Beginning with eighteenth-century enslavement of Indians to support Spanish garrisons, abetted by missionaries forcing the people to live in crowded barracks rife with disease, then the nineteenth-century wanton slaughter and continuing enslavement for immigrants' enterprises, population of California indigenous nations fell drastically, and their societies were reduced to remnant hamlets. Ethnography in the early twentieth century failed to take fully into account these historical diminutions of population and territories, instead describing California nations as "tribelets" subsisting on wild resources. Land claims filed by many of these remnant nations in the second half of the twentieth century amassed much data indicating indigenous agriculture and land management, organized fisheries, and established trade using shell monies. Prehistoric California, glimpsed by Francis Drake in 1579, resembled the present populous, busy state far more than Alfred Kroeber and other anthropologists realized when they interviewed survivors living on the margins of the rich valleys taken from their forebears.

California

Evidence for human occupations in California during the Terminal Pleistocene and early Holocene is infrequently discovered, no doubt due to sea-level rise in the Holocene and floodplain deposits deeply burying valley sites. As in the rest of the continent, a combination of millennia of population growth plus sites both more numerous, somewhat larger, and less likely to be hidden under coastal waters or deep soil overburden results in more archaeological knowledge for the Late Archaic, *c.* 4000–2000 BCE, and subsequent periods. Indications that the basic subsistence economy common in California was already utilized in the Middle Archaic, *c.* 6000–4000 BCE, come from sites in the Santa Clara Valley south of San Francisco, where metates and manos (slab rock base and hand-held stone grinder milling sets) were found. These durable artifacts are used to grind the seeds of grass-like native grains as well as, eventually, maize. Direct evidence of fish did not appear, but a shell bead and a stone that might be a net weight suggest use of aquatic resources.

Late Archaic societies in central California, like those in the Eastern Woodlands, built modest burial mounds. Graves usually include artifacts for each corpse, the bodies themselves laid with heads to the west. Many corpses wore shell necklaces made from the small marine snail *Olivella* by removing the closed end, or by turning flat pieces into squares or disks, shapes used for abalone-shell ornaments as well. Whether measured strings of these shell beads served as money, as they did historically in California (like wampum shell beads in the East), cannot be deduced from the archaeological context. Chipped stone javelin and spear points and knife blades were common, in one grave with a bone hook remaining from the wooden spearthrower (atlatl) originally placed with the javelins. Antler points for trident fish spears, along with bone fishhooks and bones from the prey, sturgeon and salmon down to small fish, attest river exploitation complementing land game. Metates and manos, for grinding seeds, stone mortars with pestles for crushing acorns, and twined baskets rounded out the subsistence toolkits.

Standing out in the California Late Archaic are hundreds of beautifully polished ground stone pendants, termed charmstones by local archaeologists. Whereas in the Eastern Woodlands, Late Archaic artistry in small ground stone sculptures was expended on weights for atlatls, in California the objects do not seem suited for use with atlatls, or any other discernible practical purpose. Nearly all the "charmstones" were perforated at one end, and a few still bear a bit of asphaltum with the impression of string that suggests they were suspended. They don't seem to have been pendants on necklaces, for which they would be rather large. Stones selected for the objects include alabaster, serpentine, steatite, and diorite, and some have small square shell beads inlaid on one face. Shapes are abstract (at least to our eyes), trapezoids, ovals, regular or elongated diamonds. The "charmstones" don't divulge their purpose, but they do tell us that, by the Late Archaic, California settlements supported artisans with the time and experience to create non-utilitarian objects out of beautiful stones. We can guess that other artisans worked in perishable materials, particularly basketry. These peoples' lives were certainly not "nasty, brutish, and short...where everyone looked after himself or perished."

During the second millennium BCE, with sea level stabilized, California societies increased in population and more intensively exploited regional resources, differentiating the coast from the inland Central Valley and the Sierra. Present-day California, the state, includes desert in its southeast, but this desert is better viewed as part of the Southwest and will be described in the next chapter. From the point of view of archaeologists, the principal regions had separate populations; their apparent distinctive material cultures, however, may reflect toolkits for different resources rather than ethnic distinctions. There was trade across regions, and individuals, families, or even villages moved to harvest seasonal products. California, with dramatic contrasts in environments as close as two sides of a narrow valley – one side dry, with chaparral, the other side shaded and filled with trees – is a good example of the complementary views obtained from history and archaeology, the latter exhibiting material culture while the former tells of linguistic and political divisions.

Linguists suggest the indigenous language stocks in California may have become established in their historic homelands around four thousand years ago, i.e., once sea level and climates similar to today stabilized. A hypothesis derived from a combination of linguistic analyses and archaeological data posits the earliest California languages to be Yuki and related Wappo, spoken historically in northwestern California. Next, groups speaking Hokan languages are hypothesized to have entered California, or perhaps to have expanded from Paleoindian societies in California: Hokan includes Pomo, Shasta (both in northern California), Yuman and Diegueño (Kumayaay) on the Southwest-California border, probably Karok (in the north) and Seri (in Baja California), and possibly Chumash (around Santa Barbara, on the south-central coast). These Hokan languages lie around a bloc of Penutian-stock languages – Wintun, Maidu, Yokuts, Miwok – in central California, which are presumed to have entered that region from the north and pushed ancestral Hokans out to the peripheries of the state during the third and second millennia BCE. A radical suggestion by a linguist familiar with Ugric languages of Asia notes a number of similarities between Proto-Ugric and Proto-Penutian estimated at roughly two thousand years ago, implying some contact or immigration of Central or Northern Asians into the Bay Area of central California. Any notion of prehistoric trans-Pacific contacts is usually dismissed without consideration by most American archaeologists and linguists, but one respected scholar has found the Ugric-Penutian similarities worth pondering, especially considering that the set of similarities includes a series of words for bows, arrows, and their component parts, while the estimated time, two thousand years ago, correlates with the earliest evidence for bows and arrows in North America. Finally, Uto-Aztecan is represented in southern California by Tubatulabal, Cahuilla, and Luiseño, presumably moving into the state from the Southwest around two thousand years ago, and Athabascan stock is represented in northernmost California by Hupa and Tolowa, probably coming into the Oregon border region about the beginning of the second millennium AD. Two languages also in northernmost California, Yurok and Wiyot, are distantly related to the great band of Algonkian languages in Canada and the northern half of the United States from the Rockies to the Atlantic. Scenarios for this finding range from supposing ancestral Algonkians came down the Pacific coast from Asia as far as northern California and then moved eastward across the continent, dropping member groups in place over many centuries, to supposing the opposite, Algonkians moving westward from the Great Lakes with the Rockies a barrier except for the vanguard Yurok and Wiyot; a middle of the road scenario (literally) sees the Algonkian homeland, at least after Paleoindian times, in north-central America, the Yurok and Wiyot migrating west and numbers of other Algonkians expanding eastward. Over all, the intriguing fact about aboriginal California is that it was home to the greatest diversity of languages in any American region, these languages representing every one of the principal language stocks of North America.

Regional differentiation in California

California was never isolated from the rest of America, but its people did not adopt the maize-based agriculture developed in Mexico and spread from there to the Southwest and Eastern America. Careful reading of historic descriptions reveals that southern Californians knew maize and would plant it on higher plots as a fall-back crop in case their own indigenous grains failed to sprout in the valleys. European explorers commented on the valleys' abundant "grasses" yielding quantities of edible seeds, without realizing that the Indians sowed the seeds on fired-over valley bottoms, not requiring tillage. Westerners also noticed that the acorn oaks so important to most California Indians tended to grow in regular rows near villages, without realizing that they had been planted as orchards. Prickly-pear cactus were planted in circles around southern villages, producing delicious fruit and acting as a fence protecting the village from surprise raids. Deer were kept near and numerous by firing hillsides to encourage browse: the replacement of Indian villages by Euroamerican ranches and settlements resulted in immense areas reverting to dense chaparral or scrub, not to mention lakes turned into barren flats when their feeder streams were diverted into urban reservoirs.

California societies thus exemplify political economies very different from the Eurasian plow-agriculture/herded livestock model. Generally speaking, North American Indian societies relied on diversification rather than intensive monocropping for economic stability. Nature was collaborated with instead of conquered, not from noble-savage spirituality but from intelligent calculations of risk and labor costs. Diversification spread risk broadly, and spread and moved families around the range of resources, creating a value upon autonomous decision-making; the economy couldn't use serfs. American Indians seemed, to European observers, to embody freedom. Leaders needed to win respect, they could not dictatorially coerce commoners. Particularly in California and the Northwest Coast where native plants and animals were managed, not replaced with imported crops, Europeans thought they were looking at unfettered people in a bounteous wilderness, the opposite of English philosopher Thomas Hobbes's conviction that only a policed society could be tolerable. Western indigenous Americans' ways of life does not fit common European assumptions about work and politics, although the underlying rationality of indigenous economies is clear enough.

Between the idealized innocently noble savage and the damned nasty, brutish, and short-lived aborigine projected alike by Europeans, lay the real indigenous Californians. They recognized social classes, from intermarrying aristocratic lineages and family lines of specialists in doctoring, crafts, hunting, or plant propagation and use, through commoner families who performed most of the subsistence tasks, to captives pressed into drudge work, and, finally, ne'er-do-well beggars. In the first millennium AD, villages of several hundred people were numerous, each with a central larger house serving the community for gatherings and men's workshop space. Homes and community halls in central California were usually built over excavated basins to enhance insulation quality, and these pithouses were supplemented with aboveground thatched granaries, open-sided sunshelters (ramadas), small saunas (sweathouses), and small houses that women occupied when menstruating, a time when they were relieved of daily chores and avoided men's gear. Elsewhere in California, families built aboveground homes of thatch, tule reeds or bark sheets over rounded sapling frames: because these left little trace in the ground, archaeologists have difficulty estimating community size compared to the evidence remaining from villages of pithouses. The substantial villages had satellite camps where people harvested game, fish, plants not found near the villages, or raw materials such as the obsidian quarried in several localities in north-central California.

Nut meal was the basic staple for most of California. Acorns and buckeyes were most frequently used, two high-protein nuts requiring laborious processing to leach out a poisonous acid. These nuts had to be crushed, dried, soaked and rinsed several times, and finally dried for storage. The meal was cooked into porridge or baked into griddle cakes. Stone mortars and pestles are ubiquitous signs of nut processing in California, sometimes mortars pecked out of bedrock outcrops near oak groves, more often made from freestanding stones. Flat metate-type milling stones and manos are less numerous, indicating hard seeds had become a lesser staple since the Archaic period. This shift from reliance on seeds to reliance on acorns signifies more sedentary, more territorial societies in which women labored at home to a greater degree, compared to men. Women were highly skilled in basketry, weaving many types and styles for collecting, storing, and serving foodstuffs, storing valuables, and wearing – they wore basketry hats exhibiting distinctive designs emblematic of their nations. Among the sets of household baskets might be an open-bottomed basket like a hopper, set over a stone mortar so that leached acorn meal would flow down into the mortar for further milling. Fine baskets were (and are yet) an art form deeply respected by California Indian men as well as among women. California is one of the few regions of America lacking indigenous pottery, a lack due to preference for basketry even for carrying water and cooking (baskets were tightly woven and, to hold water, glazed inside with natural tar). Neighbors in the Southwest had pottery, pots were occasionally traded from there into California but, like maize, the originally Mexican craft failed to attract Californians.

Marine resources gave coastal Californians the stimulus to work out particularly productive technologies. In the north, salmon runs were captured and processed in assembly-line fashion, men on board catwalks over rapids, tossing up the fish with dipnets, women gutting, filleting and hanging the slices to dry on racks. In estuaries such as San Francisco Bay and the Central Valley rivers draining into it, fish dams and traps caught large quantities, and an abundance of shellfish, from abalone to clams, oysters, and mussels, led to discarded piles of shells that look like small hills. Sea lions and seals were hunted from boats, large dugouts in the north and plank canoes in the Channel Islands area (Santa Barbara): in both areas, the boat owner was a well-to-do aristocrat, his crew recruited from the best paddlers and harpooners he could engage.

Inland, deer, smaller game, and birds were caught with traps and nets as well as thrown weapons. Extensive marshes in the river deltas and Central Valley brought millions of waterfowl, in addition to maintaining reed beds furnishing basketry materials. Foothills of the Coast Ranges and the Sierra Nevada were ideal for deer. High valleys were of course accessible only in summer; Yosemite was the most popular in prehistory as it is today. Compared to San Francisco Bay and its Delta, and to the Channel Islands coast region, inland populations were less densely settled although still populous. Historic decimation of California Indians was dramatic, with epidemic diseases spreading out into free communities from the insalubrious mission barracks and garrisons, and probably along trade routes, long before any Europeans or Euroamericans could begin general censuses. Descriptions of gold rush era Indians therefore are already descriptions of remnants of larger nations struggling to maintain the social organizations they once had elaborated.

Warfare is evidenced for the last three thousand years, through burials of skeletons with fractures and deep wounds unlikely to have happened accidentally. Skeletons also point to periodic food shortages, shown in interruptions of children's growth (which could be illness, but when common in skeletons is probably periodic malnutrition) and in an apparent greater number of deaths in winter than in other seasons – not that the people starved to death, but poor nutrition left them vulnerable to other causes of death. The bow and arrow came into California in the first millennium AD, facilitating deer hunting but escalating mortality in war raids because villages could be attacked from a greater distance than with spears and javelins. At the same time, trade seems to have been increasing, to the point that uniform shell beads suitable for money are being manufactured in quantities. Trade moved obsidian for cutting tools and weapon heads, several other types of stone, shells and manufactured shell and stone beads, ornamental feathers, yew-wood bows from the mountains, tar (an adhesive and caulk), salt, and foods. One village would have brought in items coming from the Oregon border, northern interior, central coast, Central Valley, Sierra, and the Southwest. The early historic pattern of semi-autonomous villages with recognized resource territories and a considerable degree of labor specialization managed by aristocrats aided by assistants was in place at least by the end of the first millennium AD.

Northwest Coast

North of California, American First Nations were less catastrophically affected by European/Euroamerican invasions. Spain's northernmost garrisoned missions were established, 1769–1823, from present Mexico to Sonoma on the northern edge of the San Francisco Bay area. These decimated the coastal populations herded into the confines of the garrisons, and diseases abetted by malnutrition took thousands of inland people taking in refugees from the missions, and cut off from marine and Coast Ranges resources. Missions' sheep, goats, and bushels of seed wheat and oats carried in weed seeds that invaded valleys and foothills, replacing the indigenous seed grasses depended upon by the Indian communities. Groves of acorn oaks were cut down, or Indian access to them prohibited by ranchers homesteading the land. After Mexico gained its independence from Spain, 1821, the province of California was so remote from the Central Mexican seat of government that, Chartkoff and Chartkoff remark in their history of Indian California, less money was used than before Spanish colonization when indigenous shell monies were in circulation.[5] Beginning in 1839, United States emigrants colonized the Central Valley, demolishing Indians' resource bases and enslaving the destitute. The 1849 gold rush pulled 150,000 strike-it-rich hopefuls into California, up into river headwaters, swamping even Indian families in the rugged Sierra forests. Survivors in the northern reaches unsuited to colonization, or in hamlet "rancherias" of impoverished laborers scattered on the edges of colonizers' ranches and farms, were, in the early twentieth century, only an estimated 5 per cent of the California population when Drake stopped ashore in 1579.

The west coast from northern California up and around the North Pacific Rim had a quite different postcontact history. The Russian American Company's first American post, on Kodiak Island off southeast Alaska, in 1783, led to establishing Sitka, on the mainland, 1799, and Fort Ross on the Russian River in California, 1812. The Russians relied on indigenous nations to supply post food supplies, stimulating Tlingit around Sitka to raise tons of potatoes and bring in quantities of "mutton" (mountain sheep meat?) and halibut. Siberian and Aleut men pressed into service lived with Indian wives around the Russian posts, producing a generation of Creoles with ties to Indian communities. Russian Orthodox priests evangelized these communities with limited success (mostly in coastal southern Alaska), lacking soldier backup, and tended to side with Indian converts against Russian exploitation. Canadian and United States emigrants moving into Russian America in the mid-nineteenth century found no broad well-watered valleys as in California, but narrow strips of beach backed by steep mountains broken through by swift rivers. Smallpox and other introduced diseases took a heavy toll, leaving some aristocrats with several noble titles once distributed among related lineages. Puget Sound and the Fraser Delta (around Vancouver) Indians were largely displaced by colonists, but commercial fishing and canning of salmon became sources of income for many indigenous families along the coast. Thanks to continued access to these and marine fish, Northwest Coast nations retained more of their political economies than Californians could.

Salmon and shellfish have been major components of Northwest Coast economies since the seventh millennium BCE. Rising sea level, complicated by occasional earthquakes and volcano eruptions disrupting sections of the coast or upriver zones, destroyed or hid many occupation sites, making the archaeological record sketchy until mid-Holocene stabilization in the fifth–fourth millennia BCE. After 3000 BCE, large middens of discarded shells, mostly clams and mussels, have been preserved. In southeast Alaska, where the earliest dated excavated shell midden was in use around 6500 BCE, salmon and halibut, sea lions and seals, deer or caribou, beaver, and rabbits were other components of the inhabitants' economy; presumably they collected berries, tubers, and other edible plants, but these were not preserved in the midden. On northeastern Vancouver Island, bones of dolphins and porpoises predominated in a Late Archaic site, and bones of the huge bluefin tuna occur in many Vancouver Island sites.

A considerable portion of the Northwest Coast has inlets, bays, and islands that create marked local differences in resources. Communities facing the open ocean were oriented toward deep-sea animals, both sea mammals and fish, and might send canoes as much as twenty-five miles (forty kilometers) out to sea to fish for halibut on offshore banks. Communities on the inland passage, sheltered from the open ocean by islands, sought the fish frequenting their waters, which include the bluefin tuna. These communities were better positioned to harvest salmon running up rivers to spawn. Because communities claimed rights to harvest specific resources at specific stations, many confederated into alliances for trading localized products or permitting seasonal use of localities. This practice goes back at least two millennia, as evidenced by relatively large, permanent villages at favored harbors, with both "inside" (the Inland Passage) and "outside" (on the open ocean) products found in each village. Archaeological data also indicate that war for territorial conquest was an alternative to confederation, intensifying in the last millennium AD.

Cutting tools and weapons in Alaska and the northern coast at this time were created out of tiny razor-sharp stone blades glued into slots along the sides or end of wooden or bone handles. Southern British Columbia and northwestern United States preferred leaf-shaped knife blades and weapon points chipped from single large flakes. "Microblades" were very common in northern Asia in the Late Pleistocene-early Holocene, leaf-shaped chipped blades common in most of the rest of America: the differences in technology must reflect cultural differences, given each type dominates in a large geographical area. It is purely a guess that the microblades were carried by Athabascan speakers – Tlingit, Haida, Eyak, and interior Dené – and that the central and southern Northwest Coast respectively already held ancestors of the region's Wakashan speakers – Nootka, Kwakiutl, Makah – and of Salish-speakers – Bella Coola, Fraser Delta and Puget Sound nations, and Tillamook.[6] Tsimshian, in northern British Columbia, and Chinook on the lower Columbia River and Oregon coast are considered to belong to the Penutian stock, as are most Oregon languages and Sahaptin and Nez Percé in eastern Washington-Idaho. California Penutians may be descended from people who moved down from the Northwest coast into what had been Hokan territories.

Populations had become substantial by the second millennium BCE, more intensively working the Northwest Coast's resources. Large weirs, some with several thousand stakes, were built to trap schools of fish including herring; one archaeologist pointed out that seals would follow herring, so herring traps would attract seals to be slaughtered in addition to providing quantities of fish. Another small schooling fish, a smelt called eulachon, was caught and no doubt processed as it was in historic times to render its oil. Historically, a saucer of eulachon oil accompanied every meal, for dipping dried fish and meat and mixing into nearly every dish, like olive oil in Mediterranean cuisine. Casks of eulachon oil were a principal Nuu-chah-nulth export; so were the narrow rectangular shells of dentalium, a mollusc found only in deep offshore beds mostly near Vancouver Island. Nuu-chah-nulth invented a kind of broom or rake with extension poles to entangle the shellfish and pull them up to the boat, after which they were boiled and the shells polished and strung – during a 1793–94 exploring voyage, an American captain bought strings of dentalium totaling 300 meters (or yards) from Nuu-chah-nulth, to use as money. Dentalium appear in archaeological sites in the third millennium BCE, becoming common in the first millennium BCE *except* in Nuu-chah-nulth territory on the west (outer) coast of Vancouver Island, their probable principal source! The reason for this apparent absence seems to be archaeological, in that excavations there have conscientiously avoided disturbing burials, likely to have been bedecked with dentalium, working instead in trash middens.

Rectangular planked timber houses appear in the second millennium BCE, replacing earlier round pithouses; rectangular houses would have more space to hang dried fish fillets under the roofs, preserving them in the smoke from central hearths, and room in the corners to stack boxes and baskets of other foods for the winter. It is reasonable to suppose that the houses held recognized lineages, as in historic times, and the increase in food production involved coordinating teams of residents engaged in different procurement tasks according to their strengths – the markedly larger shell middens may mean that now children and elderly remained in beach-front villages, making themselves useful collecting shellfish, while more able-bodied adults were out fishing, hunting, or cultivating beds of camas, wapato ("Indian potato," an indigenous root), or edible clover. Among late prehistoric houses were very large structures with broad pits excavated to create two or even three tiers of living and storage space, the lineage chiefly family's wealth boxed in the back of the house, commoner families with their tools along the sides, and slaves sleeping near the front.

Planked houses show that Northwest Coast people had mastered the craft of splitting cedar logs, and coffins in one site reveal skill in the art of bending planks into boxes, in this instance large ones that could become coffins. Huge canoes carved from the massive cedars of the Northwest Coast probably were being made. Adzes made of nephrite, a very hard stone like jade, testify not only to such wood-working, but also to high skill and time to specialize in working stone. In the first millennium BCE, copper was hammered into sheets and headbands. Sculpture had appeared, in stone, in the second millennium BCE, and in wood in the first millennium BCE (preservation would be a factor here, the handsome carved wooden handle that is the earliest known example having the luck of being left in a waterlogged site). Antler and bone, including whalebone that could have been salvaged from beached whales but may well have been hunted off Vancouver Island and the Olympic Peninsula, were also carved into handles and clubs. Weaving tools, often decorated, indicate this craft was practised, whether from mountain goat hair or the fine hair of specially bred dogs, used in Chilkat blankets, is not known. Stone, bone, copper, antler, and wood objects all conform to the canons of classic Northwest Coast art, one of the great art styles of human history, though development of the style, with its regional variants, can be discerned, as can differences in the skill and talent of artists. Some may already have been professionals commissioned and supported by lineage chiefs.

War was common along the northern coast, evidenced by a number of skeletons killed or once injured by blows of a club or dagger. It seems less common in the southern coast. Then, in the later first millennium AD, warfare led to fortified retreats in the north, where villagers took refuge in castle-like walled compounds on defensible ridges, while attackers might mount a siege to starve them out. Secret tunnels below the fortifications gave the besieged a possibility of escape. Historically, some fortresses guarded overland trading trails or boat passages, very likely the situation in late pre-historic times as well. Controlling trade routes brought goods and income from tariffs levied on cargoes permitted to continue on the route. An iron adz blade in use during the fifteenth century AD, long before documented European contacts, indicates North Pacific Rim trade extending west into northern Asia.

The village at Ozette, in Makah territory at the northwestern tip of Washington state, buried by a landslide about AD 1700 (before European contact), had a wealthy lineage's house and ordinary houses, the latter with more scraps and worn items on the floors, the wealthy house less littered. This house was closer to the beach, the poorer houses in a back row behind it. Probably the owner or lineage chief in the larger house owned a seagoing boat, for gear for sea-mammal hunting was stored in this house but not found in the others, and this house, not the others, had whale meat – Makah and Nuu-chah-nulth historically were the only Northwest Coast nations that actively pursued whales. Makah traded whale oil and blubber to other nations, evidenced at Ozette by the quantity of whalebone indicating processing of the animals beyond what one village would have consumed.

Ozette did not have burial mounds, but a millennium earlier, mounds were constructed over some burials in the southern sectors of the Northwest Coast. The largest excavated one, on the lower Fraser River in southern British Columbia, is eight feet (nearly three meters) high, and covered a stone cairn over a burial of a man with perforated copper disks and abalone shell pendants near his face, and seven thousand dentalium shell beads, the type used as money historically. This and other mounds were on a ridge behind a village of eighteen houses along the river. The burial mounds, like the differences in house sizes and furnishings, demonstrate social classes have been characteristic of Northwest Coast societies for at least two thousand years, quite possibly longer.

Research Puzzle

Concern for sustainable resource management, less dependent on expensive petrochemicals, helped revise estimation of indigenous

West Coast nations' development. Archaeologists are challenged not only by stereotypes based on European images and the sorry condition of survivors of massacres and dispossession, but also by Californians' considerable use of perishable materials. What's left for archaeologists may resemble a simple material culture. Northwest Coast villages with their large timber houses left more evidence, but in both regions, archaeologists who were taught that West Coast First Nations were "foragers" living off the land and runs of spawning fish tend to fill in a research puzzle outlined by that stereotype, rather than read deeply into ethnohistorians' analyses of these nations' sophisticated resource management and political institutions. The basic fact of high population densities poses the significant research puzzle, answered better by extrapolating from ethnohistoric studies than by assuming, as did British Columbia Chief Justice McEachern in 1991, that "no written language, no horses or wheeled vehicles" means primitive people "foraging" like animals.

Bibliographical Note

These volumes of the Smithsonian Institution's (Washington DC) Handbook of North American Indians series supply extensive detailed material on the West: volume 5, *Arctic*, edited by David Damas, published in 1984; volume 6, *Subarctic*, edited by June Helm, published in 1981; volume 7, *Northwest Coast*, edited by Wayne Suttles, published in 1990, and volume 8, *California*, edited by Robert F. Heizer, published in 1978. Volume 17, *Languages*, edited by Ives Goddard, published in 1996, includes an extended discussion of language histories and archaeological corollaries by Michael K. Foster, pp. 64–110. The larger portion of each encyclopedic volume is given to ethnography and ethnohistory, with the prehistory summarized in a few of many chapters; the years required to prepare volumes with so many contributors meant that most articles were written well before the publication date and could not incorporate late-breaking new data.

For the Northwest Coast, *Peoples of the Northwest Coast: Their Archaeology and Prehistory*, by Kenneth M. Ames and Herbert D. G. Maschner (London, 1999), and *Since the Time of the Transformers: The Ancient Heritage of the Nuu-chah-nulth, Ditidaht, and Makah*, by Alan D. McMillan (Vancouver, BC, 1999), and for California, Michael Moratto's *California Archaeology* (Orlando, FL, 1984) and Joseph L. and Kerry K. Chartkoff's *The Archaeology of California* (Stanford, CA, 1984) are standard overview volumes.

Notes

1. Claude Lévi-Strauss, *The Way of the Masks*, translated by S. Modelski (Seattle, WA, 1982).

2. Quoted in Robin Ridington, "Fieldwork in Courtroom 53: A Witness to *Delgamuukw*," in Frank Cassidy (ed.), *Aboriginal Title in British Columbia: Delgamuukw vs. The Queen* (Lantzville, BC, 1992), pp. 212, 213, 216. See also Kent McNeil, "Social Darwinism and Judicial Conceptions of Indian Title in Canada in the 1880s," *Journal of the West* 38(1) (1999): 68–76, Dara Culhane, *The Pleasure of the Crown: Anthropology, Law, and First Nations* (Barnaby, BC, 1998).

3. Quoted in Ridington, "Fieldwork in courtroom 53," pp. 210–11.

4. Quoted in ibid., p. 213. The Supreme Court of Canada overturned McEachern's judgment on appeal, 1997.

5. Joseph L. Chartkoff and Kerry L. Chartkoff, *The Archaeology of California* (Stanford, CA, 1984), p. 271.

6. Contemporary members of most First Nations are urging the use of their own names for their nations, rather than Anglicized versions or foreigners' nicknames such as Nez Percé (French for "pierced nose"). Nootka is now Nuu-chah-nulth, Kwakiutl is Kwakwaka'wakw, Bella Coola are Nuxalk, Tsimshian are two nations, Nisgha and Gitksan, and Nez Percé are Nimipu. See Kehoe, *North American Indians: A Comprehensive Account*, for detailed lists of the first nations in each geographic region.

References

Ames, Kenneth M. and Herbert D. G. Maschner (1999), *Peoples of the Northwest Coast: Their Archaeology and Prehistory*. London: Thames and Hudson.

Chartkoff, Joseph L. and Kerry K. Chartkoff (1984), *The Archaeology of California*. Stanford, CA: Stanford University Press.

Culhane, Dara (1998), *The Pleasure of the Crown: Anthropology, Law, and First Nations*. Barnaby, BC: Talonbooks.

Lévi-Strauss, Claude (1982), *The Way of the Masks*, translated by S. Modelski. Seattle, WA: University of Washington Press.

McMillan, Alan D. (1999), *Since the Time of the Transformers: The Ancient Heritage of the Nuu-chah-nulth, Ditidaht, and Makah*. Vancouver, BC: University of British Columbia Press.

McNeil, Kent (1999), "Social Darwinism and Judicial Conceptions of Indian Title in Canada in the 1880s," *Journal of the West* 38(1): 68–76.

Moratto, Michael (1984), *California Archaeology*. Orlando, FL: Academic Press.

Ridington, Robin (1992), "Fieldwork in Courtroom 53: A Witness to *Delgamuukw*," in Frank Cassidy (ed.), *Aboriginal Title in British Columbia: Delgamuukw vs. The Queen*. Lantzville, BC: Oolichan Books, pp. 206–20.

From Edward Sapir, *Wishram Texts*, pp. 201–5

The Wishram were dwelling at Wa'q!Emap; some of them were
dwelling at Wa'q!Emap, some of them were dwelling at the
village Nixlu'idix. Now and then a duck flew over their heads.
And then they heard it, it made a noise: shu'lulululu [very high-
pitched]. Now then one man said: "It made the noise with its
beak." One said: "It made the noise with its wings." So then they
got to arguing. And then they seized their arrows. Then indeed
they fought, both parties killed each other. They fought and
fought (until) they ceased.

And then (whenever) any one fished with dip-net, thus two
men provided with quivers remained near their friend, kept
watch over him; while he, the dip-net fisherman, caught salmon,
his two friends staid near him. Three years passed by and there
they dwelt; there they fought (until) at last they ceased. And
then (one party of) the Wishram said: "Being in some way
disgraced, let us now go off somewheres; we have become
disgraced before our friends. Now let us go to look for
(another) country." So then they took cedar planks and then
went off. Way yonder they went, among the Wallawalla. They
went on past AcnE'm. They went on past NuLla'-ik. They went
straight on past NuLla'nuLla. They went straight on past
Sts!E'mtsi. They went straight on past Wisu'm. They went
straight on past Ta'malan. They went straight on past
Txa'ianuna. Straight on they went to a small river. They went
straight on to Pô'uwankiut. They went straight on past Xit!a'i.
They went straight on past a dried-up small river. They went
straight on past SA'tAs. They went straight on past I!Lu'mEni.
They went straight on to Palā'xi. [Note: the migration was east
for a short distance along the Columbia River, then north across
the divide between the Columbia and the Yakima, and then
along the Yakima to the Wenatchee.]

Now there they remained. And then they caught Chinook
salmon, blueback salmon, eels, and suckers; they ate them. And
then they said: "Behold! the country is small. Now let us go off
yonder, let us look for another country." They went straight on
to Patixkwi'ut; now to-day white people call it "The Gap." There
they remained. Only at night do people catch salmon there,
they fish with dip-nets. The name of that same country is
IxElExtgi'dix. And again they said: "Behold! the country is

From Edward Sapir, Wishram Texts, *pp. 201–5 (continued)*

small." And again they went on, went to seek (another) country. To this day I see where those Wishram used to live long ago. Among the rocks cedar boards are standing. That is how I know that they took cedar boards with them, so that I think they are the cedar boards of them, the Wishram; perhaps some may have died there.

And again they went on, went to look for (another) country. They moved. They thought to themselves: "We will get lots of salmon; far away somewheres there is a good country, and there we will dwell." They went straight on to Wenatchee; there the Wishram arrived. And there they dwelt, dwelt long. And then they said: "Now let us all move." And then again they moved. They took a country for themselves (where there were) lots of salmon and lots of deer. To this day they dwell there and they are just nothing but Wishram.

Given in Wishram by ME'nait (Louis Simpson), 1905, translated by Pete McGuff.

Sapir, Edward (1909), *Wishram Texts.* Publications of the American Ethnological Society, vol. II. Leyden: E. J. Brill.

From Dell Hymes, "In Vain I Tried to Tell You:" *Essays in Native American Ethnopoetics*, pp. 188–9

A long time ago,
   maybe fifty years ago,
      it attacked them.
They were staying on the Clackamas river,
   one fellow climbed a pine tree,
      then she saw them.
He pulled his arrows out,
   he shot her maybe three or four times:
      nothing to her,
      she bled through her mouth.
This thing looked like a coyote on the head,
   short ears;
      teeth like a wild hog's tusks,
      long white front claws,
      long hind legs,
      short front legs.
He *tried* to do everything to her,
   then he got afraid:
      only two arrows left.
The he took one,
   he lit I don't know what,
      he put it on this arrow,
         then he shot the arrow,
         then it started to burn.
Again he did the same with one arrow,
   then this (thing) went down into a canyon,
      there it burned.
This thing is what they call At'únaqa.
   Then it really started to burn.
      Then a lot of white men ran up,
         they put it out;
         the state of Oregon put out a lot of money.
There's nothing of that sort to be seen on our side of the
   mountains.
Only on the other side could things of that sort be seen.
A long time ago,
   maybe as much as fifty or sixty years ago,
      this thing was seen.

From Dell Hymes, "In Vain I Tried to Tell You:" Essays in Native American Ethnopoetics, *pp. 188–9 (continued)*

Told in Wasco by Hiram Smith, 1956, and translated by Mr. Smith.

Hymes, Dell (1981), *"In Vain I Tried to Tell You:" Essays in Native American Ethnopoetics.* Philadelphia, PA: University of Pennsylvania Press.

7

ALASKA

When the United States annexed Alaska in 1867, it acquired the western sectors of two immense ecological zones, the Arctic Coast and the Subarctic, and the northern sector of the Northwest Coast rainforest zone. That zone, home of the Tlingit and Haida, has been described in the preceding chapter. This chapter describes the Arctic Coast and the Subarctic zones.

Arctic Coast

The Arctic Coast from Pacific Alaska across Canada through Greenland is inhabited by nations speaking Eskimo languages, and formerly called "Eskimo." Today, two of these nations are self-governing territories, Kalaallit Nunaat (Greenland) and Nunavut (Northeast Canada), their indigenous inhabitants the Inuit. Alaska's northern people are Iñupiaq (a version of the word "Inuit"), and those in the west and southwest coastal areas are Yupik. Some Yupik live on the Siberian side of Bering Strait. Aleut, inhabitants of the Aleutian Islands stretching westward from Alaska's southern peninsula, speak a language that is part of the Eskimo-Aleut stock but so different from Yupik-Iñupiaq/Inuktitut that Aleuts must have separated from the ancestral Proto-Eskimo-Aleut population several thousand years ago.

Surely the Arctic Coast is the most challenging environment colonized by humans. Half the year is ice-bound dark winter, the sun appearing only dimly, or not at all, in midday, the temperatures far below zero – centigrade or Fahrenheit! – with howling blizzards. Short summers are beset with biting insects. Few edible plants grow.

Abundance of sea mammals lured people into the zone, ingenious technology kept them alive and prospering. The pioneer anthropologist Franz Boas lived for a year, 1884–85, with Inuit in Nunavut, discovering that far from being miserable scavenging brutes, they relaxed in snug thermally engineered iglus enjoying poetry, songs, dancing, visual art, and jokes. Survival gear today follows Inuit designs for parkas, dome shelters, kayaks, cargo sleds, toggle fastenings, and snow goggles. These inventions, plus others such as composite harpoons, cargo boats (umiaks) used also for whaling, dogsleds, waterproof suits of fishskin, gutskin, or birdskin, economical lamps burning rendered seal oil that can heat and light an iglu while cooking meat, enabled Inuit to explore and settle northernmost America.

Inuit culture seems to have developed in the Eurasian Arctic, then spread across Bering Strait into Alaska, and taken off eastward across northernmost Canada in the last millennium AD. Three staging areas are implied, Eurasia to invent the basic technology and strategies to survive in the high Arctic, Alaska to add to and refine these, then filling in the Canadian Arctic within a few centuries, meeting the westward-colonizing Norse in Greenland, AD 1000. The interesting complication is that the first people came into the Canadian Northeast and Greenland about 2000 BCE, carrying a stone technology with microblades and unusually small chipped blades (the Arctic Small Tool tradition). These people had many elements of Inuit technology including toggle harpoons, kayaks, lamps, clothing, and probably bows and arrows. Initially hunting a diversity of land and sea animals, through time the descendants of these colonizers came to focus more on sea mammals during the first millennium BCE, hunting them from the ice rather than from boats on open water. A millennium later, immigrant Inuit, called Thule, coming from the west had techniques and tools for more efficient hunting of sea mammals, and dogsleds to transport meat and household goods overland. They displaced the population already in the eastern Arctic (called Dorset); DNA analyses indicate Dorset were not absorbed into Thule communities, and where Dorset went, no one knows. Looking from the east, then, successful adaptation to the High Arctic spread across northern America around 2000 BCE, and the historic Thule of the last millennium AD constitute the most effective variant developed. Whether the Dorset and their ancestors the Arctic Small Tool people spoke languages related to Inuit, no one knows.

Early Holocene occupations in Alaska are referred to as Paleo-Arctic, and are similar to those on the Siberian side of the Pacific. Most sites appear to have been campsites, often on river banks high enough to be above the worst of the mosquitoes, but not so high that shrub thicket covered them; some sites are on high overlooks commanding river valleys or the coast. Caribou bones indicate the importance of these deer, always vital to provide skins suitable for clothing as well as meat, and explain the location of campsites where caribou herds might be sighted. A few sites have been securely radiocarbon-dated to the first couple of millennia of the Holocene, fewer to the middle Holocene, because the camping episodes left small scatters of artifacts and food debris, a number of episodes on the same favored campsites, frustrating archaeologists' efforts to separate the episodes and fine-tune the dating.

During the fifth millennium BCE, approaching the climax of the post-Pleistocene warming trend, artifacts resembling those used in the Subarctic interior forests occur through much of Alaska, out into the tundra, prompting some archaeologists to posit a spread of Canadian Subarctic people north and west, other archaeologists to suggest an association between these artifact styles and greater reliance on caribou, without necessarily any ethnic migrations. People seem to have sheltered in tents, with a site on the western coast exhibiting a semi-subterranean house floor, that is, a wide pit dug into the subsoil to insulate the house, with perhaps a roof of blocks of sod over a wood frame, or simply a tent banked with sod or brush. Such a house would be a winter residence, its family using a tent to camp out on caribou-hunting excursions inland.

Suddenly – according to the archaeological record – in the later second millennium BCE, the Alaskan population appears to increase rapidly. The apparent proliferation of sites is probably an effect of the stabilization of sea level by the beginning of that millennium, because more sites and larger, longer-occupied sites chosen for winter villages have always been along the coasts where marine fish and sea mammals abound. Rising sea levels during the first half of the Holocene simply covered coastal settlements of that era. Once the sea no longer steadily encroached upon the entire coast, many sites remained accessible to archaeologists. Circumstances such as these explain why the geologist is the archaeologist's best friend.[1]

A good example of what appears sudden is the Old Whaling site on Cape Krusenstern, western Alaska. Five deep, large pithouses close together would have been the village's winter dwellings, with five similarly large, shallow-floored houses close by the summer dwellings. In front of one house was a butchered whale skull, other whalebones littered the beach by the village, and large harpoon heads and long-bladed knives point to the pursuit of whales at this time. No other whalers' villages nor whaling gear resembling theirs are known so early in Alaska. Clearly these people had seagoing boats, so they may have come a considerable distance, then decided after a year or two that beaches back home, wherever that was, better suited their needs.

In the first millennium BCE, excavations have shown a 49-foot (15-meter) oval house in one site, in another a rectangular house 26 by 16 feet (8 by 5 meters) built on the western coast of Alaska, and tents continuing in use inland, perhaps for summer caribou hunts. One interpretation of the rectangular house is that it was used for community events and the men's workshop, the village families living in smaller round structures nearby; this model from historic village layouts in Alaska would see the historic ethnographic social pattern to be three thousand years old. Supporting this interpretation is food debris within the outlines of the smaller structures, much less in the larger house, and tools for working wood and stone in the house, not on the smaller floors.

Pottery was the striking innovation of the first millennium BCE in western Alaska, as in the Eastern Woodlands. Alaska's first potters seem more skilled than those who made Early Woodland-type pots in the East; the craft dates back to the Terminal Pleistocene in Siberia, almost certainly the source for introducing ceramics into Alaska. Stone lamps, and a bit later, clay lamps, burning oil also were used. Judging from the quantities of seal bones in sites, the oil would have been rendered from seal blubber, and the pots would have been useful for this purpose. Another innovation, in southwestern Alaska at the beginning of the second millennium BCE and becoming common in northern Alaska by late in the first millennium BCE, is ground slate knife blades and weapon heads. Smooth, long ground slate blades are excellent for slicing fish and sea mammal meat and blubber. Ground slate, like ceramics, was widely used in coastal Siberia and in the Late Archaic northeastern Woodland. It's puzzling that ceramics and ground slate are not found in the vast area between Alaska and the Northeast. Coastal Alaska shared the North Pacific maritime culture with Siberia, but the idea that northeastern coastal America shared a North Atlantic maritime culture with northwestern-most Europe has been resisted by most American archaeologists.

Ipiutak

From the standpoint of a historical approach, Ipiutak may be the most significant site in Alaska. Occupied in the first millennium AD, the name site is at Point Hope on the northwestern tip of Alaska or, from the sea perspective, the northeastern coast of the Chukchi Sea (that portion of the Pacific north of Bering Strait). Related cultural material is found from Point Barrow, the northernmost tip of Alaska, to Cape Krusenstern in central western Alaska. Five hundred and seventy-five houses were mapped for the Ipiutak town on Point Hope, and 72 excavated in the archaeological project carried out between 1939 and 1941. It is supposed that not all the houses were simultaneously occupied, but they lie in two sets of long parallel rows running in from the beach, with little superposition and a wide "street" between the sets of rows. Houses had a frame of timber posts in the corners of squared shallow basins ten to eighteen feet (three to six meters) across, a hearth in the center and banquettes built along three sides for sleeping and seating platforms. Walls and roofs were constructed of logs and poles, covered with hides and/or blocks of turf, and a downsloping entrance passageway shielded the interior from drafts and retained heat within the house – basic engineering for Arctic winter houses originating in the Upper Paleolithic in Eurasia and characteristic of historic Inuit iglus. Burials were either corpses interred in log coffins, usually with few or no artifacts, or apparently on a cleared surface over which a grave house was constructed, these corpses frequently accompanied by beautifully carved objects.

Seals, probably hunted at their breathing holes, were the principal marine resource for Ipiutak, complemented by caribou, a subsistence economy continuing into the present for some Inuit. Bows and arrows and harpoons were the weapons employed and, in the interior, caribou were driven into lakes where they could be speared from kayaks as they tried to swim away. Their stone technology links Ipiutak with earlier central coastal Alaskans, except that they didn't make microblades, didn't use ground slate, and, most surprisingly, did not make pottery.

Carvings are spectacular components of Ipiutak culture. Quantities were found at Ipiutak, nearly all in the ground-level graves presumed to have been covered with wooden grave houses. Bone, antler, and particularly walrus-tusk ivory were carved and decorated with lines and dots. Many ivory carvings represent walruses, bears, humans or fantastic animals, the elements of the design dynamically curvilinear and ornamented. Some creatures have their skeletons incised, as if an X-ray were superimposed on the body, a motif used also in Northwest Coast art and around the Pacific, from which a few archaeologists have argued that there was once, maybe two thousand years ago, a circum-Pacific art style spread through coastwise trade and population movements and surviving historically in New Guinea and adjacent Melanesia, among the Ainu of northern Japan, and the Northwest Coast of America. Ipiutak carvers went beyond this semi-realistic, abstracted style for figurines, dagger handles, and harpoon sockets, to produce, in addition, linked chains, swivels, and twists each made from a single piece of ivory. Corpses sometimes were given artificial eyes of ivory, or mask-like carvings of which the ivory may be the preserved part of composite masks with a wooden or leather base. The association of the figurines, chains of links, twisted shapes, and swivels with selected corpses buried differently from most, suggested to the excavators that those persons had been shamans, like Siberian shamans across the Chukchi Sea who wear special tunics from which hang a variety of figurines and metal chains and swivels. Siberian shamans believe the objects can be useful in engaging spirits to help them in healing, divining, or retrieving wandering souls. Ipiutak carvings may have been ivory versions carved because the shamans on the American side could not obtain the metal pieces manufactured in Asia.[2] One ivory engraving tool with a tiny iron point found at Ipiutak supports this interpretation that Ipiutak was in contact, but not in regular trade, with Siberians.

What were the contacts across Bering Strait is a question less investigated than circumstances imply. First-millennium AD sites on St Lawrence Island, at the south end of Bering Strait and more or less midway between Siberia and Alaska, tie in closely with contemporary sites on the eastern Chukchi Peninsula. Looking from the Chukchi Peninsula, Ipiutak shared much of its culture, notably the effusive delight in curvilinear decorations on nearly all bone and ivory objects, with these communities. Historically, Yupik lived on both sides of the Strait, and a few traveled hundreds of kilometers into Siberia to Russian trade fairs. Iron in precontact northern America from Ozette, in northwestern Washington state, to Inuit sites across the Arctic might come from Asian shipwrecks but at least as likely came from long-distance trade around the North Pacific or across the Strait. A Japanese archaeologist argued that the innovations in Alaskan coastal cultures late in the first millennium AD, innovations that mark the Thule culture leading to historic Inuit/Iñupiaq, may have come from northeastern Asia.[3] That area, specifically the Okhotsk Sea north of Japan, exhibits many imports from northeastern China and from Japan during the late first millennium AD: the Ainu (whose art style resembles Northwest Coast) and others around the Okhotsk Sea traded furs and walrus ivory for iron and bronze manufactures, glass beads, and fine clothing. The market for North Pacific furs and ivory may be older than the Okhotsk Sea archaeology can demonstrate, possibly stimulating the big settlement and fantastic ivory carvings of Ipiutak.

Thule and Its Forebears

Coastal Alaskan societies that seem to more closely resemble historic Inuit/Iñupiag lived contemporary with Ipiutak not only on the Chukchi Peninsula but also in northernmost Alaska around Barrow. These people, called Birnirk after a site near Barrow, lived in single-family small houses, a few to a village, building the structures with driftwood timbers eked out with walrus and whalebone, covered over with sod. Sloping entrance passageways ended lower than the house floor, creating a cold trap; in one house, the lintel of the doorway into the house proper was a whale skull, under which the residents crawled into the interior warmed and lit only by an blubber-oil lamp, for there is no firewood so far north. Seals and walruses were efficiently hunted, to the degree that an implement was invented to make a scratching noise on ice that would attract seals in springtime. Birnirk people probably did not actively hunt whales, as opposed to scavenging beached whales.

Closer to Bering Strait, pursuing whales was definitely a major activity. Villages were large enough to house enough men for whale-boat crews, optimally more than one boat in order to head off whales swimming in leads in the offshore ice. Harpoons large enough to kill whales are regularly found, and an ingenious harpoon head with an offset hole for the line and an asymmetric spur that caused the head to twist in the wound at a right angle to the thrust, more effectively securing the harpooner's line in the prey. Walrus bone and ivory were made into ice picks, snow shovels, ice-creepers to fasten on to bootsoles to grip when walking over ice, and runners for hand-pulled transport sleds. Powerful bows backed with glued strips of sinew (increases the spring force of the bow), ivory wristguards, and a variety of arrows and javelins from blunt-ended bird bunts to fearsome multi-barbed arrows identified by Iñupiaq as meant for war, form the arsenal during the first millennium AD. Asian-style slat armor of rows of narrow strips of bone tied to bone frames worn over thick hide shirts confirm the interpretation of war arrows. Why did they go to war? Iñupiaq tell stories of beauteous, industrious wives kidnapped by enemies, Helen of Troy stories one might say but, as with the Greeks' Trojan War, advantageous harbors and access to resources likely were the real prizes.

From the westernmost tip of Alaska at the Bering Strait itself, north and eastward along the Arctic Ocean, the immediate forebears of the Inuit/Iñupiaq, called Thule, appear at the end of the first millennium AD. Items of dog harness and driving whips show that dogsleds came into use at that time, facilitating transporting meat, household goods, and people. Dog teams don't come free, they must be fed, creating a need for netting and storing quantities of fish for dog food in addition to what owner families eat.[4] Thule culture generally was an intensification of first-millennium AD Birnirk and neighboring north Alaskan coastal culture, with whaling developed to the point that crews tackled the huge bowhead whales in addition to the beluga and other smaller whales. The big whales feed at certain locations in the northern seas where currents concentrate plankton. These tend to be off major headlands; therefore Thule had large villages at a few major headlands and hamlets widely dispersed elsewhere. They went inland in summer and early fall to hunt caribou, as necessary to their suvival, for clothing, and they hunted whales and the seals along the ice during the long winters. When hunting inland, families lived in caribou-skin tents; during the winter, they clustered in dome-shaped sod-covered houses, of the type used in Birnirk, near sealing grounds.

The fifteenth century AD began a period of colder climate called the Little Ice Age, lasting until the mid-nineteenth century. Effects of this climate shift would be especially harsh in Thule lands, the northernmost regions inhabited by humans, and Arctic populations adapted by reducing settlement size except in the few localities still seeing bowhead whales, Point Hope and Barrow. Fishing became more important to most Alaskans, with greater use of nets to capture more fish, rather than taking them with lines and hooks or spearing. Seals remained a vital resource, one posing a difficulty for archaeologists, because for the last few centuries and possibly earlier, Inuit and Iñupiaq built snowblock houses out on the pack ice to hunt seals. These houses and any artifacts and debris in or around them disappear into the water when the ice melts or shifts, removing evidence of half each year's occupations from the archaeological record! Seals were also hunted in summer from land settlements. A study of an Iñupiaq community over a generation pointed to two critical times annually, early summer when quantities of fish and seal can be dried, and early fall when fish can be stored frozen. Any condition that affects harvesting and processing these resources, such as excessive flooding in early summer or early freeze-up in fall, can be catastrophic for a small Iñupiaq community – they would probably spend more time hunting caribou inland, but conditions that affect fishing and sealing may affect caribou populations and movements, too. Seal numbers, too, will be affected by fish numbers, since that is what seals eat.[5] Thule strategies and technology were extraordinary and, as many of their descendants in Alaska, Canada, Nunavut, and Kalaallit Nunaat know, the best-ever devised for long-term survival in the High Arctic.

Interior Alaska

The interior of Alaska and adjacent northwestern Canada is the home of the Athabascan-speaking nations, in their own languages the Dené.[6] Their economy is based on the boreal spruce forests and the rivers and lakes running through them, with excursions on to the tundra to the north and to the coasts and inlets. Herds of caribou and spawning salmon were the staples in Alaska, both processed into dried meat. To eat the lean dry meat, rendered bear oil was considered essential, unless seal oil was available. When hunting or traveling near the Alaskan mountains, people went after Dall sheep, the hides of which were ideal for winter bedding; if these could not be obtained, skins of hares, muskrats, and ground squirrels were sewn together for blankets, and ground squirrels, usually taken by women in set snares, sewn to make warm lightweight underwear. Berries and edible roots were regularly added to meals and, historically, Dené harvested these to optimize sustainable yields, to the degree that some claimed that failing to utilize useful plants would result in the plants disappearing. Historic records show that the majority of Dené births occurred in early spring because women were most well nourished in summer, therefore most likely to conceive.[7] At the opposite time of year, late winter, food supplies are running out and fat and oil, especially, may be minimal, reducing women's body fat to a level that inhibits conception. The warm half of the year would be best for babies' survival, in part because their better-fed mothers could better provide milk, so the cycle of human nutrition and of births fits principles of natural selection. The observation highlights the necessity of fat in human diets and helps the archaeologist extrapolate from the historic present to the more distant past.

Archaeology in the boreal forest zone is impoverished by acidic soils that destroy bone as well as softer organic materials. Consequently, human skeletons that might provide biological markers of affinity to early historic populations are lacking, and comparisons confined when attempted to coastal and High Arctic sites where preservation is much better (especially in the latter zone, where permafrost acts as a freezer maintaining organic matter for centuries). Exacerbating the challenge to archaeologists is the boreal forests' limited biomass, resulting in very low population densities of game animals and human populations, high mobility of game seeking forage and humans seeking game, and light, quickly built or easily transported shelters. Firewood being abundant, people relied on blazing hearths to keep them warm, rather than on heavily insulated structures such as those on the coasts that offer archaeologists solid frames, banks of collapsed sod blocks, and stone or ceramic lamps. Some pithouses have been excavated, few of them very ancient, most with comparatively shallow floors.

Adding to archaeologists' burdens, pottery is virtually absent in the western half of the boreal forest, Canada's Northwest Territory and adjacent Alaska. What is left are stone artifacts, often roughly made just to get a working edge. Looking at the crude heavy stone artifacts typical of western boreal forest sites, one wouldn't guess that the makers probably wore beautifully tailored clothing tastefully decorated with designs created with colored porcupine quills. These mobile people often left stone implements behind at campsites instead of carrying them along, an obvious reason why little effort was given to producing laboriously crafted, aesthetically pleasing stone objects. Repeated visits to campsites well situated for sighting or processing game, for fishing or berrying, or at portages could bring the artifacts into use again and again, their rough manufacture discouraging other visitors from taking them away.

The term Northern Archaic has been assigned to interior Alaskan artifacts dating from the fifth millennium BCE to at least the second millennium BCE, perhaps to the first millennium AD. Sites are often difficult to date, most of them campsites with little deposition of soil between multiple visits mixing artifacts and debris. No dramatic innovations appear until European incursions in the nineteenth century. Apparent continuity through minor changes in material culture leads to the interpretation that the Northern Archaic represents Athabascan (i.e., ancestral Dené) colonization of the region around six thousand years ago. Offsetting this straightforward linking of material culture continuity with the historic nations of the region, is the limitation of the archaeological record to utilitarian artifacts designed to take and process caribou, fish, bear, and the other resources essential to survival in the land. Iñupiaq hunting caribou inland left campsites looking much like those of Dené. Experiencing life with Dené brought anthropologist Robin Ridington the realization that their technology is basically knowledge they carry in their heads, of how to expeditiously make what they need out of generally available raw materials; weight is critical to these people who move several times a year, on foot or in spruce-frame boats covered with caribou or moose hides.[8] It is reasonable to suppose that interior Alaska was populated by Dené for as many as six thousand years, but there is no way definitely to link Dené to sites more than a few centuries old.

Research Puzzle

The premise that the Americas were populated by migrations through Beringia, and later, in the Holocene, across Bering Strait, gives Alaska the potential for disclosing the times and contents of these immigrations. Alaska's huge size, rugged terrain, thick forests, and small population mean archaeological sites are generally difficult to spot, nor often revealed by modern construction as in the Lower Forty-eight. Finds may contravene expectations, for example in Alaska Paleoindian Fluted Tradition blades seem to be no earlier than similar blades in temperate America. The state's potential conflicts with practical difficulties in carrying out research.

Metal tools, from native copper and from imported or meteoritic iron, have been revealed to have been more common in later Arctic societies than anthropologists had supposed. A Canadian researcher is persuaded that the Thule migration across the Arctic was a search for sources of iron, with Norse in eastern Canada and Greenland discovered to be one set of sources, amenable to trade. Utilization of metal tools would have kept Aleut, Alaskan, and Northwest Coast nations in the circum North Pacific trade circle: collaboration between Russian and American archaeologists following the end of the Soviet Union and the Cold War impressed both sides with the extent of this trade, leading them to title a jointly sponsored exhibit "Crossroads of Continents." Detailing movements of people, technologies, and art styles back and forth on those crossroads is the major research puzzle for archaeologists working in Alaska and the Arctic. Whether Norse and their forebears, on one side, and northeastern American First Nations on the other, will be seen to have constituted a voyaging zone in the North Atlantic is a research puzzle awaiting in-depth investigation.

Bibliographical Note

The Arctic volume, volume 5, of the Smithsonian Institution's *Handbook of North American Indians*, edited by David Damas (Washington DC, 1984), contains several detailed chapters on Alaskan Arctic prehistory; volume 6, the Subarctic, edited by June Helm (Washington DC, 1981), covers the boreal forest zone. Don E. Dumond's *Eskimos and Aleuts* (2nd edn, London, 1987) is a general survey of Alaskan prehistory, emphasizing major trends and questions of ethnic affiliations. The journal *Arctic Anthropology* is a source for recent research, for example in volume 35, number 1, 1998, papers from a symposium "North Pacific and Bering Sea Maritime Societies." Gordon R. Willey's *An Introduction to American Archaeology: North and Middle America* (vol. 1) (Englewood Cliffs, NJ, 1966), Chapter Seven on "The Arctic and Subarctic" remains a good introduction to the region, exceptionally well illustrated and containing interesting details on sites. As with any archaeological publication more than thirty years old, dating and chronological sequences cannot match the refinements developed from more recent, technically improved radiocarbon dating and further excavations amplifying the data base.

The archaeology of interior Alaska offers so little in the way of spectacular artifacts that, unlike the Yupik and Iñupiaq coastal areas, not to mention the southeastern Alaskan coast and islands with the magnificent Tlingit and Haida art, it has no coffee-table art books or volumes written for the public. There is some archaeology in *Key Issues in Hunter-Gatherer Research*, edited by Ernest S. Burch Jr and Linda J. Ellanna (Oxford, 1994), both of whom work with Alaskan First Nations. The volume brings together studies of coastal and interior Alaskan societies, Northwest Coast, Canada, Kamchatka, Tierra del Fuego, Africa, and Australia, with editors' introductions highlighting the data supporting authors' interpretations.

Notes

1. Sometimes the situation is reversed, geologists asking archaeologists to help sort out the history of local landforms according to the ages of artifacts found within or on their surfaces. The archaeologist will use stylistic attributes to link artifacts with similar ones radiocarbon-dated elswhere. Such collaboration between geologists and archaeologists is particularly common where both are working on Late Pleistocene–Early Holocene localities subject to relatively rapid physical changes.

2. Shamans are religious leaders in indigenous Siberian nations, the term coming from the Tungus language spoken by the Evenki. Inuit *angakkut* are similar to Evenki shamans and probably originated from, or learned from, northeastern Siberian shamans. Northwest Coast religious performers and doctors used many of these techniques, although Northwest Coast dance-dramas are more elaborate than Siberian performances. Diviners among Subarctic Indian nations such as the Ojibwe seem to have learned

techniques from this body of practices widespread in the North. "Shaman-ism" is not, however, a primordial religion, nor one shared by all peoples popularly called "primitive." For full discussion of shamans and of the misuse of the term even by academic writers, see my *Shamans and Religion: An Anthropological Exploration in Critical Thinking* (Prospect Heights, IL, 2000).

3. Kiyoshi Yamaura, "On the Origins of Thule Culture as Seen from the Typological Studies of Toggle Harpoon Heads," in Allen P. McCartney (ed.), *Thule Eskimo Culture: An anthropological Retrospective*, National Museum of Man, Mercury Series, Archaeological Survey of Canada no. 88 (Ottawa, 1979), pp. 474–84.

4. In the late twentieth century, many Northerners felt caught between substituting ski-doos (snowmobiles) for dog teams because the machines make no demands other than cash for gas, or maintaining dog teams as part of a relatively independent hunting way of life. Wage-earner schedules interfere with subsistence hunting, cash isn't easy to earn Up North. The dilemma of retaining "traditional," that is to say not Western capitalist, economies has been relatively successfully resolved in the Canadian James Bay Agreement of 1977 (see Ronald Niezen, *Defending the Land: Sovereignty and Forest Life in James Bay Cree Society*, Boston, 1998) and poorly so in the United States Alaska Native Claims Settlement Act of 1971 (see Norman A. Chance, *The Iñupiat and Arctic Alaska: an Ethnography of Development*, Fort Worth, TX, 1990).

5. Owen K. Mason and S. Craig Gerlach, "Chukchi Hot Spots, Paleo-Polynyas, and Caribou Crashes: Climatic and Ecological Dimensions of North Alaska Prehistory," *Arctic Anthropology* 32(1) (1995): 101–30, This paper emphasizes, through detailed discussion of several principal archaeological sites, the importance of particularities, rather than broad generalizations, for under-standing human situations.

6. Apaches and Navajos in the American Southwest are Athabascan-speakers who migrated south from western Canada, probably Alberta, around a thousand years ago. Their name for themselves, Diné, is a variant of Dené.

7. Bryan C. Gordon, *People of Sunlight, People of Starlight: Barrenland Archaeology in the Northwest Territories of Canada* (Hull, PQ, 1996), pp. 15–16.

8. Robin Ridington, *Little Bit Know Something* (Iowa City, IA, 1990).

References

Burch, Ernest S., Jr and Linda J. Ellanna (eds) (1994), *Key Issues in Hunter-Gatherer Research*. Oxford: Berg.

Chance, Norman A. (1990), *The Iñupiat and Arctic Alaska: an Ethnography of Development*. Fort Worth, TX: Holt, Rinehart & Winston.

Dumond, Don E. (1987), *Eskimos and Aleuts*. 2nd edn. London: Thames & Hudson.

Gordon, Bryan C. (1996), *People of Sunlight, People of Starlight: Barrenland Archaeology in the Northwest Territories of Canada*. Hull, PQ: Canadian Museum of Civilization, Mercury Series, Archaeologial Survey of Canada, Paper 154.

Kehoe, Alice Beck (2000), *Shamans and Religion: An Anthropological Exploration in Critical Thinking*. Prospect Heights, IL: Waveland Press.

Kiyoshi Yamaura (1979), "On the Origins of Thule Culture as Seen from the Typological Studies of Toggle Harpoon Heads," in Allen P. McCartney (ed.), *Thule Eskimo Culture: An Anthropological Retrospective*, Ottawa: National Museum of Man, Mercury Series, Archaeological Survey of Canada, Paper 88, pp. 474–84.

McCartney, Allen P. (1979), *Thule Eskimo Culture: An Anthropological Retrospective*. Ottawa: National Museum of Man, Mercury Series, Archaeological Survey of Canada, Paper 88.

Mason, Owen K. and S. Craig Gerlach (1995), "Chukchi Hot Spots, Paleo-Polynyas, and Caribou Crashes: Climatic and Ecological Dimensions of North Alaska Prehistory," *Arctic Anthropology* 32(1): 101–30.

Niezen, Ronald (1998), *Defending the Land: Sovereignty and Forest Life in James Bay Cree Society*. Boston, MA: Allyn & Bacon.

Ridington, Robin (1990), *Little Bit Know Something*. Iowa City, IA: University of Iowa Press.

Willey, Gordon R. (1966), *An Introduction to American Archaeology: North and Middle America*, vol. 1. Englewood Cliffs, NJ: Prentice-Hall.

From Julie Cruikshank, *Life Lived Like a Story*, pp. 278–81

This is our *Shagóon* – our history. Lots of people in those days, they told their story all the time. This story comes from old people, not just from one person – from my grandpa, Hutshi Chief, from Laberge Chief, from Dalton Post Chief. Well, they told the story of how first this Yukon came to be.

You don't put it yourself, one story. You don't put it yourself and then tell a little more. You put what they tell you, older people. You've got to tell it right. Not you are telling it: it's the person who told you that's telling that story.

My grandpa, one man, was Hutshi Chief. He's got two wives: one [Dené] from Selkirk, one [Tlingit] from Carcross [Caribou Crossing]; his name is Kaajoolaaxí; that's Tlingit. Oh, call him a different one: Kakhak – that's *dän k'è* [Southern Tutchone language] – that's an easy one. His Coast Indian [Tlingit] name comes from a long time ago: it was from trading they call him that way. You see, long-time Coast Indians, they go through that way to Selkirk, all over. He married first my grandma from Carcross: Däk'äläma. His Selkirk wife was K'edäma: she's the one they call Mrs Hutshi Chief.

My daddy's name was Hutshi Jim: my daddy is the oldest. Another brother is Chief Joe – Hutshi Joe – he had the same mother. One grandpa we've got, and I've got lots of cousins up at 1016 [Haines Junction] from this lady, Däk'äläma. These kids are all born around Hutshi. Hutshi is a coast name: Coast Indians call it Hóoch'i Áayi – means "Last Time Lake." That's when they go back [return to the coast]. The *dän k'è* name is Chuinagha. Lots of people used to live at Hutshi. My grandpa had a big house at Hutshi...all rotten now. Oh, it used to be good fishing spot! King salmon came that way, too. everybody came there together. Kajit [Crow clan] owns that place, but they're not stingy with it. [Mrs Ned, the narrator, is Kajit.]

Now I'm going to tell a story about long ago. This is my two grandpas' story, Big Jim's and Hutshi Chief's. I'm telling this story not from myself, but because everybody old knows this story. Just like now they go to school, old time we come to our grandpa. Whoever is old tells it the same way.

Well, Coast Indians came in here a long time before white people. People had fur, and they used it for everything themselves. Nobody knows alcohol, nobody knows sugar before

From Julie Cruikshank, Life Lived Like a Story, *pp. 278–81 (continued)*

those Coast Indians came. They brought guns, too. No white man here, nothing.

At Noogaayík, Tlingit people first saw chips coming down from upriver. People making rafts, I guess, and the chips floated down.

"Where did this one come from?" they asked. So that time Coast Indians wintertime to Dalton Post. That's the way they met these Yukon Indians. Yukon people are hunting, and they've got nice skin clothes – Oh, gee, porcupine quills [embroidery], moose skins, moccasins! Everything nice.

Coast Indians saw those clothes and they wanted them! That's the way they found out about these Yukon people. Right then, they found where we hunted. Coast Indians traded them knives, axes, and they got clothes, babiche, fish skin from the Yukon. They've got nothing, those Tlingit people, just cloth clothes, groundhog clothes. Nothing! Goat and groundhog [skins], that's all.

But people here had lots of fur and they used it in everything themselves – ready-made moccasins, buckskin parka, silverfox, red fox, caribou-skin parka sewed up [embroidered] with porcupine quills. You can't see it, this time...so pretty.

So that's how they got it. Coast Indians got snowshoes and moose-skin clothes – all warm – parka, caribou parka, caribou blanket, caribou mattress. Anything like that they want to use. Those people wanted clothes from here in Yukon...skin clothes, sheepskin, warm mitts...So they traded. They traded for snowshoe string, for babiche, for sinew, for tanned skin – all soft.

These Yukon people told Coast Indians to come back in summertime. So they did, next summer. Yukon people had lots of furs. That time they don't know money – they don't know where to sell them. So Coast Indians brought in guns. Well, they're surprised about that, Yukon people! They've been using bow and arrow! So they traded.

Coast Indians got guns, knives, axes. They came on snowshoes. They packed sugar, tea, tobacco, cloth to sew. Rich people would have eight packers [porters] each! They brought shells, they brought anything to trade. They traded for clothes.

From Julie Cruikshank, Life Lived Like a Story, *pp. 278–81 (continued)*

Coast Indians brought sugar, tea. At first these Yukon people didn't want it. But pretty soon, they went to Klukwan [on the coast]. They took their fur. They knew where to sell it now. They would go down wintertime with toboggan, Dalton Post way or by Lake Arkell.

But people here got crazy for trade goods. They traded for knives, they traded for anything, they say – shells, guns, needles. When you buy that gun, you've got to pile up furs how long is that gun, same as that gun, how tall! Then you get that gun.

I don't know those guns – that's before me. But my grandpa had that kind at Hutshi. I saw what they've been buying, though – blankets, not so thick, you know, quite light. You could pack maybe fifty blankets, I guess, from the coast. They would bring all that. Everybody bought their grandpa, their grandma a knife that time!

My grandpa, Hutshi Chief, had a trading partner, Gasleeni. We fixed up his grave, my brother and myself. Old people were satisfied with Coast Indians, what they used to bring – cloth, guns, and matches. They used flint before, and birch bark. Coast Indians taught people to chew tobacco – I never used it, me. I never used to use sugar, either.

Well, Coast Indians would rest there and then they could go anyplace, see? They go hunting; then they go back. Then these people would go down to see them. I never saw *those* ones – I know lots of Coast Indians, but they didn't bring anything in my time: I didn't see Coast Indians packing. It was before me, I guess, when my grandma was young.

Told in English by Ntthenada, Mrs Annie Ned, Southern Tutchone Dené, in the 1980s. Mrs Ned was born in the 1890s and raised by her grandparents.

Cruikshank, Julie (1990), *Life Lived Like a Story: Life Stories of Three Yukon Native Elders.* Lincoln, NE: University of Nebraska Press.

8

THE INTERIOR WEST

Between the Sierra of California and the Rockies is a vast land of broadly rolling sagebrush plains and pine-covered mountain ranges, the Great American Desert according to the United States' explorers seeking farmlands and timber. The land's indigenous people were disdainfully called Diggers, for their women were usually seen carrying a sturdy hardwood stick, grubbing up roots to take home in a woven bag tied to their waists. Population density was low, communities small and moving seasonally to their resources. When colonists' wagon trains trekked across the First Nations' valleys and passes, muddying streams and eating up forage, the land's inhabitants seldom fought off the well-armed invaders. Nearly a century later, professional ethnographers interviewed reservation-bound descendants of the First Nations, constructing a picture of family groups eking subsistence from fleet antelopes and the yearly harvest of pine nuts in the hills. So their forebears had lived – that is, two generations earlier after Mormon farmers and hundreds of wagon trains had banished them from the lakes and marshes their ancestors had relied upon.

The first extended effort, in the mid-twentieth century, to understand the archaeology of the Interior West took as its model the ethnographers' picture of people roaming the sagebrush, eating roasted grasshoppers and grass seeds, scattered like their resources. This was termed the Desert Culture, and continuities in stone artifact styles through the strata in large rockshelters led to the interpretation that the Desert Culture had been formed early in the Holocene and persisted with little change until reservations were established. Radical revision of this model by the second generation of archaeologists, beginning in the 1960s, is one of the more interesting stories of how archaeology can illuminate not only prehistoric eras but our understanding of circumstances of the more recent past.

The Great Basin Archaic

Because most streams in the Interior West flow into lakes within the region, rather than into an ocean, it has been given the term Great Basin. The warming climate trend that began in the Terminal Pleistocene and reached a climax in the fourth and third millennia BCE brought considerable aridity to the Great Basin, depleting resources needed by humans. Their response was to exploit a variety of plants, evidenced by quantities of ground-stone implements for grinding and pulverizing seeds, stalks, and roots. They wintered in villages beside lakes and marshes, families dispersing in spring to pursue game and harvest plant foods from camps at higher elevations. The pattern was elaborated in the last two millennia BCE, with pithouses in some of the winter villages, as climate became less hot and arid.

Archaeological terminology for the Great Basin Archaic emphasizes the "Archaic" mode of life, referring to the two millennia AD as "Late Archaic." The terminology implies that compared to the rest of America, Great Basin people – Diggers – would seem to have stagnated. The archaeologist who argued, in mid-century, for the concept of a persistent Desert Culture was persuaded by the work of younger colleagues that his earlier reading of the stratigraphy of his principal site, near Salt Lake City, had overlooked certain significant breaks in the record, and that the ethnographic picture he had relied upon was to be faulted for not taking into account the effects of Euroamerican colonization. His rejection of the overly simplistic interpretation won the respect of the younger researchers in the Great Basin, but earned little notice outside the region, nor did the critique of "Desert Culture" seem to extend to reinterpreting "Great Basin Archaic," in effect not much more than a new label for the old simplistic model. "Archaic" means a mode of life, goes the justification for the label, an economy of hunting and gathering natural resources, of living in small mobile family bands. This chapter will show that the justification is not warranted, that its "Late Archaic" ignores the agricultural villages of the southern Great Basin and the history of the Uto-Aztecan speakers – the intriguing and challenging fact that most of the nations in the Great Basin at the time of Euroamerican invasions spoke languages of the same stock as that of the Aztecs of Mexico.

Great Basin

Early Holocene Great Basin was cooler, with more lakes and marshes, than the region has been since. For humans, the differences between that period and later periods are amplified by changes in flora and fauna utilized for subsistence. Piñon pine, with its nuts the staple storable food for indigenous nations in the historic Great Basin, was absent from the early Holocene landscape, spreading into the region only during the middle Holocene with its warmer temperatures. Marsh and lake resources including shellfish as well as fish were the focus of subsistence during the early Holocene, with only few and small sites above valley bottoms. Animals hunted were similar to those hunted later – antelope, deer, rabbits, mountain sheep, a few bison – since the Pleistocene mammoths and sloths, and horses and llama-like camelids, were all extinct.

Burials in Spirit Cave, Nevada, dated 7400–7000 BCE, show us another important resource utilized by these people: hemp (also called dogbane), sagebrush, and juniper shredded into fiber for fabrics. Probably the earliest complete fabrics known anywhere in the world, those in Spirit Cave, include plain-plaited mats and bags, plain-twined fringed bags, plain-twined mats, and a robe of twisted rabbit skins. Feathers decorated two of the fringed bags, one also with decorative leather strips and an interwoven band of juniper or sage, and a third had only interwoven leather strips.[1] The finely woven mats were large enough to wrap the corpses deposited in the dry cave. Thanks to the desert cave, we see fabric art seldom preserved, proof that an art for which historic Great Basin people are famous was well developed by the end of the Pleistocene. It is interesting that flexible bags rather than baskets were placed with these corpses, whether because basketry was perhaps not as advanced as textiles at that time, or because the bags were considered appropriate for funeral furnishing, we cannot discover. There are even older weavings known from the Great Basin, a twined mat fragment from Fishbone Cave, Nevada, dated at 11,250 years ago (9250 BCE), and twined basketry, sandals, and cords from Fort Rock Cave in eastern Oregon, approximately the same age.

With the climate warming trend climaxing between 7000 and 4500 years ago (5000–2500 BCE), increased evaporation dried up many of the productive marshes and lakes. Piñon pine spread along the lower slopes of mountain ranges, but the disappearance of many bodies of permanent water forced humans to settle mainly adjacent to springs (which tend to support marshes, as well as provide drinking water).

In one of the few such sites excavated – in contrast to the rockshelters and caves favored by archaeologists – substantial shallow pithouses, not quite a meter deep (2.5 ft) and around eight meters in diameter (22–25 ft) had been constructed with posts around a central fireplace probably supporting roof poles over which mats and then earth were likely heaped, to make winter dwellings much like those of historic California nations such as the Modoc and Klamath in the area. Away from higher valleys with springs, a dearth of archaeological sites in much of the Great Basin during the Middle Holocene suggests that considerable sections of the desert were well-nigh uninhabitable.

People moved back into the less hospitable zones of the Basin after the Middle Holocene, around 2500 BCE, into regions much like those seen by the first Euroamerican explorers and Mormon colonists. Note that once United States agricultural colonization began, in the mid-nineteenth century, marsh drainage and diversion of water to irrigate fields rapidly changed the character of most Great Basin valleys, making the desert floors one sees today. Prehistorically, Late Archaic (up to mid-first millennium AD or even later) winter settlements lay in valley bottoms near standing water and marsh, with fall piñon-nut harvesting camps on the lower slopes of ranges and summer hunting and plant-gathering camps in upland valleys and passes.

One habitat that was important before colonist invasions and strongly affected by them is floodplains along the higher reaches of rivers, prime habitat for edible roots, tubers, and bulbs including camas, bitterroot, biscuitroot, and onion. These were grubbed up with digging sticks and peeled, then baked in large earth-oven pits lined with rocks; a fire was built on the rocks and extinguished once they were hot, with leaves or stalks lining the rocks to protect the roots (or tubers or bulbs), and earth piled on top of the over-lining to insulate the heat. Baking could continue several days, after which the food was dried, pounded into meal, formed into cakes, and stored in airtight bags, cached in pits for winter use or carried as trail food. Some roots could be dried without baking and strung together or pounded into meal for bagging. Roots, tubers, and bulbs are nutritious and most yield pleasant-tasting porridge or flatbread. Rock-filled pits, the earth ovens, around two meters (or yards) in diameter, are common in the higher river valleys where biscuitroot, camas, or similar foods would have grown. Ovens required the labor of digging the large pit and carrying about half a ton of rocks, chopping and carrying firewood (juniper was preferred but grows farther upslope), and peeling the bushels of food that by volume baking would have made the labor worthwhile. Knowledgable harvesting

practices thinned the desired plants and weeded out others, max-
imizing yields; knowledge of plant-tending was entrusted to certain
members of the family or band who felt responsible for nurturing
the plants and taught younger people.

Making baskets, mats, and twined fabrics was another process
calling upon responsible knowledge of plant nurturing as well as
craft techniques. Washo women with this knowledge advised United
States Forest Service staff that to maintain bracken fern they used
for decorative black elements in weaving, decayed brush had to be
burned off, the plants had to be thinned (harvesting accomplished
some of this), and buds replanted properly spaced. The women preferred to collect ferns in the fall when their leaves began yellowing,
because, they explained, by then the plants had stored nutrients in
their roots for next spring, and taking the stalks would not affect
next year's growth. Cut stalks are soaked in mud beside springs to
obtain the desired black color. This small aspect of the basketmaker's
art illustrates the breadth of technical knowledge developed by
First Nations women and the complexity, in overall view, of their
manufactures.[2]

Another type of rock construction found in upland zones of the
Great Basin are chutes and pens built to drive and trap mountain
sheep. Dated examples belong to the historic period, but since few
have any datable organic matter preserved in them, some may be
older. Log traps are also known, and obviously likely to be relatively
recent if preserved. Conversely, nets preserved in the remarkable
dry caves of eastern Oregon and western Nevada date as far back as
the end of the Pleistocene, and may have been used to trap waterfowl,
stretched across flyways, or rabbits or antelopes driven into them,
practices common among Great Basin First Nations in the early
nineteenth century. These practices involved several families, at a
minimum, and were directed by "rabbit bosses" or "antelope bosses,"
persons as knowledgable about long-term sustainable management
of game resources as women basketmakers are of their resources.
Fish, obtained by means of constructed stone or basket-trap weirs,
nets, and hooks and line, similarly were significant food resources
and procured by group planning.

Historically, and for nearly five millennia, the "Digger Indians"
usually built rough-looking wickiups, basically a circle of light poles
and interwoven brush with a generous smoke-hole in the center.
It was in such a wickiup that the Smithsonian anthropologist James
Mooney met the prophet of the 1890s Ghost Dance religion, Wovoka
(Jack Wilson), a Northern Paiute. Wovoka preached the value of

traditional ways, although he was employed as a ranch hand by a colonist. He and his wife wore purchased Euroamerican clothing and he carried a shotgun, yet they ate native foods and raised their children in the wickiup, refusing a cabin offered them by Wovoka's employer. It was cold on the winter day Mooney met Wovoka, snow on the ground, but coats, rabbit-skin robes, and a good fire kept everyone comfortable.[3] Born just when the first colonists, backed by a military post, took over this people's lands, Wovoka learned practical and spiritual leadership from his father, exemplifying the social structure that appeared simple and egalitarian to invading outsiders equating leadership with pomp and privilege. Some idea of the depth of respect this hereditary leader enjoyed may be gauged by the belief that an earthquake after his death signified heaven shaking upon his entrance!

Fremont

With so much of Great Basin material and social culture perishable, the residue left to archaeologists appears little changed from the third millennium BCE to well into, or even after, the first millennium AD. Quite a different type of culture is evidenced in the southern portion of the Basin during the first millennium AD, particularly between AD 1000 and 1300: termed the Fremont, it is marked by permanent stone-slab architecture, maize agriculture with storage chambers for the crop, utilitarian gray pottery, rock art and figurines, and population density reflected in villages plus small farmsteads. All of these features bring to mind the cultures of the Pueblo nations of the Southwest, leading to the initial supposition that Fremont was an expansion of Anasazi (ancestral Pueblo) northward.

More regional archaeology, and more ethnohistory, complicated this picture. Bows and arrows seem to have been introduced into the Great Basin during the first millennium AD, possibly as early as the beginning of the millennium and definitely replacing the javelin with atlatl (spearthrower board) by the middle of the millennium. Whether the bow and arrow spread as technology independent of population movements, or gave military advantage to soldiers in the vanguard of territorial conquest, we cannot tell. Maize cultivation appeared at the same time as the bow and arrow, although archaeologists don't seem to see much significance in this correlation, presumably because maize originated in Mexico and was carried northward over many centuries, while bows and arrows conventionally are seen to have come into America from the north-west (Bering Strait, because bows and arrows are millennia older in Eurasia and probable in the Arctic Small Tool Tradition, second millennium BCE [Chapter 6]). The earliest arrowpoints in the North-western Plains are no older than those in the southwestern Great Basin, undermining the assumption. If the technology was intro-duced into America on the West Coast (Chapter 5), it could have spread both northeast into the Plains and southeast into the Basin and Colorado Plateau, giving the similar early dates in both regions. Pacific Coast shells in the southwestern Basin at this time testify to trade connections with California.

Besides bows and arrows and maize cultivation assisted with ditches to bring water to the plots, stone and adobe architecture and stor-age pits appear in the southwestern sector of the Basin between the first and fifth centuries AD. During this period, ceramics became established in the Southwest, south of the Basin, and in the bordering Colorado Plateau; the art was brought in from Mexico, as maize and its cultivation had been centuries earlier. Ceramics did not come into use in the Basin until the sixth century AD, utilitarian gray ware similar to that used in the Southwest at the time. Conventionally, the Southwest's Basketmaker culture, the proto-Anasazi of the first millennium AD, is distinguished from the contemporary early Fremont in the southern Great Basin, yet the differences are not great. Basketmaker people made more substantial pithouses, some-times, other times sheltering in wickiups. Basketmaker people hunted mountain sheep and collected quantities of piñon nuts, two resources characteristic of Basin adaptation. The notion that there was a Western Archaic over the vast intermontane area from Canada to Mexico from the mid-third millennium BCE into the first millennium AD fits the data.

Given this perspective merging Arizona Basketmaker and Basin Late Archaic, we see the innovation of maize cultivation, with its con-structed storage pits or chambers, moving northward from its Mex-ican homeland until it reaches the boundaries set by a combination of aridity, lack of rivers and topography suitable for irrigation projects, and frost. This boundary fluctuated with minor climate shifts during the past millennium, retreating southward after AD 1300. Stone-slab and adobe buildings with prepared clay floors and, in some areas, impressive stone storage chambers on cliff ledges, were adopted in much of this range and, some generations later, pottery. There seems no reason to perceive an invasion of Anasazi displacing the southern Basin Late Archaic peoples.

The perspective fits ethnohistoric facts often neglected in assessing "Fremont." Hopi Pueblo speak an Uto-Aztecan language of the same stock as the languages of Utes, Paiutes, Shoshone, and Comanche. Hopi's neighbors to the north are Southern Paiutes who farmed along rivers, digging irrigation ditches where necessary for their crops. When encountered by European explorers in the late eighteenth and Americans in the nineteenth centuries, they built only wickiups or somewhat heavier pole and brush winter houses, not stone or adobe pueblos on mesa tops, hence a difference between them and Hopi impressed these explorers. Once, and where, maize agriculture was adopted, population density increased and there was incentive to invest labor in stone structures, and later to make pottery – thus, "Fremont culture." In between irrigable valleys suitable for maize, there may have been lower densities of non-agricultural people in flimsier homes, or only the excursions of Fremont people to hunt and to gather foods and plant materials from other zones. Then, probable climate changes in the thirteenth and fourteenth centuries AD forced a retrenchment southward from not only the Basin but from the bordering Colorado Plateau, maize cultivation virtually disappearing from the Basin and at least some of the Colorado Plateau Anasazi moving into the Río Grande Valley among its established, and persisting, agricultural towns.

Numic Expansion

A major debate concerns the prehistory of Basin Uto-Aztecans, that is, the Numa (pronounced "Numma"). "Numic" is the language family including Shoshone, Comanche, Ute, and Paiute. Numic itself is a branch of Uto-Aztecan; other Uto-Aztecan languages include Tubatulabal in the California Sierra, several "Mission Indian" languages in southern California (Luiseño and Cahuilla among them), Hopi, and the long series through Mexico, from 'O'odham (Pima and Papago) in southern Arizona down through Yaqui, Tarahumara (Rarámuri), Huichol, to Nahuatl, the Aztecs' language. The chain implies spread of an ancestral Uto-Aztecan population, whether from north to south and eastward, or the opposite, from Central Mexico. Aztec histories say the north-to-southeastward movement is correct, that their forebears came from the desert north and learned the arts of imperial civilization from earlier citizens of the Valley of Mexico. Fitting into this history, Numa are hypothesized to have spread northeastward from southeastern California (and Hopi eastward, Tubatulabal northward). Noting that, historically, Utes and Shoshone live in the area of Fremont sites, it was premised that the droughts of the thirteenth century AD forced abandonment of Fremont fields, and hunting-gathering Numa, able and willing to survive on collected indigenous foods, took over the deserted region. Shoshone and Utes, according to this scenario, lived over much of their territory only for about five centuries. Shoshone battles against Plains and Plateau nations in the eighteenth century, legendary because these events were remembered as the northern nations' first encounters with horse soldiers, are supposed to reflect continuation of Shoshones' aggressive efforts to expand their domains. To the south, the closely related Comanche similarly are interpreted to have used their quickly acquired skill with horses to expand against nations lacking this military advantage in the seventeenth century.

Several problems beset this neat narrative. That a more arid regime affected the interior West from the thirteenth century AD into historic time seems well established. On the western edge of the Basin along the California–Nevada border, the lakes and marshes fed by Sierra runoff were reduced although not gone. Klamath, Modoc, Washo, and perhaps some Maidu remained in their homelands, withdrawing somewhat to the still well-watered higher valleys. Paiute could then use the border zone more intensively – not exactly a take-over. The huge central Basin shows no dramatic climate change, having been basically arid for millennia, and its human inhabitants would have continued their low-density, eclectic way of life, utilizing persisting lakes and marshes, lower-slope piñon groves, and higher meadows, the way of life of historic Northern Paiutes including Wovoka. The real expansion may have been into the eastern Basin and through passes into the Plateau and edge of the Plains, replacing Fremont – unless Fremont, too, were Numa, in which case we are seeing "Fremont" reverting to the ancestral Late Archaic way of life retained by their congeners in the most arid central Basin. Realistically, "Fremont" probably encompasses both Numa who carried, and some of who eventually gave up, maize cultivation, and Anasazi who drew back to the Río Grande region. The cases of the Hopi, who became stereotypically Pueblo, and Southern Paiutes who maintained river-valley maize farming until pushed out by Mormon settlers, demonstrate that "Fremont" attributes fit quite a few US Uto-Aztecan speakers.

Focusing on the fact that people have been living in the central Basin with little change in way of life, other than using bows and arrows rather than atlatls and javelins after the early first millennium

AD, for five millennia, the "Numic expansion" may best refer to the influx of people in the third millennium BCE, after the amelioration of Mid-Holocene aridity and establishment of piñon-pine groves. The very low population density, necessitated by the low (and patchy) density of both floral and faunal resources, left meager artifact clusters, and the Numas' characteristic efflorescence of the art of basketry seldom preserved in the archaeological record, giving the impression these people were poor and dull. Comparing a museum's archaeology cases of Basin artifacts, with blocky milling stones and small arrowheads, to its ethnographic cases crammed with a diversity of beautiful baskets, trays, woven boxes and hats, vividly underscores the challenges of reading peoples' histories from archaeological remains.

The Plateau

North of the Great Basin are the uplands through which major rivers flow to the Pacific: the Columbia, the Snake, and the Fraser. Sections of these rivers are deep gorges, and steep, forested mountains fill much of the region, especially the north. Lakes and grassy valleys invite people to the mid-region, while the southern sector blends into the Basin with rolling sagebrush plains. Historically, Shoshone and Northern Paiute occupied the southern area, Sahaptin speakers (Yakama, Walla Walla, Umatilla, and about a dozen other small nations) and related Nez Percé the middle region, and Salishan speakers (Shuswap, Okanagan, Flathead, Spokan, Coeur d'Alene, and some half-dozen others) the northern sector. Sahaptin seems distantly related to Klamath and Modoc in northeastern California, the "Plateau Penutians" as distinct from the many California and West Coast Penutian nations; linguists infer that the homeland from which Penutians spread to and along the coast and through California may have been the western border of the Plateau in Oregon, possibly the Willamette Valley running south from the lower Columbia River. Linguistically, the relationships of the historic Plateau nations are to the West Coast. Who may have occupied the Plateau before upriver spread of Salish and Sahaptin and northward expansion of Numa is beyond linguists' power of inference.

Early Holocene Plateau people, like those to the south, hunted deer, elk, and waterfowl, attracted to the resources of lakes and marshes. In central Oregon, obsidian (volcanic glass, making very sharp weapon points and knives) was quarried from a quiescent volcano crater as early as 9000 BCE, and perhaps it was obsidian that was traded westward, even in the early Holocene, in exchange for ornamental seashells from California. By 6500 BCE, salmon were running up the Columbia River; from this time on, salmon caught in quantities during spring and fall runs were a staple of the region.

Mid-Holocene warmer climate was less severe in affecting humans on the Plateau than in the central Basin. Camas and probably other roots, tubers and bulbs, chokecherries, and seeds from weedy grasses were harvested, attested by the split-cobblestone choppers, ground-stone grinding slabs, and rock-lined earth ovens used to process these foods. Antelope and mountain sheep, in addition to deer and elk, were hunted with tiny sharp blades (microblades) set as armature for javelins as well as the more generally common larger blades. Fish were speared or taken with lines, and probably with nets that are much less often preserved. Pithouses, very likely a few together in small villages, were introduced on the Plateau as on the California border of the Basin, indicating the present state borders obtrude over an ancient shared cultural zone. Life was endangered at 5000 BCE when Mount Mazama, now Crater Lake in southwestern Oregon, violently erupted, spewing thick hot ash over hundreds of thousands of square miles, from Alberta into Nevada, the mouth of the Columbia east to the plains beyond the Rockies. Vegetation would have been killed, and the animals dependent on it decimated. At the time depth of seven millennia ago, archaeological techniques cannot resolve data sufficiently finely to see how people coped with the eruptions continuing intermittently for a century or more, whether they found refuges in canyons or fled the region. The Mazama eruption coincides with the Mid-Holocene climate shift, complicating our reading of the archaeological record to see responses to the catastrophe. Whatever the immediate or long-term effects, human habitation remains do lie above the ash layer through-out the Plateau.

Climate amelioration by 2500 BCE fostered population increase. Historically, winter villages lay near the major rivers, the Columbia, Fraser, and Snake, generally where tributaries entered, but archae-ology shows pithouse villages on the upper reaches of the tributary rivers, too. One historian suggests that the population decimation from smallpox and possibly other epidemics in the protohistoric eighteenth century, coupled with political-economic upsets related to that and to escalation of trade due to European entry into the indigenous networks, encouraged consolidation of surviving villages into the main-river settlements seen in the early nineteenth century.

Slaves were a significant trade item at that time throughout the Plateau, Basin borderlands, and West Coast, probably in at least late prehistoric times as well, heightening the value of defendable sites and coalitions.

The Dalles (Narrows) at the east end of the Columbia River Gorge was perhaps the most desirable site in all the Plateau. The river was here channeled through a stretch of cliffs, forcing salmon to crowd and leap as they swam upstream to spawn. Men with dip nets and spears could stand on the rocks along the water channel, scooping up bushels of fish to be passed, assembly-line style, to women for filleting. Gutted and sliced, the fish were hung on racks to dry and either stored or pounded into a highly nutritious meal that was bagged or pressed into bricks. Wishram and Wasco, Chinook-speaking (a Penutian language) towns one on each side of the river at the Dalles, sold these standard-sized bags and bricks to travelers using the river, providing also other foods such as camas meal and space for traders – and gamblers. At the Dalles, one could obtain dentalium, olivella, and abalone shells from the Pacific, furs and hides from the Plateau and Rockies, fine baskets and twined bags, and one could bet, hoping to grab the wagered heap but maybe losing even one's shirt. At the beginning of the nineteenth century, the first Europeans down the Columbia saw some three thousand people at the "great fair" at the Dalles. These included, besides travelers up or down river, other nations of the Plateau who moved seasonally to the Narrows to join in harvesting the huge runs of salmon. Archaeology reveals this use of the Narrows for ten thousand years, with lessened occupation during the mid-Holocene temperature maximum, then increasingly dense occupations with those from the mid-first millennium BCE to the protohistoric period (eighteenth century AD) demonstrating participation (or trading) in artistic stonework styles of the southern Northwest Coast.

Tsagiglalal, "She Who Watches" in Wishram, is a famous rock carving (petroglyph) at the Dalles. (Actually, there are four such petroglyphs plus small carvings of Tsagiglalal in stone, bone, and antler in cemeteries in the Dalles area.) All the Tsagiglalal carvings, depicting a grinning face with large eyes formed by concentric ovals, date to the protohistoric eighteenth century, up to the early historic period about AD 1840, and two of the petroglyphs overlook village cemeteries. Because of the dating, Tsagiglalal is interpreted to represent grinning death welcoming the thousands of Indians dying in the unprecedented epidemics charging ahead of direct visits by Europeans, carried through contacts between Indians in the protohistoric century once smallpox, measles, and other Eurasian diseases had been introduced via European invasions in Mexico and the Atlantic coast. (Horses and horse-riding, too, spread Indian to Indian ahead of direct visits by Europeans, horses reaching the Columbia region half a century before Europeans at the beginning of the 1800s.) The "great fair" operated by Wishram and Wasco at the Dalles became a hollow success in the eighteenth century when the congregation of thousands from the entire Western half of the continent brought in the deadly diseases, decimating the Plateau nations.

Other petroglyphs and rock paintings (pictographs) on the Plateau depict hunt scenes, stylized human figures, or fantastic creatures that may in some instances represent insects or possibly spirit beings such as flash in lightning. Fragments of a pictograph that spalled off a rockshelter wall and were buried in an occupation layer dated between 6000–4000 BCE, and some petroglyphs, especially when somewhat protected from weather by overhangs, might be that old, but so many show horses that the majority are not older than the protohistoric. When inquiries have been made of First Nations people living near rock art sites, many in the Plateau, as in California and the Plains, aver that the art is older than their communities' memories and suggest the art not only shows spirit beings, but was made by spirit beings to inform humans that the locality is favored by the spirit, an auspicious place to pray – in other words, a shrine. Considering the rapid decimation of villages by protohistoric epidemics and subsequent population movements forced by colonist invasions, the histories of much rock art may well have been lost even if only a couple centuries old.

Research Puzzle

Puzzling for decades whether Fremont was (note singular) Puebloan, archaeologists more recently have distinguished regional variants of "Fremont." These distinctions fit ethnohistorians' contributions describing farming by Paiutes, and also careful gathering of indigenous food plants by Puebloans. Previously assumed contrasts between "hunting-gathering Paiutes" and "agricultural Pueblos" are seen to have been overdrawn. The research puzzle now requires linking early historic First Nations to regions within the southern Great Basin, attempting to find continuities in artifact types such as styles of woven sandals.

Somewhere in the Great Basin, Apacheans, forebears of the Navajo and Apache, may have traveled. These Athabascan-speaking (Dené, Diné in Navajo) peoples migrated from northwest Canada to the American Southwest about a thousand years ago, no doubt taking several centuries to complete the move. Finds of gray pottery somewhat like Navajo pottery may indicate settlements of these Apacheans in the Basin. Alternately, the Apacheans may have traveled mainly along the eastern front of the Rockies; even so, some may have explored westward through passes such as along the Bighorn River. The hypothesis that some Fremont may have been Apacheans links the puzzle of Apachean migration to the puzzle of who were Fremont.

Another research puzzle concerns identifying who inhabited the vast areas historically homelands to the Numa, if linguists' interpretation of Numic history is correct in postulating a relatively recent spread, a thousand years ago, of these peoples through the Basin from an original territory in its southern portion. The Aztecs of Mexico said their ancestors had lived to the north in a land of caves, journeying southward until they saw the envisioned promised land of marshy lakes, the Valley of Mexico. About when the ancestors of the Mexica (Aztecs) were moving southeastward, taking advantage of political uncertainties and reformulations following the decline of Toltec power, northern Uto-Aztecan speakers – Numa – were expanding north beyond the agricultural zone. Recent DNA tests suggest migrating men may have married into local hunter-gatherer families, the children speaking their fathers' Numic languages. What their mothers' languages were, we have little clue. Tying linguistic reconstructions, legendary histories, archaeological and biological data together is a puzzle in which few of the pieces snap into a close fit.

Bibliographical Notes

Basic sources for Great Basin archaeology, at this writing, include Donald Grayson's *The Desert's Past* (Washington DC, 1993), *Models for the Millennium: Great Basin Anthropology Today*, edited by Charlotte Beck (Salt Lake City, UT, 1999), *Intermountain Archaeology*, edited by David B. Madsen and Michael D. Metcalf (Salt Lake City, UT, 2000), and *Across the West: Human Population Movement and the Expansion of the Numa*, edited by David Madsen and David Rhode (Salt Lake City, UT, 1994). C. Melvin Aikens's paper in the latter, pages 35–43, argues the scenario I find most reasonable.

For the Plateau, James D. Keyser's *Indian Rock Art of the Columbia Plateau* (Seattle, WA, 1992) provides a regional overview as well as an unusually humanistic perspective. Aikens's *Archaeology of Oregon* (Portland, OR, 1986) is an exceptionally clear, thorough, and concise survey, modestly published by the US Department of Interior Bureau of Land Management, Oregon Office.

Notes

1. The textiles from Spirit Cave were described by ethnologist Catherine Fowler in a paper presented to the 1997 annual meeting of the Society for American Archaeology, and in *Nevada Historical Society Quarterly* 40(1): 17–23, by archaeologist Amy Dansie, and in *Mammoth Trumpet* 12(2): 1, 14–17, both 1997 publications. Fowler's 1996 essay in the book edited by James B. Petersen, *A Most Indispensable Art: Native Fiber Industries from Eastern North America* (University of Tennessee Press, Knoxville), pp. 180–99, gives a good account of early textiles throughout North America. Twining, a technique in which the weft element is twisted around each warp by hand rather than thrown through alternate warps by means of a shuttle, makes a strong fabric although it takes longer to make a piece. If industrial-scale production (as demanded by the Aztec empire, for example) is not required, twining may be the preferred technique for fabrics; it was common through much of indigenous North America and is still used by women of the Plateau nations for carrying bags.

2. Illustrated monographs on Great Basin women's arts include Catherine S. Fowler's *In the Shadow of Fox Peak: An Ethnography of the Cattail Eater Northern Paiute People of Stillwater Marsh* (Washington DC, 1992), and Margaret M. Wheat's *Survival Arts of the Primitive Paiute* (Reno, NV, 1967).

3. See my *The Ghost Dance: Ethnohistory and Revitalization* (Harcourt Brace, 1989) for a detailed description of these Paiute. Michael Hittman's *Wovoka and the Ghost Dance* (Lincoln, NE, 1997) is a compendium of all that is known of the prophet and his community, commissioned by them, the Yerington Paiute Tribe.

References

Aikens, C. Melvin (1986), *Archaeology of Oregon*. Oregon State Office (Portland), US Department of Interior Bureau of Land Management.

Beck, Charlotte (ed.) (1999), *Models for the Millennium: Great Basin Anthropology Today*. Salt Lake City, UT: University of Utah Press.

Campbell, Sarah K. (1990), *PostColumbian Culture History in the Northern Columbia Plateau AD 1500–1900*. New York: Garland.

Connolly, Thomas J. (1999), *Newberry Crater: A Ten-thousand-Year Record of Human Occupation and Environmental Change in the Basin-Plateau Borderlands*. Salt Lake City, UT: University of Utah Anthropological Papers no. 121, University of Utah Press.

Dansie, Amy (1997), "Note on Textiles Associated with the Spirit Cave Burials," *Nevada Historical Society Quarterly* 40(1): 17–23.

Fowler, Catherine S. (1992), *In the Shadow of Fox Peak: An Ethnography of the Cattail Eater Northern Paiute People of Stillwater Marsh*. Washington DC: US Department of the Interior Fish and Wildlife Service Cultural Resource Series no. 5, Government Printing Office.

Fowler, Catherine S. (1996), "Eastern North American Textiles: A Western Perspective," in James B. Petersen (ed.), *A Most Indispensable Art: Native Fiber Industries from Eastern North America*. Knoxville, TN: University of Tennessee Press, pp. 180–99.

Fowler, Catherine S. (1997), "Plaited Matting from Spirit Cave, NV: Technical Implications," paper presented to Society for American Archaeology annual meeting, Nashville, TN.

Grayson, Donald K. (1993), *The Desert's Past*. Washington DC: Smithsonian Institution Press.

Hall, Don Alan (1997), "Remarkable Discovery: Though Science Sometimes Takes Time, the Consequences Can Be Spectacular," *Mammoth Trumpet* 12(2): 1, 14–17.

Hittman, Michael (1997), *Wovoka and the Ghost Dance*. Lincoln, NE: University of Nebraska Press (1st edn, 1990, Grace Dangberg Foundation, Carson City, NV).

Kehoe, Alice Beck (1989), *The Ghost Dance: Ethnohistory and Revitalization*. Fort Worth, TX: Harcourt Brace.

Keyser, James D. (1992), *Indian Rock Art of the Columbia Plateau*. Seattle, WA: University of Washington Press.

Madsen, David B. and David Rhode (eds) (1994), *Across the West: Human Population Movement and the Expansion of the Numa*. Salt Lake City, UT: University of Utah Press.

Madsen, David B. and Michael D. Metcalf (eds) (2000), *Intermountain Archaeology*. Salt Lake City, UT: University of Utah Press.

Wheat, Margaret M. (1967), *Survival Arts of the Primitive Paiute*. Reno, NV: University of Nevada Press.

**From Sarah Winnemucca Hopkins, *Life Among the Piutes,
Their Wrongs and Claims*, pp. 5–15:**

I was born somewhere near 1844...I was a very small child when
the first white people came into our country....The third year
more emigrants came, and that summer Captain Fremont, who
is now General Fremont. My grandfather met him, and they
were soon friends. They met just where the railroad crosses
Truckee River, now called Wadsworth, Nevada. Captain Fremont
gave my grandfather the name of Captain Truckee, and he also
called the river after him. Truckee is an Indian word, it means
"all right," or "very well." A party of twelve of my people went to
California with Captain Fremont.

I do not know just how long they were gone....When my
grandfather went to California he helped Captain Fremont fight
the Mexicans. When he came back he told the people what a
beautiful country California was....That same fall, very late, the
emigrants kept coming. They could not get over the mountains,
so they had to live with us. You call my people bloodseeking. My
people did not seek to kill them, nor did they steal their horses,
– no, no, far from it. During the winter my people helped them.
They gave them such as they had to eat. They did not hold out
their hands and say: –

"You can't have anything to eat unless you pay me." No, – no
such word was used by us savages at that time; and the persons I
am speaking of are living yet; they could speak for us if they
choose to do so.

The following spring, there was a great excitement among my
people on account of fearful news coming from different tribes,
that the people whom they called their white brothers were
killing everybody that came in their way, and all the Indian
tribes had gone into the mountains to save their lives. So my
father told all his people to go into the mountains and hunt
and lay up food for the coming winter. Then we all went into
the mountains. There was a fearful story they told us children.
Our mothers told us that the whites were killing everybody and
eating them. So we were all afraid of them. Every dust that we
could see blowing in the valleys we would say it was the white
people. In the late fall my father told his people to go to the
rivers and fish, and we all went to Humboldt River, and the
women went to work gathering wild seed, which they grind
between the rocks....

From Sarah Winnemucca Hopkins, Life Among the Piutes, Their Wrongs and Claims, *pp. 5–15 (continued)*

Oh, what a fright we all got one morning to hear some white people were coming. Every one ran as best they could. My poor mother was left with my little sister and me. Oh, I never can forget it. My poor mother was carrying my little sister on her back, and trying to make me run; but I was so frightened I could not move my feet, and while my poor mother was trying to get me along my aunt overtook us, and she said to my mother: "Let us bury our girls, or we shall all be killed and eaten up." So they went to work and buried us, and told us if we heard any noise not to cry out, for if we did they would surely kill us and eat us. So our mothers buried me and my cousin, planted sage bushes over our faces to keep the sun from burning them, and there we were left all day.

Oh, can any one imagine my feeling *buried alive,* thinking every minute that I was to be unburied and eaten up by the people that my grandfather loved so much? With my heart throbbing, and not daring to breathe, we lay there all day. It seemed that night would never come. Thanks be to God! the night came at last. Oh, how I cried and said: "Oh, father, have you forgotten me? Are you never coming for me?" I cried so I thought my very heartstrings would break.

At last we heard some whispering. We did not dare to whisper to each other, so we lay still. I could hear their footsteps coming nearer and nearer. I thought my heart was coming right out of my mouth. Then I heard my mother say, "'Tis right here!" Oh, can any one in this world ever imagine what were my feelings when I was dug up by my poor mother and father? My cousin and I were once more happy in our mothers' and fathers' care, and we were taken to where all the rest were.

Well, while we were in the mountains hiding, the people that my grandfather called our white brothers came along to where our winter supplies were. They set everything we had left on fire. It was a fearful sight. It was all we had for the winter, and it was all burnt during that night. My father took some of his men during the night to try and save some of it, but they could not; it had burnt down before they got there.

This whole band of white people [the Donner party of emigrants] perished in the mountains, for it was too late to

From Sarah Winnemucca Hopkins, Life Among the Piutes, Their Wrongs and Claims, *pp. 5–15 (continued)*

cross them. We could have saved them, only my people were afraid of them. We never knew who they were, or where they came from.

Early in the following spring, my father told all his people to go to the mountains, for there would be a great emigration that summer. He told them..."Within ten days come together at the sink of Carson [Carson River oasis]."...During that day one could see old women getting together talking over what they had heard my father say. They said, –

"It is true what our great chief has said, for it was shown to him by a higher power. It is not a dream. Oh, it surely will come to pass. We shall no longer be a happy people, as we are now; we shall no longer go here and there as of old; we shall no longer build our big fires as a signal to our friends, for we shall always be afraid of being seen by those bad people."

"Surely they don't eat people?"

"Yes, they do eat people, because they ate each other up in the mountains last winter."

This was the talk among the old women during the day.

Written in English, edited for publication by Mrs Horace Mann, by Sarah Winnemucca, daughter and granddaughter of the principal chiefs of the Northern Paiute, "Truckee" and Winnemucca.

Hopkins, Sarah Winnemucca (1883), *Life Among the Piutes, Their Wrongs and Claims.* Edited by Mary (Mrs Horace) Mann. New York: G. P. Putnam's Sons. Facsimile reprint 1969, Bishop, CA: Sierra Media.

Figure 4 Chetro Ketl pueblo, Chaco Canyon. Photo by Alice B. Kehoe

9

THE AMERICAN SOUTHWEST

The American Southwest – Arizona, New Mexico, and the adjoining border sections of Utah and Colorado – fits geographically more into northwestern Mexico than temperate United States, and indeed until the annexation of Texas stimulated United States ambition to expand to the Pacific through a southern route, the Southwest had politically been part of Mexico. Underlying cultural continuity is as obvious today as when the first Spanish, in 1540, christened "Nuevo México" after journeying for months through nation after nation speaking Uto-Aztecan languages.

Archaeologists conventionally divide the American Southwest into three provinces, Hohokam in southern Arizona (including the Phoenix and Tucson Basins), Mogollon in southwest New Mexico (south of Albuquerque) and southeast Arizona into Chihuahua, Mexico, and Anasazi in northern Arizona and New Mexico and adjacent Utah and Colorado. A fourth sector would be the western Arizona–southeastern California zone along the Colorado River, generally considered peripheral to the Southwest. Much of the Southwest is semi-arid, real desert in southern Arizona, but elsewhere extensive uplands and mountain ranges supporting piñon and other conifers. From the standpoint of economics, Southwesterners should have always made their living by seasonal movements of small bands harvesting relatively sparse but varied wild foods; contrary to common sense, for three thousand years most Southwesterners have farmed, investing much labor in nurturing maize on land alien to it. This determination to construct agricultural societies makes the history of the Southwest intriguing.

Paleoindian sites in the Southwest include mammoth kills with Clovis blades in southeastern Arizona, and giant bison (*Bison antiquus*) kills with Folsom spearpoints in eastern New Mexico. The latter lie near the valleys and ranges of the mountains, the open high plains – prime habitat of the bison – before them to the east. Paleoindians may well have wintered in sheltered low basins, harvested wetland and upland plants and game in the spring, and slaughtered the huge bison on forays on to the shortgrass plains when weather and herd movements were most favorable. This economic pattern (if the data are correctly interpreted) persisted to the historic period, modern plains bison replacing their larger ancestors in the early Holocene.

Archaic sites have failed to attract much interest among South-western archaeologists, in contrast to the attention the Archaic gets in the Great Basin: everything in Basin prehistory looks "Archaic" with small camp occupations and no striking artifacts other than stone blades, while in the Southwest an archaeologist's eye is quickly caught by the building ruins and painted pottery of the last millennium. One synthesis of Southwest archaeology informs its readers that "the Archaic way of making a living was extremely con-servative, remaining remarkably stable until the introduction of corn from Mexico."[1] The authors do realize there was "archaeologically invisible cultural change hidden beneath" the artifacts of seasonally transhumant resource harvesting. Milling stones – flat or shallow stone slabs on which seeds were ground with a handheld cobblestone in a circular motion, unlike the trough metates with shaped long-oval manos for grinding corn in a back and forth motion, later in the Southwest – occur in sites beginning with the sixth millennium BCE. Dry rockshelters have provided Southwestern archaeologists with good samples of human paleofeces (that's right, dried ancient feces) that when examined under a microscope proves Archaic people ate seeds of chenopods, amaranth, and sunflower, cactus fruit, eggs (bits of shell consumed, too), roasted insects, lizards and small mammals whose tiny bones were sometimes crunched with the meat, or the animals, presumably gutted, dried whole and then pounded into a high-protein, calcium-enriched powder for storage or journey food.

Up to the end of the second millennium BCE, when maize first comes into the Southwest, it was culturally part of an intermountain West, although with regional distinctions. Basketry and twined fabrics, including blankets or winter robes made by binding fur strips or feathers with yucca cord and then weaving them, were similar, and these similarities in fiber artifacts continued much longer, until cotton came into cultivation in the Southwest about AD 700. A difference has been noted between Early Archaic sandals in the southern Colorado Plateau (northern Arizona and New Mexico) and those in the northern sector of the Plateau (southern Utah and southwestern Colorado) and the Great Basin. After 6000 BCE, the southern style was adopted on the northern Colorado Plateau, implying more intercourse between communities in the two sectors.[2] Animal figurines made of basketry-material split twigs have been preserved in dry sites in northern Arizona; some may have been duck decoys.

Introduction of maize and squash about 1000 BCE added a valuable new resource to the existing Late Archaic Mogollon and southern Southwest subsistence base of seasonal harvests, without apparently radically changing Southwesterners' life. A curious archaeological observation is that maize and squash are evidenced in a number of rockshelter and habitable caves during the first millennium BCE, but open-air habitation sites with maize seem rare until the beginning of the first millennium AD. This observation reflects the Late Archaic cultivators' practice of caching stores of maize in rockshelters. Some may have slept during planting and harvesting seasons near their plots in wickiups or tents that left no discernible traces on the landscape. Near Tucson, in a creek valley suited to farming, salvage excavation along a pipeline trench revealed two oval pithouses, possibly more beyond the pipeline right of way project, with bell-shaped storage pits inside and also outside the houses. Maize, chenopod, amaranth, and a Southwestern grass seed, plus walnuts and hackberries, were stored in these pits, with slab millingstones and manos to grind the seeds – the maize was related to the Chapalote flour corn raised by 'O'odham (Pima and Papago) historically, nearly three thousand years later.

Two thousand years ago, bows and arrows came into the Southwest, and open-air villages of pithouses with maize storage pits were built on the Colorado Plateau. To raise maize there, farmers not only needed to select for resistance to cold nights and frosts, but also for varieties that can germinate in spring in soil retaining some moisture from winter and then grow vigorously later when summer rains come. On the Plateau, maize kernels are planted deep, where winter moisture will be held. Northwest Mexican and southern Arizona Uto-Aztecan indigenous farmers instead plant in early summer on floodplains, placing the kernels only half as deep as Plateau Pueblo farmers do and relying on the accumulation of moisture where canyons disgorge water on to floodplains. Their late planting can be successful because frosts do not curtail maturation in the fall. Hence, maize agriculture on the higher, cooler Colorado Plateau required several sophisticated adaptations, the threat from frosts in the fall inducing earlier planting to obtain a full growing season, this depending on knowing the soil and topography that contains moisture before summer rains begin, and developing cold-resistant races of maize even more drought-tolerant than the southern races. A Hopi cornfield today startles a visitor from the East or Midwest: the maize plants are widely spaced with more bare dry earth than plants in the field, very different from the thick rows that make a solid green of cornfields in the humid east.

Bows and arrows entered the Southwest, presumably from the north (presumably, because bows predominate in Anglo America but atlatls with darts continued in general use in Mexico to Spanish conquest, as many Spaniards wounded by atlatl-propelled darts penetrating their chainmail could attest). For their first millennium in the Southwest, bows were simple self-bows, sending the projectile at twice the speed of an atlatl dart; then about AD 1300, sinew-backed recurved bows appear (in the Great Basin also), a complex type that shoots arrows faster than the self-bow. It is not surprising that during the first millennium AD, Southwesterners frequently built villages (of pithouses) on defendable hilltops, sometimes with series of low stone encircling walls, or if suitable hilltops near farmland were not available, building log stockades around villages.

Maize and squash agriculture reached the southern Southwest at the end of the second millennium BCE and the Colorado Plateau somewhat more than a millennium later, expansion to the higher and cooler Plateau demanding innovations both in agricultural technology and in the genetics of the plant. Judging from continuities in basketry and sandal styles, the colonization of the southern Colorado Plateau was by farmers from farther south in Arizona and New Mexico, while the first farmers on the northern Colorado Plateau seem to have been local people taking up the practice from their new neighbors. Bows and arrows exacerbated conflicts as arable land became more valuable and increased population harvested wild resources as well.

Hohokam: Agricultural towns in the desert

Civilization, in the form of agricultural towns with large public buildings and plazas, developed in the fertile lake basins of interior western Mexico in the first millennium BCE, preceded in the second millennium by villages with platform constructions and chamber tombs at the bottom of deep shafts. Furnished with fine pottery, handsome ceramic figurines, and jewelry, the tombs reflect societies already marking social class and honoring their defending soldiers. Although much less archaeology has been conducted in the western half of Mexico than in the more densely populated eastern half, societies in the west seem to have paralleled those in the east. By the beginning of the first millennium AD, Teuchitlán in Jalisco was building pyramidal platform mounds around circular plazas, ball courts, and extensive water-management systems, ditching and constructing raised fields along its lake and terraced fields with check dams for water retention on adjacent slopes.

Far to the north, in southern Arizona, the beginning of the first millennium AD saw villages of shallow pithouses along the Gila and Salt Rivers, extending maize fields through irrigation ditches. These communities were not much different from the preceding Late Archaic, except that they made pottery, at first a plain unpainted type. After a couple of centuries, red-slipped pots (surfaces covered with fine red-firing clay wash) were also made, and by the seventh century AD, red-painted light-brown pots. With pottery, the sites are labeled Hohokam.

Continuing contact with northwest Mexico, evidenced by Gulf of California shells in Hohokam sites, and population increase in the river floodplains gradually led to more and larger villages, by the end of the first millennium AD in most of the irrigable floodplains of southern Arizona. Rectangular pole and brush houses built in shallow pits were by then clustered around courtyards with cemeteries close by, suggesting these were extended-family households. Cremation came to be the custom for disposing of the dead, burning pottery, palettes for preparing body and face paints, and ornaments with the corpse. Examination of Hohokam skeletons, from the minority who were buried or left in abandoned sites, or bones not thoroughly consumed by cremation, shows closer similarities to northwest Mexican population characteristics than to people of the northern Southwest. Culturally, similarities in textile techniques and designs, in rock art, in platform mounds and ballcourts, and the practice of cremation point to northeastern Michoacán (west-central Mexico) just prior to Hohokam emergence, i.e., 100 BCE–AD 200, as a source of colonists.

A few real towns grew, for example at the locality called Snaketown, on the Gila about thirty kilometers (twenty miles) south of Phoenix. In the lower Salt River valley, platform mounds were built three miles (five kilometers) apart, implying an overall organization or confederation of their villages. Miles of irrigation ditches watered maize, squash and cotton fields that fed and clothed hundreds of townspeople

who built rectangular houses grouped in neighborhoods, large platform mounds, and ballcourts for the fast Mexican game that used a
hard rubber ball, hit soccer-style no hands, probably through a high
ring, basketball-style, as in Mexico. Five hundred spectators could
have sat on the earth-embankment bleachers to watch Snaketown's
games. Archaeologists suggest that tournaments between Hohokam
towns and villages visibly linked the communities, complementing
the links maintained by trade and military alliances.

Marine shell imported from the Gulf of California was worked, in
quantities, within Hohokam towns such as Snaketown. Craftsworkers
mastered difficult techniques to cut, carve, and etch the delicate
surfaces of shells. Lizards, frogs, and horned toads were often
depicted, as well as birds, snakes, and humans, in clay figurines and
masks and in stone, as well as in shell. A particularly precious Pacific
shell, the rose-colored spiny oyster (spondylus), is found associated
with the wealthiest burials and buildings from Peru through
Mesoamerica and, though rare, in Hohokam, proof of Hohokam's
continuing links to the civilizations to the south, bringing in tropical
macaws alive from southeastern Mexico, copper bells from West
Mexico during the eleventh century, mirrors made of iron pyrites
set as a mosaic to produce a reflecting surface, and marine shell
trumpets.

Hohokam probably was not a single ethnic group. Its ceramics,
irrigation agriculture, town styles with plazas, platform mounds,
and rectangular houses, and many craft technologies place it at
the northern end of Mexican civilizations, yet variations between
Hohokam sites in the several river basins of southern Arizona, and
continuities with Late Archaic especially outside the Gila heartland
hint that some indigenous communities acculturated to the Hohokam
agricultural economy and trade system established by colonists from
the south. Hohokam also was not the simple settlement of a group
of farmers then isolated from further innovations. The eleventh
century especially witnessed significant changes, with cotton apparently being stored in central town facilities rather than solely in
family residences as earlier, introduction of Mexican-type spindle
weights and production of finespun thread, and quite complex,
elegant fabrics such as figured gauzes and, in the twelfth century,
brocades (technically, tapestry weaves). These fabrics required not
only great skill but also would be very time-consuming, expensive
in terms of labor; recovered specimens seem to have been woven
in the Southwest but copied from examples worn by Mexican
aristocrats.

About AD 550, an outpost town was built on the eastern side of the Sierra Madre mountains in northwest Mexico precisely on the Tropic of Cancer latitude, to make astronomical observations: this unusual colony was probably sent by the great Valley of Mexico state Teotihuacán to enhance its calendar calculations (used to cast horoscopes as well as to regulate civic life). Teotihuacán encouraged mining, too, in the west, stimulating more colonization or development of local economies into the trade systems. These way-stations on the thousands-of-kilometers-long routes between Arizona and central Mexico, and the substantial agricultural towns in valleys along Mexico's Pacific coast, reinforced Hohokam trade. At the same time, second half of the first millennium AD, the defensive siting of most outposts and local capitals, and the hundreds of young men's skeletons in many of them, collected and sometimes displayed as trophies, indicate the western frontier of Mesoamerica was roughly contested. Such evidence of battles and/or sacrifice (as later by the Aztecs) is lacking in Hohokam during most of its duration – Arizona was too far from imperial centers to warrant their attacks.

Of all the raw materials utilized, directly or for trade, by Hohokam, the most telling for archaeologists is turquoise. Many outcrops of turquoise, some both extensive and with excellent quality nuggets close to the surface, occur in a broad zone from southern California–Nevada in the northwest, through New Mexico, into Sonora and interior northwest Mexico to Zacatecas. Exact mineral content varies between outcrops, so, if source samples are available, chemical assays can pinpoint the origin of turquoise ornaments. High-quality turquoise was commercially mined by the late first millennium AD. Near the Tropic of Cancer astronomical observation outpost are the rich Chalchihuites turquoise mines, tapping deep into the lodes with tunnels as much as a kilometer long and numerous underground chambers from which the miners broke out the ore, littering the landscape with immense spoil heaps. The earliest civilizations in Mesoamerica, in the second and first millennia BCE, had valued green jade above all, but during the first millennium AD, turquoise became increasingly prized, surpassing the use of jade for ritual and wealth objects. This may relate to the mythic birth of our present cosmic age, when a god threw himself into the fire burning in "the turquoise enclosure," his self-sacrifice transforming him into the Fifth World Sun giving light and life to our world. We know this myth from Aztec priests at the time of the Spanish conquest in the sixteenth century, but it probably goes back to Teotihuacán a millennium earlier. In the eleventh century, coinciding with the greatest

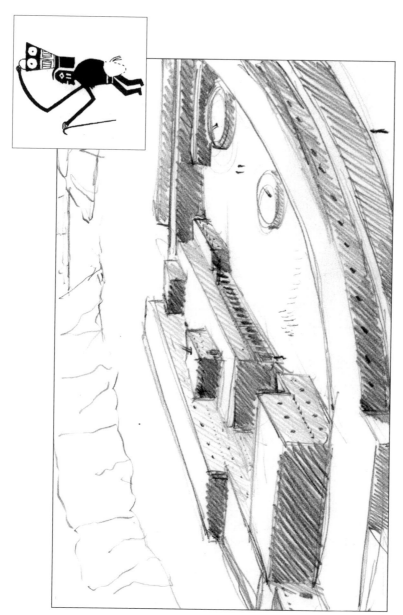

Figure 5 Chetro Ketl pueblo, Chaco Canyon, AD 1100. *Inset*: Woman carrying burden basket with macaw tied to rim (Mimbres pottery painting). Drawn by Anne Chojnacki

extent of Hohokam, Central Mexican artisans made mirrors with reflecting faces of iron pyrites mosaic and backs of turquoise mosaic, embodying "the turquoise enclosure" in this potent object emitting sparks when its pyrites face is struck. Possibly the Hohokam learned this cosmic myth when they imported iron pyrites mirrors.

The Toltec state in central Mexico fell in AD 1168, according to Aztec historians, which is about when Hohokam retrenches back to its Phoenix Basin core. They stopped using ballcourts (perhaps shifting to a game played on a field), and constructed adobe houses on ground surface in compounds instead of the pole and brush homes formerly built in shallow pits. Leaving more substantial ruins, adobe buildings are visible on the platform mounds, too. Despite distinctions appearing in the outlying regions of maximum Hohokam, implying independence from earlier dominance, Hohokam farmers in the core Gila and Salt valleys maintained and extended irrigation canals. By this time, agricultural towns were common in the Anasazi and Mogollon areas north and east of Hohokam; indeed, the largest Anasazi town, Chaco in the San Juan Basin (on a thin tributary of the San Juan River), flourished at the same time as Hohokam's greatest extent, and also fell in the late twelfth century. Chaco seems to have controlled the Cerrillos turquoise mines in New Mexico, some of which reached central Mexico, and like Hohokam, it imported copper bells and tropical macaws, raising additional macaws in pens. Enough differences in details of imports, and particularly in textile techniques, exist between Hohokam and Chaco to draw two principal routes for contacts into Mexico, a western route taking in the Pacific coast but perhaps cutting through the Sierra north from Culiacán to southern Arizona for Hohokam, and an eastern route through Zacatecas and Durango (Mexico) for Chaco, enabling the two Southwestern nations – or confederations, perhaps – to coexist. What wiped out the major Hohokam towns in the core Phoenix Basin was, ironically for a desert society, a devastating flood, AD 1356, that destroyed the network of irrigation canals and carefully tended fields, as well as homes. A generation later, floods wiped out what had been rebuilt. Nothing on the scale of Hohokam would be seen in the Sonoran Desert until twentieth-century Phoenix.

Mogollon

The earliest pottery in the Tucson Basin, plain ware associated with pithouses and floodplain maize farming in the early centuries AD,

would be classified as Mogollon. This leads archaeologists to postulate
that Mogollon, in higher elevations above the Sonoran Desert home
of Hohokam, once lived also in the desert basin but left it when
Hohokam invaded, about AD 400. Southwestern specialists will cry
"ouch!", but from an outsider perspective, "Mogollon" seems to
encompass most of the variations in Southwestern societies that don't
clearly fit into either Hohokam or Anasazi, and mostly occur between
the ecologically distinctive Sonoran Desert lowlands and Colorado
Plateau. A maverick Southwestern archaeologist remarked, of the
Mogollon Mimbres

> Mimbres, at AD 1000, looks like "Anasazi" with the addition of
> longer growing seasons and a nice little creek to irrigate from,
> and the absence of sandstone to build with. It's all the same
> thing – people making a living in the piñon–juniper zone –
> with a few local twists.[3]

Of the several named regional variéties of Mogollon, Mimbres
stands out, its marvelous stylized-realism paintings on ceramics
carrying it into the realm of world-class art. These black-on-white
slip bowls, most deposited in graves after being ritually "killed" by a
hole punched in the bottom, depict the people, animals, and plants
of southwestern New Mexico with a flair that doesn't mask the details
revealing Mimbres life. For example, from the paintings, a fisheries
expert identified by species numerous marine animals, most native
to the Gulf of California. To the surprise of archaeologists, he
explained that bowls with "fishes" bigger than the people beside
them are not mythical fantasies but pictures of whales, probably
beached – the details were clear to him.

Mimbres Valley people began constructing masonry multi-roomed
"pueblos," that is, apartment-block buildings[4] housing a number of
families along with storage rooms and plazas, around AD 1000.
At the same time, Mimbres turned from rainfall-based upland or
creek-fed valley agriculture beside villages of the earlier pole and
brush houses in shallow pits, to canal-irrigated fields in the valley
bottom. Pueblos and canal irrigation were equally costly in labor,
compared to the preceding lighter houses and agriculture sustained
by small check dams and channeling runoff. Probably the investment
in canals paid off by supporting more people in the locality, and
that induced the people to invest labor in the permanent masonry
houses. Aggregation within a more compact, long-term set of buildings may reflect, also, greater economic control by community

officials; they could better supervise the upkeep of the irrigation system and the granaries holding the harvests from pooled labor.

Mimbres masonry pueblos were abandoned about AD 1150, the same time as Chaco was abandoned and Hohokam shifted to adobe house compounds, some multi-storey; these approximately coincide with the collapse of the Toltec state according to Aztec history. What seems to have happened in the Mimbres Valley is that the population dispersed into hamlets small enough to live off limited plots watered by adjacent streams or the flow through alluvial fans, plus hunting and harvesting wild foods. In many cases, what had been seasonal shelters at outlying fields, occupied by pueblo families during planting and harvesting, became the base home – the masonry pueblos were emptied in favor of returning to the earlier pattern of family or hamlet autonomy. Then, after about a century, families congregated again in pueblos, now constructed of adobe; burned farmhouses have been noticed, whether burned because the family moving to the pueblo village wanted to clear the site, or because enemies attacked and the family fled to a pueblo, cannot be discerned. Nor do we know why, after mid-twelfth century, the people ceased painting their remarkable and beautiful representations of their world on their bowls, instead blackening them and burnishing them to a sheen – blacking out the past?

The Pueblo Period

About AD 750, people on the Colorado Plateau decided to live in surface-built rectangular rooms joined in rows, much resembling the mom-and-pop little motels once common along highways before the Interstate freeways and multi-storey chain motels. One or two deep pithouses would be built alongside the condo-type line of rooms, usually identified as "kivas," retreat chambers for religious sodalities in historic pueblos. Historic kivas also are used as men's workshops, where vertical looms have been set up for men weaving blankets and wide cloth, while women work in their households grinding cornmeal and preparing meals. The earlier surface dwellings were pole and brush. In the tenth century, solid masonry dwellings, still in the little-motel style, replaced lighter ones and, by the thirteenth century, these amalgamated into large blocks of rooms, often two or even three stories high. Designated trash heaps outside the blocks or in older abandoned rooms kept the village neat. Plazas and round underground masonry-walled kivas, assumed to represent persistence of ancestral pithouses now functioning as chapels where spirits of ancestors could be invoked, complemented the residential and storage rooms. It is notable that nothing like a palace, no richly ornamented buildings nor expensively furnished rooms, can be recognized in Anasazi pueblos, although a few burials displayed a wealth of ornaments.

From AD 900 to 1150, Chaco Canyon in northwestern New Mexico contained a town with eight really large masonry pueblos (the largest had 700 rooms, including the storage units) plus many little-motel pueblo blocks, strung out on both sides of the canyon floodplain for a couple of miles. Possibly close to two thousand people lived in the canyon. At the southern entrance to the canyon stands a pillar-like landmark butte, and on the plateau above the canyon straight roads run out for miles to satellite pueblos. Logs were required to frame and roof the pueblos, and these had to be transported, presumably overland, from distant mountain slopes because Chaco Canyon is arid, watered by a minor stream. Counting the labor of bringing in the thousands and thousands of logs, a lot of manpower went into Chaco Canyon. Why? Why build in this semi-desert with marginal rainfall for maize and no potential for Hohokam-type massive irrigation systems?

Archaeologist Stephen Lekson startled his colleagues with a bold hypothesis: Chaco Canyon is in the center of a basin that could support many farmsteads using channels and check dams to maximize rainfall and intermittent stream moisture. Somehow, these families paid (literally) homage to the central place where all roads led, where great kivas and imposing piles of rooms and connecting walls formed a theater of power. Astronomical alignments of buildings and roads harmonized the human landscape with the cosmos; straight north runs a 30-mile (50 kilometers) roadway, with kivas and shrines at stations beside it, to a stairway into a canyon, and southwest from Chaco runs a 36-mile (57 kilometers) roadway to the tower Kin Ya'a ("Tall House" in Navajo) and the peak of a butte – altogether, from the depths in the north, through the surface human center, to the heights reaching toward the heavens in the south.

Chaco apparently controlled the rich Cerrillos turquoise mines, it imported marine shells from the Pacific and scarlet macaws from Mexico. These and turkeys, a Southwestern domesticate, were bred in pens for their feathers prized for ceremonial paraphernalia. The ruling clans at Chaco (if that was what they were, on analogy with historic Pueblos that privilege aristocratic clans rather than private individual wealth or power) organized an entire region economically and politically, perhaps in a federal system whereby the outliers retained local governance. Then Chaco collapsed. Lekson sees it reincarnated, as it were, directly north nearly 100 kilometers (60 miles) at Aztec Ruins on the Animas River. "Great houses" like the eight major buildings at Chaco were constructed at Aztec[5] beginning in the early twelfth century and continuing for a century and a half, until 1275. Aztec's collapse may have resulted from a prolonged drought, since most of its outlying farms depended on rainfall, and drought would have reduced stream and water-table flow, too. Upon the collapse of Aztec Ruins, a new impressive center was built far to the south, in what is now Chihuahua, Mexico, at Paquimé (also called Casas Grandes). Lekson points out a striking alignment: Aztec, Chaco, and Paquimé all lie on the same north–south meridian. Were Aztec and then Paquimé located to draw on whatever cosmic power these people believed to reside in that heavenly alignment?

Paquimé flourished from the end of the twelfth century to AD 1450. Its cultural pattern covered societies from south-central New Mexico to Presidio on the Río Grande in west Texas, west to the Arizona border and across northern Chihuahua. Part of its pattern was constructed by what is called coursed adobe, adobe walls built up with successive big gobs of clay smoothed on to the preceding course, working along the length of the wall. This building method was used in the twelfth century in Mimbres and the Chaco Basin as an alternative to the more popular coursed sandstone slab masonry, then became the dominant technique in much of the Southwest in the thirteenth century and survives historically – Paquimé looked much like today's Taos Pueblo, only larger, with ball courts, platform mounds and several plazas. Paquimé ceramics are in the red-on-brown Mogollon tradition rather than the black-on-white of Mimbres – which is usually considered Mogollon, however – and Colorado Plateau Anasazi Pueblo. Innovations into the Southwest at this time, fourteenth century, include the "shoe-form" pot, shaped like a big bootie, which functioned to simmer food, its "toe" end in the embers and its wide offset mouth allowing steam to escape, and stone griddles for baking tortillas ("pikis" in the Southwest), both cooking innovations familiar in Mexico at the time. Basically, Paquimé was on the border between the American Southwest and West Mexico, supporting itself with extensive canal-irrigated fields in one of the Southwest's most favorable basins for agriculture, and admirably positioned to intersect east–west trade routes to Sinaloa and the Pacific, and northwest–southeast routes into central Mexico. Like Chaco, but on a larger scale, Paquimé raised turkeys and tropical macaws for feathers, imported copper bells and sheet copper for tinklers, and quantities of Pacific coast and Gulf of California shells. With its massive blocks of thick adobe rooms, four or possibly five storeys high, Paquimé was a major hub, and it was also a manufacturing center, especially for shell ornaments.

During the period of Paquimé's dominance, AD 1300–1425, religious symbols of Mexican origin come into the Southwest. Paquimé has a large square "kiva" with paintings of a feathered serpent and a figure resembling a one-horned katsina. Most of the turquoise recovered from Paquimé lay in one red-painted jar placed in a pit covered with a stone slab sealed with adobe, at the bottom of a water reservoir within the pueblo: this strongly suggests the cosmic "turquoise hearth" from which our present world was said to have been regenerated. Another Mexican icon may be picturing flowers and birds, representations that become popular only at this time and may signify the Mexican metaphor for worship, "flower and song."[6] The katsina figure, if that is what the painting represents, would reflect the development of katsinas (also spelled kachinas) in Pueblo communities. Particularly in the east-central Arizona Little Colorado River region, rock art and kiva mural pictures resembling historic katsinas appear beginning at the end of the thirteenth century; historically, katsinas are spirits who come into the pueblo periodically from their underground homes. Some katsinas are souls of the dead, others are purely spirit beings; they travel as rainclouds from the mountain peaks that are their portals to the human world. Tourists know the katsinas for their colorful public dances in pueblo plazas, and for the little wooden figurines portraying the various named katsinas. Hosting the katsinas – technically, their masks which Pueblo men don for their dances – is believed to enhance the likelihood of rain and good harvests. Living humans must do their part, maintaining water retention and dispersal systems, caring for crops, keeping order and respect as taught by the priests who invoke the katsinas' visits. Depictions of katsinas thus suggest that, by the fourteenth century, Pueblo societies worked through the indirect rule of priests managing work parties, community storage and distribution, and trade and visits by outsiders, all in the guise of hewing to the sanctions from the foundational spirit world.

Among the contemporary Pueblos, such as Hopi, Zuni, and Acoma, legendary and documented histories tell of a number of groups moving into the pueblo communities in which they now live. Each group usually has its own ritual, or is asked to take responsibility for one of the regularly enacted rituals, producing a community calendar of ceremonies incorporating a series of kiva sodalities or clans. Katsina sodalities are integrated into the calendar, and legendary histories mention opposition by some of the other sodalities ("medicine societies") to the innovation of katsinas. The fourteenth century was a period of movements in the Southwest, the Four Corners region of the Colorado Plateau (where four states meet, Utah, Colorado, New Mexico and Arizona) virtually abandoned and groups moving into the Río Grande Valley, joining or settling between pueblos already along the Río Grande. Pecos and Gran Quivira were large pueblos established in New Mexico east of the Río Grande near the edge of the southern Plains grasslands, with Pecos becoming a trade hub and over-wintering site for Plains bison hunters and other travelers. There was considerable interaction throughout the Southwest, evidenced by the spreading popularity of polychrome (multi-colored paintings) and glazed ceramics. Offsetting trade was an obvious concern with defense, inducing communities to cluster about three miles (five kilometers) apart, a distance that permitted alerting each other by signal fires on hilltops or towers if enemies were sighted; between the clusters of a few villages were zones about twenty miles (thirty kilometers) wide without permanent residences. This is the period of the spectacular cliff dwellings of Mesa Verde, pueblos built into large rockshelters as last-ditch defenses after mesa-top villages had been abandoned, the cliff dwellings themselves deserted after a few generations.

Paquimé was attacked and its people driven off by 1450. They very probably were one, or part of, Uto-Aztecan-speaking nations encountered by the Spanish a century later, and mostly surviving today, but which one of the Northwest Mexican Uto-Aztecans is difficult to figure out. Paquimé's enemies probably were neighboring nations to the west in Sonora, little city-states that were aggressively hostile obstacles to Spanish entradas in the 1530s, before epidemics scattered decimated communities into the ranchería homesteads recorded by Jesuit missionaries in the seventeenth century. Judging from fifteenth-century Pueblo trade along the lower Colorado River and, on the other side of the Pueblo domain, into the southern Plains, Paquimé was being bypassed by a Pacific coast route for Mexican goods such as shell and macaws, and by the creation of Pecos for direct Plains trade. The preponderance of large (over 100 rooms), multi-storey pueblos, well sited for defense and presenting high blank thick adobe walls to the outside, in the fifteenth century betokens serious competition, conceivably for both arable land and trade profits.

Into this final prehistoric period for the Southwest came entirely foreign invaders, Diné originally from the Canadian Northwest. Their forebears formed a frontier of Dené (see Chapter 7, Alaska) steadily advancing southeastward over centuries until the vanguard reached the edge of the Canadian forests where the Rockies meet the Plains in Alberta. A few settled there, allying with the powerful Blackfoot alliance native to the Northwestern Plains, and are the Tsuu T'ina (T'ina = Dené, Diné, "People"), formerly called the Sarcee (Sarsi), the Blackfoot name for them. Other families continued moving south, along the foothills of the eastern Rockies. They may have picked up knowledge of maize farming in Colorado, or not until they settled on the Colorado Plateau region of the Southwest and began interacting with Pueblos. Today known as the Navajo and Apache, the Diné in the Southwest added limited maize, squash, and beans farming to their hunting and wild food harvesting economy, building wickiups and, later, log-crib hogans away from the principal rivers used by the Pueblos. Besides farming, the Diné learned spinning and weaving and pottery making, ritual sandpainting and religious concepts from their Southwestern neighbors. Following the only temporarily successful Pueblo Revolt of 1680, many Puebloans, especially priests, took refuge in Navajo communities. With Spanish reconquest and colonization, Diné took up herding sheep and goats and making silver jewelry. Strange are the twists of fate in history: today the Navajo Nation is the largest, fastest-growing Indian nation in the United States, bounding back from their Trail of Tears imprisonment during the US Civil War (the Union feared they would cut its access to California via the Santa Fe Trail).

Fremont and Pueblo Frontiers

Looking for traces of Diné before they incorporated Pueblo imperishables into their culture, we find they must have traversed Fremont country. Fremont are Puebloan communities in the northern Colorado Plateau and eastern Great Basin, mostly in Utah. They were maize farmers from the beginning of the first millennium AD until 1400, living in Basketmaker type pithouses with storage pits until into the tenth century, when pithouses became almost rectangular and adobe or masonry storage chambers were built adjacent to them, on the ground surface, then in the eleventh century aboveground adobe or masonry dwelling rooms, too. Most Fremont fields were watered through irrigation ditches, so their villages are located where perennial streams come down from the mountain ranges; between zones of Fremont settlement are the region's dry valleys with little or no evidence of habitation.

Fremont are the northern frontier of maize agriculture in the interior West. Their pueblos were small compared to the principal towns in Arizona, New Mexico, and adjacent Chihuahua, but contrast with the camps of wickiups north of the Fremont frontier. It is tempting to premise that the abandonment of Fremont farming settlements and their Puebloan cultural pattern at the end of the fourteenth century would have been forced by climate shifts rendering maize farming too precarious to rely upon for subsistence, but direct data for such climate shifts seems elusive. One scenario has this picture of crop failures and drastic retrenchment of the Puebloan Fremont to merge with New Mexico Pueblos. If Fremont were dependent on the Chaco–Aztec Ruin pattern of trade, then the apparent collapse of that trade pattern and rise of Paquimé in the south might account for Fremont termination, but archaeological data for trade, in imperishable items or regional raw material exploitation, don't make it appear that crucial. Another scenario has the Fremont adapting to the supposed climate shift by taking up the Great Basin pattern of seasonal camps for wild harvest. Diné moving southward west of Great Salt Lake in the fourteenth and fifteenth centuries, making a distinctive, rather crude-looking (compared to the fine Pueblo ceramics) gray pottery and replacing Fremont in the region is a scenario that doesn't quite explain the end of Fremont since there is not a great deal of evidence for hostilities. Finally, yet another proposed scenario relates the end of Fremont to the "Numic expansion" (see Chapter 7), Paiute replacing Fremont, although again, why Fremont left their pueblos isn't explained: neither Diné nor Paiute, being dependent on wild harvests in semi-arid country, could have had populations matching the strength of established farming settlements, and both sides were armed with bows and arrows.

Río Grande Glaze Ware, pots decorated with a lead glaze derived from lead mined from a source halfway between Albuquerque and Santa Fe in northern New Mexico, near the Cerrillos turquoise mines, was traded widely through the Southwest and into the Southern Plains as far east as Oklahoma. The glaze was invented about AD 1325, and a number of Río Grande villages produced the pottery, obtaining the lead from the miners. Big shields made from bison bull hide may have been exchanged for the handsome pots by Plains nomadic bison hunters, and the shields traded farther west by the eastern Río Grande pueblos, to judge from kiva mural paintings in the Albuquerque area and in Hopi, and rock art that depict men with the large round shields mentioned by the sixteenth-century Spanish invaders. The Pueblos traded maize and cotton *mantas* (large cloths used as blankets and cloaks) for bison and elk meat and hides. Two Wichita ("Quivira" to the Spanish) men from Kansas were at Pecos when Coronado rode in, 1541, and hired them to guide him to fabled Cibola. The man Coronado called The Turk, because his hair style reminded them of Turks, tried to convince Coronado that Cibola must be a Mississippian town, describing the pomp of a Mississippian king. The other Wichita argued that the party should go more northeastward, which would take them to his own land in Kansas. He was more persuasive: Coronado followed him after executing The Turk and never saw anything more than thatch-roofed villages. A century or so earlier, Pueblo mantas and Cerrillos turquoise were interred with other wealth in the tomb of the lord of Spiro, on the Arkansas River in eastern Oklahoma and, further west in Oklahoma, a burial contained hundreds of beads made of turquoise and of Pacific shell, and a turquoise pendant.

At the other end of the social spectrum, many very ordinary gray Pueblo cooking pots, greasy and sooty from use, occur on Southern Plains sites, in west Texas and into Oklahoma, after AD 1450. These probably were made and used by eastern Pueblo women living in the villages, women who may have moved with their families on long hunting trips or who were escaping hard times in home pueblos, or who may have been sold as concubines and slaves. Spanish observers in the sixteenth century recorded slaves in Pueblo towns, and raiders, Diné ("Apaches") and Plains nations, capturing women and children to sell as slaves; Spanish markets for slaves may have escalated the practice but it seems to have existed before their entradas. Spiro lost its power after 1450; the east–west trade route to the south across the Red River gaining over Spiro's Arkansas River route. How that move fits into the evidence for Pueblo women in the Southern Plains after 1450, the attacks ending Paquimé's dominance, and the incursions of Diné, remains a question.

Connecting the historic Pueblos with ancestors faces these changes in the Southwest after 1450. Hopi, Zuni, and Acoma Pueblos have occupied their mesas for over a thousand years, originally as clusters of villages and then consolidating in the fifteenth century into the towns we see. Hopi, being Uto-Aztecan speakers, may have been related to the Virgin Anasazi (in the Virgin River Basin) north of Hopi and/or to some of the Fremont beyond the Virgin Basin.

Hopi history recounts the migrations of a series of communities to the Hopi mesas, to become clans in the nation. Such histories, told by Zuni and other Pueblos, make it clear that no single series of site occupations will encompass the origins of all the members of a Pueblo nation. The Río Grande pueblos that survived Spanish conquests and epidemics took in refugees, and similar ingathering took place in the thirteenth and fourteenth centuries as the Colorado Plateau pueblos were abandoned. These pueblos speak languages in the Keresan stock, with no apparent connections to any other language stock, or the Tanoan stock, distantly related to Uto-Aztecan. Kiowa, the language of that nation historically on the Plains, is linked with the Tanoan languages, implying that Kiowa was once closer to the eastern Pueblos. One ethnohistorian postulates that the Kiowa are the same as the Jumano described by the Spanish on the southern Plains in the seventeenth century as a bison-hunting people living in *ranchería* farmsteads in southeastern New Mexico, regularly trading with Pecos. A notable Jumano leader, Sabeata, was interrogated by Spanish officials in 1683 at El Paso when he led a delegation requesting Spanish troops to reinforce Indian settlements along the Río Grande south of El Paso that were being raided by Apaches. Making his case for an alliance, the Jumano reminded the officials that he had spoken with other Spaniards at Parral in northwest Mexico, and was familiar with Europeans (French) sailing to trade with Caddoans in East Texas, 1200 miles (2000 kilometers) from the Jumano *rancherías* and even farther from Parral. Whether the Jumano, who disappear by that name after the seventeenth century, were overcome by the Apache or fled to the north, to reappear half a century later on the Southern Plains as Kiowa, can't be determined. Sabeata's well-documented trading relationships with Hasinai Caddoans in Texas and Río Grande pueblos in New Mexico are a historic example of centuries-old trade.

The Pueblos' westernmost frontier was (and is) occupied by Yuman speakers, a branch of Hokan, along the Colorado River. Pai nations including the Havasupai in the Grand Canyon farmed the Colorado floodplain and hunted mountain sheep, deer, and antelope on the plateau above. Mojave and other Yumans farmed along the lower Colorado and its delta, extending into northern Baja California. Depending on the annual river floods, the Yumans planted their maize, squash, and beans as the water subsided, and fished in the pools renewed by the floods. Better known for basketry than pottery, the Yumans needed only brush shelters in most of their hot country, producing little that would remain for archaeologists. Not much threat to colonizers and ignored by Fred Harvey's railroad-based tourist development that made the Pueblo Southwest "America's Indian Theme Park" (Lekson's phrase[7]), the Yumans' history appears as marginal as their border territory.

Research Puzzles

The American Southwest is the region most intensively studied by archaeologists, for more than a century. Its dry climate and relatively few, and recent, urban developments preserved huge quantities and varieties of prehistoric data. The many vigorous debates over its prehistory indicate that abundance does not automatically provide answers.

A fundamental puzzle asks whether the Southwest is better understood from the perspective of Mexico, or more specifically, northwest Mexico, or as a self-contained region. Researchers examining Mexican relationships had to delve into the significant differences between inland and coastal northwest Mexico, neither region as well known as more glamorous Central Mexico or the Maya; the presence of tropical macaws in the Southwest, and Southwestern turquoise in Central Mexico, raises the further possibility that trade directly linked the Southwest to the eastern half of Mexico. Against these definite proofs of contact between the later Southwest and Mexican empires, some archaeologists focus on dynamics of adaptations to localities in the Southwest, for example in the Mimbres Valley. The two approaches should be complementary and mutually strengthening, but the local focus allies archaeologists to ecologists and may handicap recognition of data stemming from foreign contacts. The ecological emphasis has been favored, resulting in studies relating, for example, the movement from pithouses to above-ground pueblos to climate shifts, without discussion of alternate interpretations, such as that the shift reflects admiration of Hohokam lifestyles.

A simmering controversy flaring up from time to time concerns the notion of gentle hardy earth-people, pictured by tourist agencies since Fred Harvey advertised the romance of the Southwest to attract passengers on the Santa Fe Railroad. When archaeologists came on the scene, all the Southwestern nations, conquered and subjected to United States domination, appeared peaceful and secluded. Even some Pueblo citizens are disturbed to admit their ancestors pursued war. Excavations revealed instances of brutal killing, echoing stories in pueblos' own histories. Recognizing wars in Southwestern prehistory makes these nations' histories more conventional, and undermines the more popular emphasis on adaptations to local environments, as well as tourists' image of peaceful farmers outside the sweep of history.

Bibliographical Notes

Linda Cordell's *Archaeology of the Southwest* (2nd edn, San Diego, 1997) and *Ancient Pueblo Peoples* (Washington DC, 1994) are the most accessible and reliable general sources. Jefferson Reid and Stephanie Whittlesey's *The Archaeology of Ancient Arizona* (Tucson, AZ, 1997) treats only that state but is well written, combining descriptions of archaeological cultures with a narrative of questions and debates pursued by archaeologists over a century of research.

Because the Southwest is the only section of the United States with standing masonry ruins, and these in landscapes of stark beauty, it attracts tourists and retired people, spawns hundreds of photograph books, and incubates archaeological projects taking advantage of long field seasons and the high visibility of sites where vegetation is sparse. Most of the archaeological literature is introspective, delineating ceramic styles by region and time and seeking environmental changes to account for apparent societal changes. "The Southwest is a natural laboratory," claim some, where geographic diversity and climate shifts can be correlated with the charted artifact styles and changes to reveal, it is hoped, critical factors in cultural developments. Thus there is an abundance of monographs and conference volumes proposing models, very little of it of interest beyond the profession.

Beyond Cordell's sound and balanced syntheses, these volumes rise above the mass: Baker H. Morrow and V. B. Price (eds), *Anasazi Architecture and American Design* (Albuquerque, NM, 1997), taking the archaeological studies into the present with papers on contemporary applications of Anasazi structural principles; Michelle Hegmon (ed.), *The Archaeology of Regional Interaction: Religion, Warfare, and Exchange Across the American Southwest and Beyond* (Boulder, CO, 2000), presenting a diversity of topics and issues with full references; and Lynn Teague's *Textiles in Southwestern Prehistory* (Albuquerque, NM, 1998), documenting the range of fine textiles from the prehistoric Southwest and, most unusual, tying the technologies and styles to roots in the Interior West Archaic and in Mexico.

For the period of Southwestern history with Mexican ties, Davíd Carrasco, Lindsay Jones, and Scott Sessions (eds), *Mesoamerica's Classic Heritage: From Teotihuacán to the Aztecs* (Niwot, CO, 2000) gives a fascinating and detailed background, although it is orientated toward the rich kingdoms of tropical Mexico rather than to the West.

Notes

1. Jefferson Reid and Stephanie Whittlesey, *The Chaco Anasazi: Sociopolitical Evolution in the Prehistoric Southwest* (Tucson, AZ, 1997).

2. Archaeologist Phil Geib ("Sandal Types and Archaic Prehistory on the Colorado Plateau," American Antiquity 65(3) (2000): 520) remarks that both styles of sandal are easily woven, in ten minutes, with yucca leaves,

KING ALFRED'S COLLEGE
LIBRARY

and both are comfortable. He points out that people – hunters – who were accustomed to observing animal tracks would have instantly recognized neighbor or stranger by the imprint of the sandal style.

3. Stephen H. Lekson in *Understanding Complexity in the Prehistoric Southwest* (Reading, MA, 1994), p. 213, n. 13. See also his pp. 174–5 in *The Prehistoric Pueblo World, AD 1150–1350*, edited by Michael A. Adler (Tucson, AZ, 1996).

4. Block buildings of family apartments around atriums were typical of Teotihuacán, AD 200–650, in central Mexico. These residential units organized a city of about 200,000 within a valley ringed by mountains. The Anasazi and Mogollon pueblo apartment blocks served villages and small towns where logistics of supply and sanitation would not have been difficult, therefore their compact aggregation of families is more likely designed to facilitate management of village enterprises, especially farming. The several centuries gap, not to mention thousands of kilometers, between Teotihuacán and the Southwest pueblos, and this fundamental difference in needs make it unlikely that Anasazi-Mogollon copied the architecture of the great far-distant city long before it was destroyed. There is a connection with the architecture of western Mexico, notably Jalisco and Michoacán, where similar masonry styles can be seen, and many artifacts testify to trade.

5. The site has no connection with the Aztecs who came into power in the mid-fourteenth century in central Mexico. The name was bestowed by a New Mexico local booster.

6. "Flower and song," *in xóchitl in cuícatl* in Nahuatl, refers to poetry and religious worship, psalms. Mexico's national saint, the Virgin of Guadalupe, appeared in 1531, only ten years after Cortés defeated the Aztecs, on a hilltop that burst into flowers and birdsongs heralding the Holy Mother's apparition. Since the hilltop had been the shrine to the Aztecs' similar deity Tonantzin, "Our Lady Mother," some Mexicans believe the apparition to a Nahuatl Indian signified an assertion of the continuing worth of Aztec deities, calling forth *in xóchitl in cuícatl*, traditional "flower and song" hymns.

7. Comment in *Understanding Complexity in the Prehistoric Southwest*, edited by George J. Gumerman and Murray Gell-Mann (Reading, MA, 1994), p. 228, n. 26.

References

Adams, E. Charles (1991), *The Origin and Development of the Pueblo Katsina Cult.* Tucson, AZ: University of Arizona Press.

Adler, Michael A. (ed.) (1996), *The Prehistoric Pueblo World, AD 1150–1350.* Tucson, AZ: University of Arizona Press.

Baugh, Timothy G. and Jonathon E. Ericson (eds) (1994), *Prehistoric Exchange Systems in North America.* New York: Plenum.

Carrasco, Davíd, Lindsay Jones, and Scott Sessions (eds) (2000), *Mesoamerica's Classic Heritage: From Teotihuacán to the Aztecs.* Niwot, CO: University Press of Colorado.

Cordell, Linda S. (1994), *Ancient Pueblo Peoples*. Washington DC: Smithsonian Books.

Cordell, Linda S. (1997), *Archaeology of the Southwest*. 2nd edn. San Diego, CA: Academic Press.

Ericson, Jonathon E. and Timothy G. Baugh (eds) (1993), *The American Southwest and Mesoamerica: Systems of Prehistoric Exchange*. New York: Plenum.

Geib, Phil R. (2000), "Sandal Types and Archaic Prehistory on the Colorado Plateau," *American Antiquity* 65(3): 509–24.

Gumerman, George J. and Murray Gell-Mann (eds) (1994), *Understanding Complexity in the Prehistoric Southwest*, Proceedings vol. XVI, Sante Fe Institute Studies in the Sciences of Complexity. Reading, MA: Addison-Wesley.

Gumerman, George J. (ed.) (1994), *Themes in Southwest Prehistory*. Santa Fe, NM: School of American Research Press.

Hawley, Marlin F. (2000), "European-contact and Southwestern Artifacts in the Lower Walnut Focus Sites at Arkansas City, Kansas," *Plains Anthropologist* 45(173): 237–55.

Hegmon, Michelle (ed.) (2000), *The Archaeology of Regional Interaction: Religion, Warfare, and Exchange Across the American Southwest and Beyond*. Boulder, CO: University Press of Colorado.

Hickerson, Nancy Parrott (1994), *The Jumanos: Hunters and Traders of the South Plains*. Austin, TX: University of Texas Press.

Kantner, John and Nancy M. Mahoney (eds) (2000), *Great House Communities Across the Chacoan Landscape*. Tucson, AZ: University of Arizona Press.

LeBlanc, Steven A. (1999), *Prehistoric Warfare in the American Southwest*. Salt Lake City, UT: University of Utah Press.

Lekson, Stephen H. (1994), "Comments," in George J. Gumerman and Murray Gell-Mann (eds), *Understanding Complexity in the Prehistoric Southwest*. Reading, MA: Addison-Wesley, p. 213, n. 13, p. 228, n. 26.

Lekson, Stephen H. (1999), *The Chaco Meridian: Centers of Political Power in the Ancient Southwest*. Walnut Creek, CA: Altamira.

Matson, R. G. (1991), *Origins of Southwestern Agriculture*, Tucson, AZ: University of Arizona Press.

Morrow, Baker H. and V. B. Price (eds) (1997), *Anasazi Architecture and American Design*. Albuquerque, NM: University of New Mexico Press.

Neitzel, Jill E. (ed.) (1999), *Great Towns and Regional Polities in the Prehistoric American Southwest and Southeast*. Albuquerque, NM: University of New Mexico Press.

Nelson, Margaret C. (1999), *Mimbres During the Twelfth Century: Abandonment, Continuity, and Reorganization*. Tucson, AZ: University of Arizona Press.

Reid, Jefferson and Stephanie Whittlesey (1997), *The Archaeology of Ancient Arizona*. Tucson, AZ: University of Arizona Press.

Schaafsma, Curtis F. and Carroll L. Riley (eds) (1999), *The Casas Grandes World*. Salt Lake City, UT: University of Utah Press.

Sebastian, Lynne (1992), *The Chaco Anasazi: Sociopolitical Evolution in the Prehistoric Southwest*. Cambridge: Cambridge University Press.

Spielmann, Katherine A. (1991), *Farmers, Hunters, and Colonists: Interaction Between the Southwest and the Southern Plains*. Tucson, AZ: University of Arizona Press.

Teague, Lynn S. (1998), *Textiles in Southwestern Prehistory*. Albuquerque, NM: University of New Mexico Press.

From Donald Bahr, Juan Smith, William Smith Allison, and Julian Hayden, *The Short Swift Time of Gods on Earth*, pp. 251–3:

The Wooshkam people made camp there [Snaketown, Arizona] and asked another medicine man to work for them. He had the power of the bluebird, He: wacud Namkam.

The bluebird man found out that ahead of them lived a chief with many people, at a mound that is somewhere a little north of Yaqui Village [Guadalupe, Arizona]. (The medicine man sang two songs, but Juan [narrator] has forgotten them.) The house at this mound was destroyed.

The bluebird man worked some more and looked in the same direction and saw that it was raining very hard at a spot just across the river from where the previous enemy man was [Guadalupe]. This spot was where Yellow Buzzard used to live [Pueblo Grande].

This man had made his house from solid rock, so it seemed impossible for the Wooshkam to hurt it. He had done this because he didn't want any of his people to run off and leave him. They must all stay in this house with this medicine man.

It wasn't really a stone house, but the leader made it look like solid rock.

The bluebird man fooled himself by saying that the house was made of rock, and he couldn't do anything with it, so they asked another man who had the power of thunder to see what he could do. He sang:

> It is a hard house
> It is a hard house
> It is a hard house
> Do you see the foundation?
> It is made of rock.

Then he told the people that it would be easy for him, and he sang:

> I saw that he is
> Too light for me.
> It is like a windbreak
> Made out of these ocotillos [cactus].

From Donald Bahr, Juan Smith, William Smith Allison, and Julian Hayden, The Short Swift Time of Gods on Earth, *pp. 251–253 (continued)*

It was true. The thunderman came down over the house and smashed it to pieces. When this happened, the earth quaked and it knocked down a house that was close to the city of Phoenix.

Told in Pima by Juan Smith, translated by William Smith Allison (also Pima), and recorded by archaeologist Julian Hayden at Snaketown on the Gila River Reservation, near Chandler, Arizona, 1935. Pimas today are known by their preferred name, 'O'odham. Juan Smith's traditional narrative describes the 'O'odham conquest of earlier people, whom they call Hohokam ("Finished Ones"), living in the large adobe buildings archaeologists call "Great Houses," in contrast to the modest ranchería homes of 'O'odham.

Bahr, Donald, Juan Smith, William Smith Allison and Julian Hayden (1994) *The Short Swift Time of Gods on Earth: The Hohokam Chronicles.* Berkeley, CA: University of California Press.

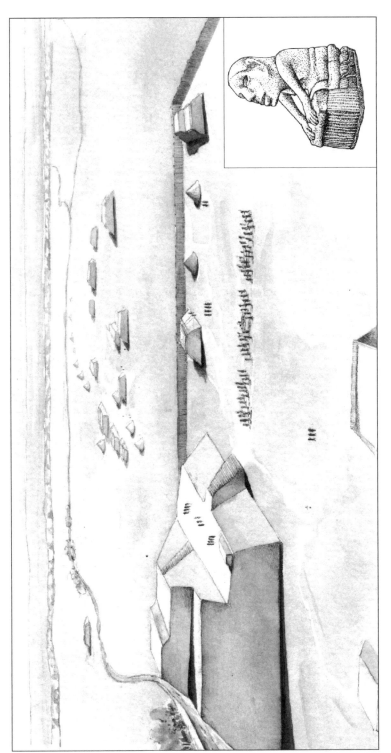

Figure 6 Cahokia, AD 1100. *Inset*: Cahokian carved stone figurine of woman weaving, probably making a covering for a shrine. Drawn by Anne Chojnacki

10

THE MISSISSIPPIAN PERIOD,
AD 950–1600

After Hopewell diminished, in the fifth century AD, with no more great geometric embankments built and the distinctive ceramic styles no longer made, societies around the Gulf of Mexico continued to live in towns, constructing burial and platform mounds and manufacturing sophisticated pottery. Classic Maya kingdoms flourished in the first millennium AD, during and after Teotihuacán's glory in central Mexico, undergoing political and economic shifts in the tenth and eleventh centuries that prompt archaeologists to designate the centuries after AD 900 the Postclassic. On the north side of the Gulf of Mexico, in the United States, the decline of Hopewell during what was the Early Classic in Mexico led to more modest societies. Those in the South, still committed to public ceremonies displaying rank, contrasted with those in the temperate Midwest and East who no longer honored rank with extravagant outlay. Then with the beginning of the Mexican Postclassic, in the tenth century, Midwesterners flared up with the Mississippian, an American Postclassic with an early climax at Cahokia, a truly impressive city where St Louis now stands, and balkanized kingdoms after Cahokia collapsed, AD 1250. The astute reader notices that the dates for Cahokia parallel those for Chaco in the Southwest.

Several questions challenge us when we examine data for this Late Prehistoric period. Why did the cosmological vision embodied in the Hopewell works, and reflected in the tombs of their mighty, no longer drive Late Woodland societies to such monumental labor? Conversely, why did the temperate-latitude Late Woodland change in this way while those in the South retained a considerable semblance of Middle Woodland achievements? What spurred Cahokia? What caused its collapse? What were the kingdoms De Soto disrupted in his ill-fated entrada into the Southeast, 1539? Answers to the questions have been handicapped by America's Manifest Destiny conviction that the European colonists' predecessors were inferior, doomed to be a vanishing race because they hadn't evolved private property laws and a money economy.[1] In spite of De Soto's and John Smith's (at Jamestown) descriptions of small kingdoms comparable to those in much of Europe (as late as the mid-nineteenth century, e.g., in Italy and Germany), many American archaeologists write of "chiefdoms" and calculate how few people might have managed to construct mounds. Ohioans squared the Circleville Hopewell had bequeathed them, and citizens of southern Illinois built a subdivision of ranch homes on the Great Plaza the Cahokians had so kindly made perfectly level. At Cahokia, at least, this is now reversed, thanks to a determined band of avocational archaeologists and local historians who lobbied for years to have Cahokia listed as a UNESCO World Heritage Site, and the State of Illinois to accept its obligation to protect that heritage.

What The Turk Described

Coronado's Wichita guide, the man he called The Turk, described a Mississippian kingdom in the American South, on a wide river upon which the lord of the realm rode in a flotilla of large canoes, the lord seated under a canopy at the stern of one boat with a large "gold eagle" on the prow. "Fish as big as horses" (alligator gar) swam in the wide river. The Turk continued

> The lord of that land took his siesta beneath a large tree from which hung great quantities of gold jingle bells which in the breeze soothed him. He said further that the ordinary table service of all in general was made of wrought silver and the jugs, plates and bowls of gold. He called the gold Acochis.[2]

"Acochis" probably is the Wichita word *ha:kwicis* "metal." The Turk told the Spaniards, in a mixture of sign language and broken "Mexicano" (Nahuatl), how the "acochis" was extracted, heated and "washed," an account that fits copper processing. Thus, given the value placed on copper by Midwestern First Nations, The Turk presumably spoke about the yellow metal, copper, but his Spanish interlocutors jumped to the conclusion he meant gold. When Coronado finally reached Wichita country, the farthest he would go, a chief there presented him with a copper pendant. He was not pleased.

Copper tinklers (not bells; rolled cones of sheet copper) have been found in Mississippian sites. The Turk described, in sign language, structures of "many stories" that Coronado interpreted to mean houses, rather than the platform mounds The Turk had seen. The Turk told Coronado that in the eastern kingdoms, there were quantities of *mantas*, large shawls or cloaks, and indeed Coronado's contemporary, De Soto, did receive many *mantas* from the South-eastern towns he threatened. De Soto's party, when they reached the Mississippi River, were awed by the salute they received from the vassals of the Lord of Aquixo,

> 200 vessels [canoes] full of Indians with their bows and arrows, painted with ocher and having great plumes of white and many colored feathers on either side [headdresses?], and holding shields in their hands with which they covered [protected] the paddlers, while the warriors were standing from prow to stern with their bows and arrows in their hands. The vessel in which the cacique [chief] came had an awning spread in the stern and he was seated under the canopy. Also other vessels came bearing other Indian notables. The chief from his position under the canopy controlled and gave orders to the other men.[3]

Survivors of De Soto's entrada reported that the big canoes and oars were polished and colored, and that the oarsmen sang rhythmically of military glories as they rowed in formation.

Such matching accounts from the Coronado and De Soto entradas of 1540, marching into the Midwest from southwestern and south-eastern approaches, corroborate the picture of Mississippian kingdoms full of pomp. Between these first, sixteenth-century, entradas and seventeenth-century colonization came severe epidemics, wars and displacements, obscuring the Mississippian civilizations. De Soto himself and nearly all his several hundred Spaniards died in America, many from fevers, leaving as legacy the famous razorback hogs of Arkansas, descended from the pigs herded along by the would-be conquistadors.

The Deep South

The Gulf Coastal Plain and interior plateaus of the South never abandoned the practice of constructing burial and platform mounds, that practice now realized to have persisted for nearly six millennia. Near Lake Okeechobee in central southern Florida, a large circle and ditch was constructed at the Fort Center site (actually, three such circles, in succession) in the late first millennium BCE, when sand-tempered (rather than the earlier fiber-tempered) ceramics appear, and maize pollen in paleofeces, the ditch, and in the paint on carved wooden birds that probably topped posts around a mortuary house in the first millennium AD. After AD 400, the decline of Hopewell in the Midwest broke off the South's extensive trade into that region, without diminishing the South's own towns. Not until the eighth century did population concentrations and public works apparently lessen, to be invigorated again a century or two later as Mississippian.

Much of the Southeast in the first millennium AD manufactured distinctive ceramics decorated by stamping the damp clay with elaborately curvilinear designs, reminiscent of the tattooing seen on people's bodies by the sixteenth-century Spanish expeditions. Picturing the first-millennium people displaying on their skin the designs adorning their serving bowls is probably valid – in the warm, humid South little clothing was worn, making tattoos very visible ornamentation. The sinuous curves of their designs, preserved for us only on the pottery, would have flowed with people's movements if they were tattoos. For graves in the burial mounds, animal and human effigy vessels were crafted. These vessels' artistic excellence reflects the elaborate rites attending the death of high-status persons: first a log tomb would be built in a pit and covered with a layer of stones and an earth mound, on the east side of this mound was placed an offering shrine with the special pottery and cremated human remains, the entire mound then burned and capped with stones, and finally more mound built over that, often including "bundle burials" of principal bones from previously buried or desiccated dead. Other, platform mounds were constructed beside these first-millennium villages, some of the platforms supporting wooden buildings and others the community's charnel house, screened off from view, where bodies were prepared and kept for burial at ritual times. Wooden posts five or six feet (two meters) high were set up around temples and mortuary houses, the posts topped with carved wooden or ceramic effigy animals – eagles, panthers, foxes, herons, bears, otters, alligators[4] – and perhaps human-face masks and painted wooden panels such as were found in the waterlogged site Key Marco. Early European travelers reported that the skeletons of ancestors of the ruling lineage were retained on platforms of mortuary houses, a priest tending a perpetual fire under the platform. Enemies attacking a village would target the aristocrats' mortuary house for destruction, signaling victory over them.

At the McKeithen site in northern Florida, a leader who died about AD 475 seems to have lived in a house on one of the site's mounds, been buried in the floor of that house along with the remains of forebears taken from their mortuary house, fine ceramics and food. The house tomb was burned, 36 people, presumably sacrificed, spaced evenly around the border of the platform, and the mound covered with sand. Intriguingly, the principal personage was slightly built, probably a woman, and died from infection following being shot in the buttock with a ten-inch-long stone-pointed arrow. At Kolomoki in southern Georgia, the largest site of this first-millennium cultural pattern, 86 people accompanied the central personage, and some if not all had been sacrificed for him. After about AD 800, such honors were no longer given, only small burial mounds built, with a few special pots left with the deceased.

Maize agriculture was established in northern Florida about AD 750, a couple of centuries after it was apparently given up in the central Florida Lake Okeechobee basin, and the same time that the Early Late Woodland mound-building culture pattern shifted to modest burial mounds in place of mounds built for ostentatious funeral rites. Villages sought out the most fertile arable land, no longer looking primarily for the most efficient siting for obtaining wetlands foods. Similarity in houses from earlier periods may indicate ethnic persistence, or equally likely, managing in the Florida climate: winter houses were constructed of poles bent inward and lashed at the top to carry thatch or palmetto roofing, a hearth near a door for ventilation, benches around the walls for sleeping, and little smudge fires under the benches to discourage mosquitoes (yes, Florida mosquitoes can get that bad!). During summers, people used open-sided pavilions, like the Seminoles' chickees tourists can see today in Florida. Once maize agriculture became the mainstay, farmsteads became the most common type of settlement, clustered as outliers to villages that in turn clustered within a day's walk, more or less, of a larger town; at historic contact, most of the Southeast was organized in this manner, with the headpersons of village–farmsteads communities considered to be vassals of the town's governing lineage. Town lords might themselves be vassals of a nobler lineage, paying tribute and contributing soldiers when required. After AD 1000, platform mounds were again constructed for aristocrats' residences, temples, and mortuary houses.

The economics of late first-millennium Gulf Coastal people, called Weeden Island by archaeologists after a Florida site, was strongly orientated to the Gulf and interior wetlands: fish, including sharks, and shellfish, sea and land turtles, alligators, snakes, waterfowl, and in the interior, deer, bear, turkeys and small game, persimmons and plums, nuts, and seeds. Settlements were placed on hummocks, and the larger villages maintained clean plazas, relegating trash to designated disposal areas. Accumulation of shells from eating shellfish continued, with favored coast or river sites coming to be mounds of shells several hundred feet (about one hundred meters) long by fifteen high (five meters), and dozens of such shell middens around a bay. Some shell middens in Tampa Bay, Florida, are nearly entirely conchs, which not only contain a couple of pounds of meat per shell but the shells were in demand for ceremonial drinking chalices, trumpets, and necklace pendants throughout the eastern United States. (In Mexico across the Gulf, the columnar spiral center of the conch shell was the icon of dynamic spiraling vital power attributed to Quetzalcoatl, the Plumed Serpent, god of the wind, whose dancing brought into being our present world.) South (peninsular) Florida apparently never took up maize agriculture, although they may have raised squashes; the country was too waterlogged and soils poor. To compensate, south Florida had the ocean, estuaries, streams and lakes, with manatees, dolphins and, off the southeastern coast, whales, as well as sharks, alligators, and big turtles. Canoes scooted around the mangrove swamps and between harvesting camps and base villages. At Pine Island, on Florida's southwest coast, a canal was dug, six to seven yards (meters) wide, one to two deep, an astonishing two-and-a-half miles (four kilometers) long across the island, so travelers could cut across rather than paddle around it. To overcome the rise in elevation as the canal reached across the middle of the island, the Indians – probable ancestors of the historic Calusa – made a series of small dams, functioning like canal locks: each section of impounded water was a little higher than the adjacent one, and by lifting canoes over the narrow dams, the boats floated on progressively higher stretches until the crest was reached and the water levels lowered to return the canoes to sea level.

The Interior South and Midwest: Cahokian Period

Mississippian societies flourished in the rich, broad valleys of the major rivers of the physiographic Gulf Coastal Plain, the head of which lies at St Louis where the Missouri flows into the Mississippi. Below that, the Ohio flows in, creating the immense river celebrated by Mark Twain. Frequent floods and shifting channels give the Central and Lower Mississippi Valley rich soils, sloughs, and wetlands. Uplands above the valley wall bluffs were forested, inviting hunting camps and backwoods hamlets. Pine barrens, poor in edible resources and unsuited to sustained maize agriculture, cover much of the interior Coastal Plains, from the Fall Line of the Piedmont to tidewater (section of rivers, up from mouths, affected by daily ocean tides). This zone discouraged Interior South nations from colonizing toward the coasts, and vice versa, settlement and trade finding principal routes to be the river valley corridors.

Following several centuries of apparently small-scale subsistence-orientated societies in the first millennium AD, after Hopewell, intensive maize agriculture associated with large towns and conspicuous display of power materializes in the major valleys between the Appalachians and the western border of the Midwest, from Illinois to the Gulf. That there was continuity between earlier populations and those we label Mississippian is amply demonstrated, in icons such as hawks seen in Hopewell and again in Mississippian, in mounds, in utilitarian artifacts; that there was significant difference is shown in the quantities of maize and the political economy it supported. Mississippians grew maize on labor-intensive raised ridge and ditch fields, where fertility is replenished every year when the farmers clean out the ditches, throwing the rich muck up on to the planting ridges. Hundreds of acres (or hectares) of Mississippian ridge and ditch fields have been identified in the Midwest and South – corn hills described much later by European colonists may be a less laborious version, with the soil heaped up just at the planting spot rather than in a continuous ridge. Earlier Eastern Woodlands domesticates, the indigenous chenopods, knotweed, little-barley, and maygrass, were still cultivated, giving the Mississippians a series of harvests, the nutrition of the higher-protein native grains, and some hedge against crop failure.

Mississippian towns, marked by their platform mounds and plazas, dominated the flat river valleys, a number of them located to control the confluence of a tributary with a main river. Ironically, this siting led to the destruction of many in the nineteenth century, because railroads were sited in the same major transport corridors and used the handy unoccupied mounds for railbed ballast. United States towns were built on top of Mississippian towns for the same reason the Mississippians chose, to facilitate controlling an agricultural zone and trade routes. Only by digging into local archives to find historic mention of "Mound Builders" preceding the pioneers can many Mississippian towns be put on a map.

The Mississippian period has two phases, that of Cahokia, ninth to mid-thirteenth century, and then that of many small kingdoms. Cahokia's heyday was the time of climatologists' Medieval Warm Episode, climate ideal for the Southern race of maize grown at Cahokia. Cahokia's collapse roughly correlates with the onset of climate shifting bringing about the northern hemisphere's "Little Ice Age," three centuries (AD 1550–1850) of somewhat colder climate. Thus, Cahokia's rise and fall could be explained by an advantageous climate for maize-growing, bracketed between the colder period of the mid-first millennium AD and that beginning in the mid-thirteenth century. Likewise, Chaco's rise and fall in the Southwest can be linked to the same northern hemisphere climate episodes. Conversely, the favorable medieval climate can be said to have supported these exceptional political–economic centers but not to be sufficient explanation why people labored to construct imposing urban centers.[5] Mexico's series of major centers, each waxing strong and then weakening, to be superseded by another region's ambitious nations, cannot be explained as adaptations to climate shifts.

Underlining the importance of ideological goads in the formation of Cahokia are a pair of figurines associated with what seems to have been a suburban community temple near the city. Fine ceramic serving bowls, mica, galena, red cedar, and hallucinogenic jimson weed, and lack of ordinary domestic debris, indicates the special function of the building. Half of a red fire-clay[6] figurine of a woman, named the Keller figurine, was found in a shallow pit inside this building, the other half lay in a garbage pit outside (south of) the building. A second red fire-clay figurine of a woman, the Birger figurine, had been deliberately buried in a small pit also outside, and east of, the building. Three other fire-clay figurines of women, and fragments of possibly more figurines, were recovered from a comparable temple in another suburban site. The Keller figurine sits, legs folded under her, on a folded pad, her outstretched arms grasping a rod-like object on top of what looks like a box. With her lips slightly parted and her face uplifted, she looks as if she may be singing. The stylized object in front of her may be a cane box or basket such as historic Muskokee Beloved Women, aristocratic women community leaders, kept to hold tokens of each clan in the community, symbolic of their shared concerns. The object might, on the other hand, represent a loom on which the woman weaves a fabric symbolic of the interwoven families, another ritual practice recalled by Muskokee. Or the object may be meant to invoke both symbols. In contrast, the Birger figurine has a strained expression on her face. She, too, kneels, tugging a stone-bladed hoe or possibly hide-scraper. On her back, gourd plants twine up around her from a burden basket. Around her is coiled a double serpent, and her hoe or scraper is digging into his back. Some archaeologists glibly write off the figurines as fertility fetishes, but surely they are better inter-preted as a pair, Keller inside the temple symbolizing the commun-ity bound together, Birger outside, with her plants and serpent, symbolizing the power of the natural world. Birger could well be she whom the Siouan-speaking Hidatsa call Grandmother-Who-Never-Dies, female power nurturing the Corn Maidens in her earthlodge over the winter, sending them out with the migrating geese in spring to invigorate the maize plants in Hidatsa women's fields. Grand-mother-Who-Never-Dies lives with her consort, the Underwater Panther with the long serpent tail, a male power that roils up bodies of water and eats unwary bathers. Often pictured with stag's antlers in the Midwest, there was a large petroglyph of this icon on the rock bluff at Alton, Illinois, at the narrows where Mississippi river traffic en route to Cahokia could be controlled.

Cahokia is bigger by far than any other archaeological site north of central Mexico. It filled the Mississippi River floodplain at what is now St Louis with well over one hundred monumental mounds and thousands of homesteads on raised foundations. Urban planning is obvious at Cahokia, the plazas, platform mounds, and commoner residences laid out orientated to the cardinal directions. Conical mounds, a few on the terraces of massive Monks Mound, and great circles of huge wooden posts balance the angularity of the overall layout, and some small oval mounds lie southeast–northwest, possibly solstice orientated. Cahokia's urban plan is Mesoamerican, based on rectangular plazas bounded by platform mounds elevating temples and elite residences; its homesteads also fall within a common Mesoamerican plan of three structures around a courtyard, a basic plan that persisted into the historic period among the Creeks (Muskokee), who customarily erected three structures, called the man's house, the woman's house, and storage house. During the eleventh-century height of Cahokian urban growth, neighborhood clusters of small rectangular houses replaced courtyard homesteads in the center of the city. No other pre-European site in the United States is anywhere as large as Cahokia (an estimated twelve square kilometers [five square miles] without including present St Louis on

the opposite side of the river), none other can have held its population (twenty thousand is a conservative figure), and no other exhibits
such an overarching design. Erection of such a well-thought-out city
at the nexus of the midcontinent waterways and the river highway to
the Gulf of Mexico was a political act.

Monks Mound at the center of Cahokia (now Cahokia Mounds
State Park at Collinsville, Illinois) was the third largest structure in
the Americas before the modern era. (Teotihuacán's Pyramid of the
Sun is the largest, Cholula's Man-made Mountain pyramid second.
Egypt's Gizeh pyramids are smaller and were not platforms.) Monks
Mound, so called because in the nineteenth century a community of
Trappist monks built their house and gardens on part of it, is slightly
over one thousand feet (316 meters) long north–south, nearly eight
hundred feet (241 meters) wide east–west, and a bit over one hundred feet (30 meters) high: even the top, fourth, terrace platform is
bigger than a football field. Excavations on the top terrace revealed
a great timber building more than 135 feet (forty-five meters) wide,
its full extent never determined due to lack of further archaeological investigation. The Great Plaza stretching south from Monks
Mound is 900 feet long by 1200 feet wide (300 by 400 meters), made
level by infilling and capping the original ground with up to thirty
inches (75 cm) of selected soil. To prevent the hulking Monks Mound
from slumping, its knowledgable engineers ordered layers of different types of earth and internal drains. Other mounds at Cahokia
show sequences of smaller mounds and special clay caps, often a
pair of round and flat-topped mounds on a low platform eventually
coalesced into one by the later additions. Satellite centers, suburban
villages and hamlets and farms filled the floodplain. Late in Cahokia's
history, near the end of the twelfth century, a timber palisade with
bastions was raised around the central plazas and mounds.

How many of the mounds in the Cahokia floodplain were monuments to ruling lords can no longer be determined. Destruction of
mounds has been extensive for a century and a half, and frequently
human bones and fine artifacts were reported, in newspapers and
by archaeologists a century ago whose crews of laborers worked like
miners to pull out treasures. The Big Mound in St Louis, pulled
down in 1869 for railbed fill, contained a tomb chamber described
as having a ceiling of logs and plastered walls and floor. Dozens
of bodies lay in rows, torsos covered with thousands of shell beads
presumably originally sewn on cloth mantas; in another part of the
mound, two bodies were given conch shell spine pendants, marine
shell beads probably strung on a necklace, and a pair of small copper

masks (pendants) with long noses, symbol of the Siouan superhero
He-Who-Wears-Human-Heads-As-Pendants (the legendary stories
make it clear these are not war-trophy real heads but magical little
faces that laugh and stick out their tongues). Other mounds now
long gone had similar contents. Hindsight provided by the only
reasonably carefully excavated and published mound, the surprisingly small Mound 72 south of the Great Plaza in Cahokia, suggests
the rows of bodies in Big Mound and others may have been sacrificed
to accompany their lord in death.

Mound 72 was only nine feet (three meters) high, 150 feet (45
meters) long by nearly fifty feet (fifteen meters) wide, oval in shape
and lying northwest–southeast along the solstice lines – small by
Cahokia standards and orientated diagonally to the principal
north–south/east–west grid. Like other mounds at Cahokia, it was
constructed in sections, or stages, first a pair of small square platform
mounds, one extending over where a large wooden post had been
set, the other covering another post pit and a typical Mississippian
building of wooden poles set in a foundation trench. A number of
burials were placed and covered, the resulting line filled in so that
the west mound was extended to the east one, then a large pit was
dug in the center of the now-single elongated mound and 53 young
women deposited in it, a smaller pit dug and four young men placed
in it, and finally all this covered to make the oval mound seen by
historic visitors. Huge cypress logs like those at the site of Mound 72
have been discovered at other locations in Cahokia, too, and hypothesized to have been solstice-observation markers, but between the
destruction of so much of ancient Cahokia and the overwhelming
scale of the principal mounds and plazas, defying the puny crews
and funds allocated to conduct archaeology there, not enough data
exist to evaluate the hypothesis definitively – the putative great circles
of massive posts might have been cathedral-sized forerunners of
historic Sun Dance ceremonial lodges and the circles of posts
with dancing maidens depicted in sixteenth-century engravings of
Eastern Indian villages.

Sometime in the eleventh century AD, a nobleman, very possibly
Lord of Cahokia, had been buried in the southeast of the two first-
stage mounds of Mound 72. A commoner or slave man was laid down,
covered with an earthen platform draped with a magnificent rug or
cloak in the shape of a hawk with folded wings, sewn with thousands
of glittering shell beads, and the Lord laid on that (over his bearer,
we may surmise). His head was toward summer solstice sunrise.
At his head and left side two adults were laid out, at his right

a bundle of bones from a young adult, and next to that another young adult lying as if thrown down: the three articulated skeletons are assumed to be retainers or bodyguards, the bundle burial may be one of the Lord's family previously deceased. Four yards (or meters) away was an offering cache with five young adults, two of them probably women, and two adults more poorly preserved, covered with valuables, and then three more bodies, one partially disarticulated adult and a pair of young adults, man and woman, were laid over the previous set and at a right angle to them. The non-human offerings included neat bundles of hundreds of perfectly flaked arrows of the best-quality stone from distant quarries, fifteen polished disk-shaped chunkey stones for the bowling-type game popular in the Southeast, a variety of necklaces of shell beads, rolls of sheet copper, and a pile of sheets of shiny mica. No doubt fine cloth was there, too, no longer preserved for us to note. Everything was completely covered with a black clay mound topped with a white clay and sand mix.

The second original mound platform, at the northwest end of the final mound, was constructed over the foundation of a wooden building open at the east end where one of the massive log posts had been installed. On the platform, over the former south wall of the building, the disarticulated bones of about thirteen adults were arranged in three piles, long bones, flat bones, and skulls with small bones. A pair of small, burnished black jars were placed with these piles. West of the piles were four bundle burials, apparently four persons, and on the east side of the platform were the bodies of two men, one wearing a shell hair ornament. A man and woman about thirty years of age were buried south of the piles of bones, man on the east and face down, woman to the west, face up, both wearing chokers of shell beads, and a pot of Lower Mississippi Valley style next to the woman. Where the massive post had been, east of the former building, a large north–south rectangular pit was dug, its floor covered with clean sand, and 22 women in their twenties were neatly laid in the pit, heads to the west, in two layers separated by mats. South of the former building, a similar pit orientated east–west held nineteen bodies, young women except for two children, ten on the bottom and nine above them, layered with two kinds of mats. All these were covered, a capping layer applied, and over their pit placed a treasure offering of conch spine pendants, over 36,000 shell beads, a pile of 451 arrowpoints of local chert, unhafted, a burnished black ceramic bottle and five red-slipped jars. Another rectangular pit like the preceding was dug into the southeast corner area, orientated like the final Mound 72 northwest–southeast, and filled with two layers of young women, 24 in all, laid on matting or cloth.

Finally, literally capping this ostentatious exhibition of power, yet another rectangular pit was prepared for, this time, 53 young women in two double rows with two women on top of the layers, across the bodies below them. One of these women wore shell beads; none of the others had ornaments, unless some had decayed away. Northwest of this largest set of sacrificed young women, only six feet (two meters) beyond as if guarding them, was a pit with four young men, their heads and hands removed. South of this set of two pits, in the middle of the south side of the final mound, a deep rectangular pit was dug and 39 people both men and women, a few middle-aged, were forcibly thrown into it, not laid neatly; three of these people had their heads chopped off and dropped into the pit, two had arrowpoints in their bodies (possibly old wounds). These sacrifices were covered with matting and above them were placed, in a careful row, bodies carried on litters of cedar poles: on one, a young man, a young woman, and an adolescent, all disarticulated; next, an adult with a child on top of it; then a woman; then a woman with two children; then an adult with its head cut off and placed on its chest; and lastly, one after another, another woman, an adult of undeterminable sex, and two adolescents who seem to have died somewhat earlier and become partially decomposed. Northwest of this pit was a smaller one with eight persons including a child, and next to that, a pit with six disarticulated people. The last mass burial pit, in the center of the final Mound 72, had sixteen mostly disarticulated skeletons (nine of them in bundles) over a couple of whole bodies, plus one little child about three years of age – the only very young child in the whole mound. Finishing off were six separate pits with a total of five bodies and four bundle burials. A last covering and capping completed the homage to the Lord Hawk of Cahokia. Two hundred and sixty youths and adults, and one small child, had been arranged in his monument, nearly all of them sacrificed.

Mound 72 and Monks Mound trumpet Cahokia's singularity: the awesome bulk of Monks Mound is unmatched anywhere in America except Mexico, and there only by two capitals of great states, and the terrible number of sacrifices unmatched except, again, in the capitals of the great Mexican states. Surely eleventh-century Cahokia was the capital of a state more powerful than any other north of central Mexico's broad valleys. Noting the distribution of Cahokia's fine-quality ceramics, of eleventh–twelfth century towns with platform mounds, of principal Indian travel routes in the Midwest, and of petroglyphs of hawk/falcon/thunderbirds associated with pecked crosses in circles – these last territorial markers in Mesoamerica – archaeologist Patricia O'Brien calculated the Cahokian state to encompass 52,000 square kilometers (approximately 20,000 square miles) of America's heartland.[7] This was difficult land to control, forested outside the settlements and their farms, populations knowledgable about wild foods so able to retreat into the woods to escape state demands, all the men trained and equipped to hunt deer and therefore humans if politics induce them to do so. The wonder is not that Cahokia could not maintain its power over the generations, but that so imperious a state could be instituted at all.

Cahokia's Mesoamerican-style urban plan would imply a Mexican stimulus, except that so little else is distinctively Mesoamerican. Two hundred and sixty adults in the mound tomb of their lord echoes the same number sacrificed in the Feathered Serpent Pyramid in Teotihuacán, centuries earlier; there, the number matches Meosamerica's 260-day ritual calendar,[8] but the elaborate calendar reckoning of Mesoamerican astronomer-priests isn't known for United States First Nations. A few individuals with filed front teeth, popular among Mesoamericans, have been excavated from Cahokia-period graves in the Cahokia area – and a few from the contemporary Chaco period and region – and these may have been visitors, possibly architects and traders, from Mexico because filed teeth are not otherwise known in United States sites. Mound 72 had no Mexican valuables, no feathered serpent designs, no goggled warrior masks, no macaw bones. Of course, any manner of perishables such as macaw feathers might have quickly decayed in the humid Mississippi Valley, but it is striking that all the treasures given to that Lord of Cahokia were Midwest manufactures or, in the case of the conchs, imports from the American shore of the Gulf.

Weighing the contemporaneity of Chaco and Cahokia, the lack of indications of direct contacts between them, and the contemporaneity of the Toltec imperium in Mexico, we may postulate opportunities in the late tenth and eleventh centuries for ambitious leaders in the Southwest and Midwest to engage in lucrative trade with Mexico. Chaco could export turquoise, Cahokia could export maize, expertly tanned deer hides, perhaps dried meat, and slaves, taking advantage of its prime water route to southern markets. Thus more advantaged than Chaco in its desert, Cahokia's ambition to match the glory of its Mexican emporia materialized in its grandiose capital. The funerals of its lords, the wanton sacrifice of so many of the fairest maidens and young men its minions could command, were calculated to make its power seem cosmic. It was, in reality, chimerical: when the Toltecs fell, it seems the frontier states at Chaco and Cahokia lost their power base, their capitals emptied and the territories tenuously held quickly became independent little kingdoms.

The Interior South and Midwest: Post-Cahokian Period

During Cahokia's prime in the eleventh century, its heartland was rimmed by towns that were either outposts – Aztalan in south-central Wisconsin at the headwaters of the Rock River which flows into the Mississippi – or more numerous, entrepôts such as that at the confluence of the Platte River with the Missouri, near Kansas City, where bison products from the Plains met the deer and maize of the Midwest. Cahokia's thirteenth-century demise correlates with population movements, some into towns strongly fortified with palisades, others into substantial villages sited in the best farmlands. Dependence on maize agriculture expanded during and after the Cahokian era, strengthened by a new, hardy flour corn, adapted to short growing seasons, called eight-rowed Northern Flint, developed from a variety probably introduced into Florida from the Caribbean. Beans were also introduced from the south, their cultivation spreading quickly around AD 1000 as far north as upstate New York and into the central Ohio Valley. Oddly, Cahokia-era Mississippians did not accept beans. Only after AD 1300 do they appear in central Midwest Mississippian sites, completing the famous "Three Sisters" of Eastern American agriculture, corn, beans, and squashes. Because beans fix nitrogen in their roots, by planting beans between maize plants, not only do the maize stalks serve to support the bean runners, the beans replenish the soil nitrogen taken up by the maize. Beans also provide protein, deficient in maize, balancing a farm-based diet. All Mississippians harvested deer and fish, very likely maintaining deer parks beyond their farms by regularly burning browse areas, so protein may not have been a problem, and the Cahokians' ridge and ditch fields replenished nitrogen when the ditch muck was shoveled on to the planting ridges, lessening the role beans could have played. Cahokia's eastern frontier might be marked by a "bean line," beyond which independent societies pursued their own economic regimes.

Conventionally, archaeologists distinguished "Mississippian" from concurrent "Late Woodland," assigning the Mississippian label if a site had platform mounds, reliance on maize, and shell-tempered

Figure 7 Etowah (Mississippian period site in Georgia), view of top of largest mound, looking at second-largest mound. Photo by Alice B. Kehoe.

pottery. Late Woodland was the label for sites, usually small and on uplands, with grit-tempered pottery and less evidence of maize. Obviously – and archaeology is increasingly demonstrating this – "Late Woodland" sites could be Mississippians' seasonal camps for hunting deer, harvesting nuts or other wild foods, or cutting wood. Other "Late Woodland" sites may be small nations taking refuge from Cahokian dominance in bush country unsuited for Mississippian intensive agriculture. "Mississippian" sites such as Toltec Mounds[9] near Little Rock, Arkansas, sometimes challenge archaeologists by, as at Toltec, having more than a dozen platform mounds and a plaza, but (1) beginning construction of the mounds in mid-seventh century AD, "too early" to be Mississippian, (2) cultivating the indigenous Midwest small grains, that is, chenopods, maygrass, knotweed, and little-barley, rather than depending on maize, and (3) making pottery tempered with hard clay particles. Toltec Mounds is an Arkansas River town sharing the ancient Lower Mississippi Valley mound-building tradition, continuing the Midwest indigenous-plants agriculture developed in the Late Archaic, and in its later phase trading downriver with "true" Mississippian, evidenced by some shell-tempered pots. Cahokia's frontiers were ringed by independent societies like these, living their own trajectories of history.

Smaller kingdoms and confederations of towns become very visible in the fourteenth century, freed of Cahokia's shadow. Moundville in Alabama, Etowah in Georgia, Angel in Indiana and Kincaid in Illinois on the lower Ohio River, are towns with a plaza, a few up to two dozen mounds, usually a palisade, many single-family pole and thatch houses, and plenty of maize. Historically and still today, the Creeks (Muskokee) distinguish between *etulwa*, "town," having a ceremonial ground (plaza) and sacred fire, established and formally named with the proper ritual, and *talofa*, "village," simply a settlement and affiliated with a "mother town" *etulwa* politically and to participate in rituals.[10] The difference in scale between Cahokia and even the largest of the post-Cahokian towns, Moundville, is dramatic. These were the kingdoms described by De Soto's chroniclers, not so different from the many kingdoms and principalities in fifteenth-century Europe.

As Christianity provided a set of symbols overriding the political divisions in medieval and early modern Europe, so post-Cahokia Mississippians shared a set of symbols referred to as the Southeastern Ceremonial Complex. Elements of the Complex have been recognized at Cahokia, but the full-blown Complex post-dates it, seems to have borrowed from contemporary Late Postclassic Mexico but, like the Aztecs claiming legitimacy through a link to the Toltecs before them, the Late Mississippian rulers treasured icons from Cahokia: the Lord of Spiro on the Arkansas River was buried with some heirlooms already four centuries old. Archaeologists recognize the Southeastern Ceremonial Complex from preserved stone, ceramic, shell, and copper objects, ranging from full-sized battle-axes laboriously made from single pieces of stone, through conch-shell chalices engraved with themes of war and conquest, fine shell-tempered ceramic serving wares, to repoussé copper plates similar to the "coppers" worn on headdresses by Northwest Coast nobles. That cloth and well-tanned deerhides also were decorated with motifs of the Complex, rarely preserved even in fragments, may be inferred from Europeans' sixteenth-century accounts of the pomp and gifts displayed by Southeastern *caciques*, as the Spanish termed the aristocratic leaders they met.

Southeastern Ceremonial Complex motifs center on a pair of personages, we do not know whether conceived as deity or apotheosized dynasty founders, with winged arms and human bodies. One version seems to have hawk wings and sometimes a beak mask over the lower face, the other has tobacco-moth wings and a moth proboscis, and the design may add disks that probably represent stars in the sky. Hawks as symbols of bellicose power of course go back to Hopewell and continued in Cahokia; tobacco moths are large night-flying insects that pollinate tobacco, which was cultivated in the Hopewell as well as Mississippian eras. Historically among Eastern Woodlands First Nations, tobacco was used in rituals but not for private pleasure – it was a strong South American variety probably introduced via the Caribbean. Tobacco Moth was to Night as Hawk was to Day, a highly visible denizen of the air. A third holy personage is a dancing man wearing, as a pendant on his chest, the spiraling spine of the conch shell. Late Postclassic Mexicans used the spiral conch pendant to signify Quetzalcoatl, Lord of our present Fifth World, and derived from his power, signaling legitimate rulers.[11] The necklace of large shell beads with conch spiral pendant is frequently worn by the personages engraved on the conch cups and embossed on copper plates. Personages often brandish weapons or scepters, and these may be in the form of serpents. In his other hand, a personage may carry a trophy human head. A few engravings depict chunkey players poised to roll their stone disks. Serpents, some clearly rattlesnakes and others monstrous, with horns and wings, are common and may be shown as four intertwined to make a swastika symbol of dynamic power. The common Mesoamerican cross in circle symbol of the world, or of territory, is another frequent motif. Eastern Woodland roots for the Southeastern Ceremonial Complex are obvious, and so are Mexican motifs generally by around the Late Postclassic Gulf, of which two striking examples from Spiro are depictions of a man wearing the diadem set with star disks that is the emblem for Venus the Morning Star as War Captain, and a conch cup showing two serpents as canoes bearing a pair of paddlers each with his banner beside him – the Maya image of the celestial ecliptic, two gods eternally paddling around the heavens.

Historical linguistics presents groupings and relationships suggestive of political developments, especially for the Mississippian, most recent precontact period. Muskogean (languages of Muskokee including Creek, Choctaw, Hitchiti, Alabama, and Koasati) appears to have its homeland in the middle Mississippi Valley and expanded eastward into Alabama and then south into Georgia and Florida, and southwest into (the state of) Mississippi. Siouan languages lay in a band from the mouth of the Ohio eastward through Tennessee into the Carolinas. This mapping lets either Muskogean or Siouan be adduced as the language of Cahokia, and whichever may have been spoken in the capital, both would have been so close they would have been culturally similar. Much earlier, in the Late Archaic,

Proto-Siouan, Proto-Iroquoian, and Proto-Caddoan may have been developing from a mid-Holocene common ancestral group in the Mid-South, from Tennessee to the Mississippi Valley. Iroquoian would have then moved east and northeast, Caddoan south and southwest.

Congruent with archaeological differences, the Lower Mississippi Valley is linguistically distinct from Muskogean and Siouan, its languages being Natchez, Tunica, Atakapa and Chitimacha. Natchez, in particular, is said to show similarities to Mesoamerican languages, whence some may have spread farther north to Muskogean, Tunica, and (Siouan) Quapaw, through contact with Natchez, if not more directly with Mexico. Among semantic similarities between Mesoamerican usages and Choctaw are calling mano "child of metate" and, in the Southeast, pestle "child of mortar" – Southeasterners pounding corn in mortars with pestles rather than grinding it on metates; using the same word for "feather" and "fur," which makes one think of how common feather cloaks were in both Mesoamerica and the Southeast; and the same word to mean "to kiss," "to suck," and "to smoke."[12]

Beautifully engraved conch shell cups, or chalices, very possibly used to serve the purgative "black drink" to men ritually preparing for war, were found in abundance in burials in the mounds at Spiro, in eastern Oklahoma on the Arkansas River, commanding a narrows of this major river. Historically in Caddo territory, Spiro is assumed to have been built by ancestral Caddo, although an argument has been made that it more closely fits ethnohistoric descriptions of the Tunica.[13] The site has a large pyramidal mound on one side of a plaza outlined, in a somewhat irregular hexagon, by six small mounds, with another offset, plus three mounds in a line, lower and closer to the river. Sightlines from the large platform mound across other mounds mark summer solstice and the equinox, and distances between the set of mounds around the plaza are multiples of 150 feet (47.5 meters), a unit of measurement identified also at Toltec Mounds. The mounds were drastically looted during the 1930s, treated as a mine of objects that could be sold by the impoverished graverobbers hard hit by the Depression, and then more systematically excavated by federally funded relief labor crews, unfortunately of course not up to today's standards for scientific archaeology. The principal burial mound, in the group near the river, began with a cemetery at the end of the tenth century AD, then a series of mound layers were constructed, with burials including a body placed in a large twined fabric sack, and finally, in the beginning of the fifteenth century, a large platform on which were placed a great number of burials of which many had been exhumed from previous interment, a circle of tall cedar poles, and at last a rounded cap of earth. The early fifteenth-century event is reminiscent of Cahokia's Mound 72 funeral in that an important person was interred with bodies carried on cedar-pole litters and many more tossed together, plus piles of valuables, but there is no clear evidence of human sacrifices; instead, bones of long-deceased Spiro people together with offerings left in their graves were assembled to lie with the newly dead lord. Many of the valuables such as conch cups were broken from pressure of the earth overburden on their original graves. Other valuables such as textiles could not have been previously buried, although some may have been antiques already, and the carved wooden masks and human effigies probably, like those in Florida, were set up ringing the consecrated space.[14]

Among the valuables amassed in this newly created cemetery are figurines probably from Cahokia, a handsome young man, an older man, and a woman with a mortar, all two centuries older than the tomb in the Spiro mound. As in Mound 72, thousands of marine shell beads were deposited in the Spiro tomb, piled on textiles, and there were woven cane boxes, some with cremated or exhumed fragments of skeletons, some with copper axe heads, copper beads, and embossed copper plates. One archaeologist extrapolates from early historical documents the possibility that the lords of Spiro became wealthy by controlling production of bows made from Osage orange trees (bois d'arc), the very best bow wood in America (comparable to English yew), obtainable only in a limited region in northeast Texas south of Spiro. On the edge of the Southern Plains, this region would have served to transmit bison products, as well: in 1541, de Soto's men noted plenty of "beef" and "cowhides" in the Spiro area, and men working to process the hides to be used or traded as winter bed covering.[15] Archaeology and radiocarbon dates at Spiro seem to indicate diminution of its political–economic importance in the later fifteenth century, but the de Soto chronicles challenge this. Spiro's position on the western boundary of Mississippian societies stemmed from its geographical advantages as an entrepôt, and this location continued to be advantageous, as attested by the Spanish explorers, in the sixteenth century and into the eighteenth when horses that flourished in the Osage-orange country were traded by Indians to the French in Louisiana.[16]

Archaeological distinctions correlate with linguistic boundaries on the East, also, along the eastern foothills of the Appalachians, where a Mississippian cultural pattern, dependent on maize agriculture in the floodplains, appeared in the eleventh century, changing in the mid-thirteenth century as Mid-South societies east of the Mississippi display stronger regional characteristics. Atlantic Coastal Plain societies took up maize agriculture in the Mississippian period, without large towns and platform mounds; the easternmost Mississippian-type site with platform mounds is in the piedmont. Northeastern-style longhouse villages extend along the Atlantic Coastal Plain into North Carolina; these societies will be described in the next chapter.

Research Puzzles

There has been a tendency for American archaeologists to explain cultural changes as "natural" responses to climate shifts, and apparent institutional innovations such as towns as inevitable concomitants of population increase. In one word, American archaeologists have tended toward a *provincial* outlook, not considering political and economic movements impinging on a locality from outside the region. This tendency, to be fair, is reinforced by the need for an archaeologist to know minute details of thousands of artifacts just to write a basic local history. Wide-ranging comparisons are discouraged and disparaged as speculation. As a result, Mississippian is conventionally explained according to a supposed evolutionary trajectory carrying local populations from hunting–gathering to small settlements to "chiefdoms."

Related to uncritical acceptance of a seventeenth-century European logical construct (the "tribal" or "chiefdom" stage in a conjectured universal history) is an unfamiliarity with living First Nations. The United States policy of exiling them beyond the frontier and subsequently to reservations blocked most Americans, particularly in the East, from mingling with Indian contemporaries. Archaeologists training in standard, that is, Western scientific methods had little incentive to hang out with Indian people or study indigenous knowledge. The 1990 Congressional Native American Graves Protection and Repatriation Act (NAGPRA) is having some impact on the provincialism of many archaeologists, mandating in many instances negotiation with First Nations that may be affiliated with archaeological sites. Only a minority of Midwestern and Eastern archaeologists perceive that their standard categories derived from Western philosophers' logic are stereotypes fed by nineteenth-century racism.

Growing up in segregated communities, educated in schools teaching that American Indians were no match for "civilized" Europeans, American archaeologists are generally comfortable with terminology and interpretations that segregate First Nations into a truncated history failing to achieve "civilization."

The provincial outlook sets the puzzles of Mississippian research. Without texts such as Mesoamerican archaeologists read, nor indubitable Mexican imports such as macaws and exports such as turquoise as found in the Southwest, Mississippian archaeology can be a playground for coldly "scientific" interpretations minimizing the economics and politics of the Late Prehistoric Eastern Woodlands. For example, one archaeologist published calculations purporting to demonstrate that a population of only eight thousand people in the American Bottom would have been sufficient to raise all of Cahokia's (surviving) mounds, ergo, Cahokia was only a "chiefdom" of simple farmers. The same archaeologist refused to consider as possible evidence of Mexican contacts, the filed teeth of a few Cahokia-area skeletons, dismissing their intriguing similarity to Mexican fashion of the period. It is as if, for a jigsaw puzzle, a player arbitrarily discarded several pieces.

The great research puzzle for the Mississippian is Cahokia. How did it happen that a city of unprecedented, and never later equaled, size and architectural grandeur was relatively quickly built and then, two centuries later, collapsed? What was its relation to the mound-building tradition of the Lower Mississippi Valley? Whence its Mesoamerican-style urban plan? How large was its state? How did it influence the other nations of America, from the Rockies to the Atlantic, during its time and afterward? Cahokia is unique in America north of central Mexico. If we could understand its history and society, we would be in a position to better interpret the histories of all the nations of Late Prehistoric eastern America.

Bibliographical Notes

Judith Bense's *Archaeology of the Southeastern United States* (San Diego, 1994) is a balanced and reliable outline for the region. Jerald Milanich has published extensively on Florida prehistory and contact-period peoples, for example in *Archaeology of Precolumbian Florida* (Gainesville, FL, 1994), *Florida's Indians from Ancient Times to the Present* (Gainesville, FL, 1998), and *Florida Indians and the Invasion from Europe* (Gainesville, FL, 1995). *Indians of the Greater Southeast Historical Archaeology and Ethnohistory* (Gainesville, FL, 2000) edited by Bonnie McEwan covers the contact period and subsequent histories, nation by nation, while Marvin Smith's *Archaeology of Aboriginal Culture Change in the Interior Southeast* (Gainesville, FL, 1987) presents a powerful interpretation of shifts in Muskokee societies congruent with European disease epidemics and invasions. Robert Neuman's *An Introduction to Louisiana Archaeology* (Baton Rouge, LA, 1984) is detailed and well illustrated. Half a dozen books focus on Cahokia, but each argues a particular perspective not evident to the non-specialist; the most accessible book (other than Roger Kennedy's lively *Hidden Cities*) is *Cahokia: The Great Native American Metropolis* by Biloine Whiting Young and Melvin L. Fowler (Urbana, IL, 2000), a collaboration between a journalist friend (Young) and one of archaeologists working at Cahokia (Fowler).

Notes

1. Historian Roger G. Kennedy, retired Director of the Smithsonian's National Museum of American History, writes in *Hidden Cities* (Penguin, 1994) that Manifest Destiny became a slogan in the 1840s' propaganda for the Mexican War. He contrasts the interest Jefferson and Gallatin had in recording American ruins, including Hopewell and Cahokia, with later general obliviousness to even the stupendous mounds of Cahokia.

2. Quoted in Mildred Wedel, "The Indian They Called *Turco*," reprinted in *The Wichita Indians 1541–1750: Ethnohistorical Essays* (Lincoln, NE, 1988), p. 43.

3. Quoted in Wedel, "The Indian," p. 42.

4. These may have represented clans making up the community. The Timacua in northern peninsular Florida during the sixteenth century were reported to have matrilineal clans called White Deer, Panther, Bear, Fish, Buzzard, Quail, and Earth. It would have been appropriate for effigies of the clan symbols to have surrounded the community's mortuary house.

5. A comparison with Europe can be thought-provoking. Since the Medieval Warm Episode was felt in Europe, too, political-economic events there should be subject to the same influences that affected North America. Is the spread of Christianity and of Islam to be attributed to the Medieval Warm Episode? Kiev Rus flourished, like Cahokia and Chaco, during that Episode and fell like them at its end. Were Mongol victories over Byzantium and Rus in the early thirteenth century due to the shift toward the Little Ice Age? A general principle adduced as explanation for an American First Nation's history ought to be applicable to European history, too.

6. Fire-clay, also called ferruginous mudstone, is a relatively soft stone occurring in central Missouri.

7. O'Brien, "Prehistoric Politics: Petroglyphs and the Political Boundaries of Cahokia," *Gateway Heritage* 15(1) (1994), pp. 30–47.

8. Rubén Cabrera Castro, "Teotihuacán Cultural Traditions Transmitted into the Postclassic According to Recent Excavations," in Davíd Carrasco, Lindsay

Jones, and Scott Sessions (eds), *Mesoamerica's Classic Heritage: From Teotihuacán to the Aztecs* (Niwot, CO, 2000), p. 208.

9. No connection with the Toltecs in central Mexico. In the 1880s, a Smithsonian researcher recording the mounds theorized that Toltecs commanded the construction, employing "Aztecs" as laborers. Local businessmen took the name for a proposed town. Similarly, Aztalan, Wisconsin, was named for a supposed connection to the Aztecs' legendary place of origin, Aztlán, and Aztec Ruin in New Mexico after the same supposed Aztec connection.

10. John H. Moore, "The Mvskoke Ethnogenetic Engine," paper presented February 10, 1992, American Association for the Advancement of Science annual meeting, Chicago.

11. Conchs were used as trumpets and of course, if you put one to your ear, you hear the roar of wind. Some contemporary Creek (Muskokee) communities still have conch trumpets, now used in their churches, and some conch cups traditionally used to serve the "black drink" ritual purgative are kept as heirloom relics. The spiral continues to be a major cosmic symbol for Muskokee, seen as a dance figure and today also on Creek town letterheads (Moore, 1994: 140).

12. T. Dale Nicklas, "Linguistic Provinces of the Southeast at the Time of Columbus," in Patricia B. Kwachka (ed.), *Perspectives on the Southeast,* (Athens, GA, 1994), pp. 1–13.

13. Frank F. Schambach, "Spiro and the Tunica: A New Interpretation of the Role of the Tunica in the Culture History of the Southeast and the Southern Plains, AD 1100–1750," in Robert C. Mainfort, Jr and Marvin D. Jeter (eds), *Arkansas Archaeology: Essays in Honor of Dan and Phyllis Morse* (Fayetteville, AR, 1999), pp. 169–224.

14. James A. Brown, *The Spiro Ceremonial Center* (Ann Arbor, MI, 1996).

15. Schambach, "Spiro and the Tunica," pp. 180–1.

16. Ibid., p. 208.

References

Bense, Judith A. (1994), *Archaeology of the Southeastern United States.* San Diego, CA: Academic Press.

Brown, James A. (1996), *The Spiro Ceremonial Center.* Ann Arbor, MI: Memoirs of the Museum of Anthropology, University of Michigan, no. 29.

Cabrera Castro, Rubén (2000), "Teotihuacán Cultural Traditions Transmitted into the Postclassic According to Recent Excavations," trans. Scott Sessions, in Davíd Carrasco, Lindsay Jones, and Scott Sessions (eds), *Mesoamerica's Classic Heritage: From Teotihuacán to the Aztecs.* Niwot CO: University Press of Colorado, pp. 195–218.

Carstens, Kenneth C. and Patty Jo Watson (eds) (1996), *Of Caves and Shell Mounds*. Tuscaloosa, AL: University of Alabama Press.

Coe, Joffre Lanning (1995), *Town Creek Indian Mound: A Native American Legacy*. Chapel Hill, NC: University of North Carolina Press.

Dent, Richard J., Jr (1995), *Chesapeake Prehistory: Old Traditions, New Directions*. New York: Plenum.

Fowler, Melvin L., Jerome Rose, Barbara Vander Leest, and Steven R. Ahler (1999), *The Mound 72 Area: Dedicated and Sacred Space in Early Cahokia*. Illinois State Museum Reports of Investigations, no. 54. Springfield, IL: Illinois State Museum Society.

Green, Wiliam (ed.) (1994), *Agricultural Origins and Development in the Midcontinent*. Report 19, Office of the State Archaeologist, University of Iowa, Iowa City.

Hall, Robert L. (1997), *An Archaeology of the Soul*. Urbana, IL: University of Illinois Press.

Kwachka, Patricia B. (ed.) (1994), *Perspectives on the Southeast*. Southern Anthropological Society Proceedings, no. 27. Athens, GA: University of Georgia Press.

Larson, Lewis H. (1980), *Aboriginal Subsistence Technology on the Southeastern Coastal Plain during the Late Prehistoric Period*. Gainesville, FL: University of Florida Press.

McEwan, Bonnie G. (ed.) (2000), *Indians of the Greater Southeast Historical Archaeology and Ethnohistory*. Gainesville, FL: University Press of Florida.

McGoun, William E. (1993), *Prehistoric Peoples of South Florida*. Tuscaloosa, AL: University of Alabama Press.

Mainfort, Robert C., Jr and Marvin D. Jeter (eds) (1999), *Arkansas Archaeology: Essays in Honor of Dan and Phyllis Morse*. Fayetteville, AR: University of Arkansas Press.

Milanich, Jerald T. (1994), *Archaeology of Precolumbian Florida*. Gainesville, FL: University Press of Florida.

Milanich, Jerald T. (1995), *Florida Indians and the Invasion from Europe*. Gainesville, FL: University Press of Florida.

Milanich, Jerald T. (1998), *Florida's Indians from Ancient Times to the Present*. Gainesville, FL: University Press of Florida.

Milanich, Jerald T. (ed.) (1991), *Earliest Hispanic/Native American Interactions in the American Southeast*. New York: Garland.

Moore, John H. (1994), "Ethnoarchaeology of the Lamar Peoples," in Patricia B. Kwachka (ed.), *Perspectives on the Southeast*. Southern Anthropological Society Proceedings, no. 27. Athens GA: University of Georgia Press, pp. 126–41.

Nassaney, Michael S. and Kenneth E. Sassaman (eds) (1995), *Native American Interactions: Multiscalar Analyses and Interpretations in the Eastern Woodlands*. Knoxville, TN: University of Tennessee Press.

Neuman, Robert W. (1984), *An Introduction to Louisiana Archaeology*. Baton Rouge, LA: Louisiana State University Press.

O'Brien, Michael J. and W. Raymond Wood (1998), *The Prehistory of Missouri*. Columbia, MO; University of Missouri Press.

O'Brien, Patricia J. (1991), "Early State Economics: Cahokia, Capital of the Ramey State," in Henri J. M. Claessen and Pieter van de Velde (eds), *Early State Economics*, New Brunswick, NJ: Transaction, pp. 143–75.

O'Brien, Patricia J. (1994), "Prehistoric Politics: Petroglyphs and the Political Boundaries of Cahokia," *Gateway Heritage* 15(1): 30–47.

Pauketat, Timothy R. (1994), *The Ascent of Chiefs*. Tuscaloosa, AL: University of Alabama Press.

Riley, Thomas J., Richard Edging and Jack Rossen (1990), "Cultigens in Prehistoric Eastern North America," *Current Anthropology* 31(5): 525–41.

Smith, Marvin T. (1987), *Archaeology of Aboriginal Culture Change in the Interior Southeast*. Gainesville, FL: University Presses of Florida.

Ward, H. Trawick and R. P. Stephen Davis Jr (1999), *Time Before History: The Archaeology of North Carolina*. Chapel Hill, NC: University of North Carolina Press.

Wedel, Mildred Mott (1988[1982]), "The Indian They Called *Turco*," reprinted in *The Wichita Indians 1541–1750: Ethnohistorical Essays*, Reprints in Anthropology, vol. 38, pp. 38–52. Lincoln, NE: J & L Reprints.

Young, Biloine Whiting, and Melvin L. Fowler (2000), *Cahokia: The Great Native American Metropolis*. Urbana, IL: University of Illinois Press.

From Günter Wagner, *Yuchi Tales*, pp. 144–7

Long time ago the Yuchi were engaged in wars all the time. Once when they were in the wilderness they saw that somebody had been there; so they made themselves ready, built a bark fence and went in there. In the night when they all slept two people said to each other that they would not sleep; and then before it was dark they saw a very long track, and they said to each other that "Long Track" must have been there. "Long Track" was a very strong enemy, and he ran very fast. When "Long Track" gets killed all wars will be ended, they said. So they watched, and right there they discovered his tracks. They all slept inside the bark fence, but two people were lying there and did not sleep. When it was late in the night they could hear that the enemies surrounded the bark fence. Then "Long Track" pointed a gun at them over the bark fence. The two people who were together shot at the man about where his stomach would be. And then they shot at each other, the Yuchi and their enemies, and the enemies ran away, they said. They followed them and kept on shooting while they chased them away. When they came back to the bark fence some people were lying there, and blood was running; they looked over the fence and went along. One was lying by the way; they took his hand, rolled him on the other side and asked, "What has happened?" Nothing was the matter with him; he was lying there asleep; he woke up, and then he said, "If I had seen Long Track I should have killed him; he took off his clothes and hit the ground," they said. In the morning they trailed his track, close by the bark fence they had shot him, the beads on his belt had fallen down and blood also had dropped; this they trailed. While they were going one of them got behind. Under many little pines he saw something shaking hard, but he did not tell anything. He did not catch up with them, so he turned and went home. After long time they got back to the place where they had trailed his track, and while they were going there, the one who had dropped behind, said, "I saw those little pines shaking but I did not tell." When he told this, they all went there and saw that Long Track had died there; his bones were piled up, they saw. He had seen his enemies coming, but he was wounded and could not get up; he had been pulling the little pines so that they were tossing about, and then he had died, they found out.

From Günter Wagner, Yuchi Tales, *pp. 144–7 (continued)*

A very tall person measured his shin bone and it reached to his hip, they said. Thus the Yuchi killed Long Track, it is said.

Told by Maxey Simms, Sapulpa, Oklahoma, 1928–29, in Yuchi, translated by Mr Simms and recorded by German linguist Günter Wagner; Mr Simms's mother was Creek [Muskokee] and he also spoke Creek.

Wagner, Günter (1931), *Yuchi Tales.* Publications of the American Ethnological Society, vol. XIII. New York: G. E. Stechert.

11

LATE WOODLAND, TO AD 1600

Dense deciduous forests covering eastern North America from the Mississippi Valley to the Atlantic seaboard were the backdrop for dozens of Indian nations making a living by long-fallow farming and deer hunting, the two sources of food interdependent in that cornfields fostered browse for deer, drawing them toward settlements. Over and above similarities due to ecologically linked economics, the nations of the Eastern Woodlands traded and traveled extensively, in peace and for war. The Late Woodland period takes these peoples from the decline of Middle Woodland Hopewell, in the fifth century AD, to European invasions intensifying in the seventeenth century. Descriptions of indigenous nations left us by these invaders help archaeologists interpret Late Woodland sites, although it is often surprisingly difficult to identify the sites of historically named towns. This chapter considers Northern Midwest, Northeast, and Middle Atlantic regions during the Late Woodland period, the Southeast having been covered in the preceding chapter as Mississippian.

The Northern Regions: Effigy Mounds

A prime enigma in the prehistory of the northern Midwest are the effigy mounds throughout southern Wisconsin, built in the early Late Woodland period, mid-eighth to mid-eleventh centuries AD. Low, not more than two meters (six feet) high, they are earth sculptures of birds, bears, panthers, lizards, turtles, two known human effigies, cones, and linear ridges. They lie in clusters, reportedly as many as 174 effigies plus several hundred simple mounds in one site, more usually a dozen or two. Biggest is a bird with outspread wings stretching 624 feet (190 meters), more common are figures twenty to forty feet (six to twelve meters). Most sit on bluffs or terraces overlooking water, the best known high on the Mississippi River bluff near McGregor, Iowa (Effigy Mounds National Monument). Many, but not all, contain burials, few burials have any grave offerings, no village sites have been directly associated with effigy mound clusters – the people must have lived in small communities, in lightly built wigwams, raising a little maize and probably indigenous small grains but moving seasonally to resource locations.

To best view the clusters of effigies, one should be in a helicopter and the site cleared of trees, but of course the Late Woodland people couldn't do that, deepening the mystery of constructions their makers could never see to full advantage. Were the effigies representatives of the totems (symbols) of clans in the community? Ojibwe (Anishinaabe) who may be their descendants have clans named after Bear, Turtle, and other animals, but why would there be sometimes many duplicates of the same animal, and what would the round and linear mounds represent? Were the animals meant to be constellations, stars anchored down to earth? Again, duplications within sites and the differences between sites render that interpretation dubious. If there is any regularity or pattern, other than clusters of animals, round and linear constructions, it has yet to be discerned.

After Effigy Mounds

Aztalan, the northernmost distinctly Mississippian town, intruded into south-central Wisconsin in the beginning of the eleventh century, about the end of Effigy Mound constructions. Whether Aztalan caused change in the Late Woodland societies of the Rock River region, we cannot state; we do know that Aztalan was well situated for defense, on the bank of a tributary to the Rock and fortified with a stout bastioned palisade. Gardens inside the palisade and extensive maize fields along the floodplain outside the palisade sustained the population. Within the town are trash pits filled with food processing debris and, in a few, bones of young men butchered like deer. Aztalan's soldiers standing on the bastions may have taunted attackers, "Dogs! Little deer! We'll shoot you down and drag you in and cut you up for our cooking pots!"

The principal platform mound inside the palisade at Aztalan was built upon a natural ridge, halving the labor cost to achieve the desired height. The other platform mound was constructed in its entirety, as were a line of tall conical mounds coming down the valley wall behind the town. The conical mounds look Hopewellian but don't seem to have been tombs and date later than Hopewell. Elsewhere in Wisconsin, there are Mississippian platform mounds built upon natural ridges, for example on the Upper Mississippi River at Trempealeau, Wisconsin, overlooking an agricultural village with, as at Aztalan, fine pottery from Cahokia in addition to local manufactures. Whether or not Cahokia ever exercised political control so far north, it certainly had economic outreach.

Northern Midwest Mississippian, or Upper Mississippian (in relation to the river), depended on maize agriculture using labor-intensive ridge and furrow fields, but did not raise platform mounds, contenting themselves with villages rather than ambitious towns. There are many sites with quite modest-sized round mounds, in some locations in series of dozens, and generally the mounds contain graves, as modest as the sizes of the mounds. In the earlier phase, tenth through twelfth centuries, homes were either wigwams or rectangular pole-walled structures built in dug-out basins, that is, pit-houses. These were no longer constructed beginning in the thirteenth century, wigwams then predominating.

Oneota is the name archaeologists use for the dominant type of northern Midwest agricultural villages: whether they were colonists coming up the Mississippi, Illinois, and Rock Rivers, or local Late Woodland societies taking up intensive maize agriculture with its "sisters" squashes and beans, or both, can't always be deciphered. Shell-tempered, polished pots decorated with the abstract curvilinear designs characteristic of Cahokia's fine ware indicate direct trade with Cahokia and use of its style in ceramics made along the Upper Mississippi, while to the east, in the Lake Michigan region, local styles are seen. Oneota avoided Aztalan, if the absence of Oneota pottery from the town is a clue, then when Aztalan and its parent power Cahokia fell in the thirteenth century, Oneota blossomed, to dominate southern Wisconsin and Minnesota, northern Illinois and Iowa until the seventeenth century. From the fourteenth century on, Oneota communities hunted bison, probably on long treks west onto the prairies, as well as deer and smaller game locally; hoes were made of bison scapulae (shoulderblades) rather than the stone hoes employed farther south. Catlinite was first commonly used for pipes by Oneota, the famous red catlinite quarries in southwestern Minnesota a point to visit when trekking to the bison herds available from there westward.

Oneota expanded from the fourteenth century throughout the upper Midwest into Indiana on the east and through Iowa on the west, associated with Midwestern prairies that they, in fact, were instrumental in maintaining through agricultural clearing and regular burning for bison range forage. Historically, this broad region was home to the Chiwere and Dhegiha Siouan-speaking language groups, including Iowa, Oto, Missouri, and Hochungara (Ho-Chunk) (Winnebago) (the Chiwere group), and Omaha, Osage, Ponca, Kansa, and Quapaw (Dhegiha group), all agriculturalists familiar with hunting bison. The pattern may have been initiated along the lower Missouri and its tributaries in the twelfth century, when intensive maize agriculture on ridge and furrow fields and compact villages appear, the villages with an abundance of butchering and hide-processing stone blades implying surplus production of dried meat and hides. Occasional Mississippian ceramics and ornaments such as the carved shell faces reminding Hochungara of their legendary hero He-Who-Wears-Human-Heads-As-Pendants, reached lower Missouri communities, likely in exchange for dried bison meat and hide robes carried down to Cahokia: besides canoes and rafts, Missouri River people stretched bison hides over round willow frames to make "bullboats," rather ungainly looking but, with their shallow draft, quite serviceable for the Missouri. A string of bullboats tied to a lead boat, the way barges are pulled by a tug, could transport a ton of meat and hides downstream. After Cahokia declined, meat and hides could be brought by boats from Plains hunting grounds to the prairie villages for their own consumption.

Out beyond the prairie borders of the western side of the Mississippi Valley, maize agriculture can only be practised in valley bottoms, where the water table is close to the surface and fields sheltered from the ever-blowing strong dry Plains wind. From the close of the tenth century, agricultural villages colonized the Missouri trench and lower reaches of its tributaries, first with rectangular houses – Mississippian style, but longer than the squarish houses common around Cahokia – in open villages, then, beginning in the fifteenth century, some fortified towns of circular sod-covered earthlodges, the historic type, while small open villages continue here and there. Bison hunting is important to these communities, supplemented with deer, elk, and antelope for clothing leather as well as meat (bison hide is too thick to be tailored into clothing).

Because the agricultural towns were stable and on the main river, they attracted trade, exchanging their corn for dried meat and hides produced by grasslands nomadic bison hunters, and passing along more expensive items such as catlinite pipes and marine shell beads. Knife River "flint," a translucent brown chalcedony ideal for arrowpoints and knife blades, was quarried in central North Dakota near the most westerly of the major agricultural towns, and would have been a steady incentive for people to come to the North Dakota towns for trade. When French traders reached the Plains in the mid-eighteenth century, they made the Missouri River towns their headquarters, building on the existing trade structure and, in the early nineteenth century, Lewis and Clark wintered over in one of these towns, engaging a guide there for the westward journey. Their guide's young wife, a Shoshone girl captured near the Rockies and sold downriver, came along, with their baby, as every schoolchild knows: Sakakawea. Slaves, especially young women, may well have been a prehistoric trade item, too.

North Dakota Missouri River towns spoke Siouan languages, Mandan and Hidatsa. Both recount origins to the southeast and migrations up river to their promised lands. Some Hidatsa bands not only hunted but even overwintered in camps on the upper Missouri into present Montana, coming to be known as the Crow (Absaroke); their High Plains territory lacking habitat suitable for maize, they no longer had farms, other than small plots to grow tobacco for ceremonies. Downriver – south – from the Mandan and Hidatsa in North Dakota were the Arikara of South Dakota, Caddoan-speakers related to the Pawnee who farmed in stream valleys in Nebraska. Arikara and Pawnee archaeological remains differ from those of the Siouan speakers only in details, as do the protohistoric sites in the Dakotas used by the Algonkian-speaking Cheyenne after they gave up their agricultural settlements in western Minnesota, pushed by eighteenth-century colonization pressure on their neighbors to the east, and pulled by availability of horses giving a margin of comfort and security to Plains bison hunters. Once the use of horses spread over the Plains, the Missouri River towns added the sale of the animals to their stock in trade.

There have always been people on the High Plains, subsisting primarily by driving bison herds into corrals built against bluffs or in ravines, and complementing the meat with camas and prairie turnip, a parsnip-like root growing in many locations on the Plains. Women harvest the prairie turnip, as they do camas, with care to maintain optimum conditions for the plants (I use the present tense because the cultivation of these traditional foods continues among families both on the Plains and in the Plateau). Before horses were obtained, initially from the Spanish ranches in New Mexico and then, in the later seventeenth and the eighteenth centuries, from other Indian nations, High Plains nomadic communities bred two kinds of dogs, animals the size of German shepherds or huskies to carry packs on their shoulders and pull small travois (pair of poles fastened across their shoulders, with a cargo net or hide across the lower, dragging portion of the poles), and small fat dogs for feast meat. Moving camp by driving packs of loaded dogs, prone to yelp and nip at each other, and killing enough meat to feed the dogs in addition to people, made docile, grass-eating horses a real boon to Plains people, even aside from horses' much greater load-bearing capacity and opportunity for riding. The basic adaptation to the High Plains, corralling bison herds and harvesting root, bulb, tuber, and berry foods, was developed in the Archaic, reinforced in the Late Prehistoric period when agricultural colonies pushed up the Missouri trench, creating a steady market for processed bison, and finally widened, as it were, when horses substantially increased the range and speed of nomadism and amount of goods that could be moved, while substantially reducing the cost (in animal food) of this way of life.

North of the Oneota in Wisconsin and Minnesota, wild rice substituted for maize. A boundary for reliable maize agriculture runs through the center of these states: north of it, the expectable frost-free growing season is too short. That wild rice was indeed a substitute for maize, not merely a regional crop independently utilized, as indicated by the appearance of new styles of shell-tempered (i.e., "Mississippian") pottery in the region during the same time, eleventh–twelfth centuries, Oneota appears south of the maize-growing boundary. Along the boundary zone, Oneota potsherds have been recovered in sites where the northern styles predominate, demonstrating contact between the maize agriculturists and the wild-rice harvesters. Wild rice is an indigenous seed-bearing grass flourishing in shallow lakes. Ojibwe (Anishinaabe) and Dakota harvesters are very careful to glide their canoes through the stands of rice, lightly knocking ripened grains into the boat without breaking the stalks that still bear ripening seeds. The shallow-water stands are usually thoroughly harvested, in the process dropping enough of the light seeds into the lakebed to maintain the stand. Dried, parched, and hulled, wild rice can be stored like other grains. Whether the Late Prehistoric northern ricers were expanding Oneota adapting, by necessity, to another carbohydrate staple, or were indigenous people intensifying their dependence on rice on the model of maize agriculturists they had observed, we cannot tell; the northern people were congregating in larger, palisaded villages in this Late period, contrasting with earlier more numerous smaller camps. Oneota presumably were the threat, as they were to each other. They may have coveted their neighbors' deer and bison, beaver, furs, and processed stores of rice, even though they could not raise maize on these neighbors' lands.

The Northeast

During the seventeenth century, the Northeast was a battlefield where the Five Nations of the League of the Iroquois (Haudenosaunee) fought other Iroquoian nations, and Iroquoians fought Algonkians. Was it ever thus? or were the European colonists witnessing enmities precipitated by more than a century of European intrusions? For, Norse aside, Western European fishing boats and whalers had been numerous in the Canadian Maritimes since early in the sixteenth century, and there is tenuous evidence that this traffic goes back to the late fourteenth century, kept secret by Basque entrepreneurs. Greenland Norse excursions to Labrador for timber and furs, continuing from initial Greenland settlement at AD 1000 until late in the fifteenth century, were another element in the Northeast trade picture, reaching beyond the Maritimes. There is, in addition, discovery of a relatively lengthy inscription in Norse runic writing far to the west in central Minnesota, indicating a mid-fourteenth-century Norse expedition, possibly seeking new sources for furs after the German Hanseatic League closed off Scandinavian kingdoms' access to the European fur trade.

Origin of the Iroquois has been long debated in the Northeast. One school of archaeologists sees continuity of artifacts from Middle Woodland, positing Iroquois in their Northeast homelands for two thousand years. Opposed archaeologists are more impressed with apparent discontinuities: a shift in pottery technique from coil-built to patched-on clay in early Late Woodland, substantial maize–beans– squash agriculture appearing in the twelfth century, and fortified towns in the later thirteenth century. Apparent discontinuities tend to resolve with additional archaeological excavations. Although historic Iroquois agriculture dependent on the "Three Sisters" maize, beans, and squashes[1] does contrast with earlier cultivation of indigenous grains, maize was generally grown in southern Ontario during the latter three or four centuries of the first millennium AD, perhaps not so intensively. It seems definite that during that time, Northeastern Algonkians took up cultivating maize and modifying their pots to cook it better. Seventeenth-century Algonkian-speaking Mahican in historically documented villages of the upper Hudson Valley used styles of pottery indistinguishable from those made by neighboring Iroquoian Mohawks; their crops were the same, and most artifacts.

A hypothesis on Iroquoian origins must take into account the Iroquoian-speaking nations including Susquehannock in Pennsylvania and Tuscarora and Nottoway in North Carolina at historic contact, and the linguistic link between Iroquoian and Cherokee. Looked at from large perspective, Iroquoians and Cherokee lay along the frontier between Eastern lands and the Midwest, along and in the east-draining valleys of the Adirondacks–Alleghenies–Appalachians mountain chain. With Algonkian speakers to their north and east, and distantly related Siouans in the Midwest, Iroquoians and Cherokee appear to have been pushing into the East. Relying on maize agriculture and long-distance trading backed by military forces, Iroquoians seem to prefigure European colonization of the Northeast. Like the European colonists, the several Iroquois nations warred among themselves for farmland and control of trade, allied, intermarried and adopted with both other Iroquoians and with Algonkian-speakers. Their trade forays distributed their goods well beyond their territorial borders. Thus archaeology cannot pinpoint Iroquois territories simply by noting artifact styles, and analyses of skeletons does not differentiate an Iroquois genetic type contrasted with an Algonkian type, but the opposite, lack of any sharp distinctions.

Related to the Iroquois history question is that of the affiliation of the eastern Ohio Valley societies termed Fort Ancient. With a series of settlements, some well fortified with palisades, in southwestern Ohio to West Virginia, Fort Ancient began in the thirteenth century and continued into the protohistoric seventeenth century. Embankments on top of the bluff overlooking the "type site" in southern Ohio were built a thousand years earlier by Hopewell; the large Fort Ancient villages with plazas generally were preceded, from the tenth or eleventh centuries, by small ones of a few rectangular semi-pithouses each with a generous storage pit for maize. By the thirteenth century, substantial in-ground storage chambers holding up to thirty-five bushels of maize ringed the village plaza. Beans, squashes, sunflowers, and tobacco were raised, and food prepared and served in shell-tempered pots. Using crushed shell to temper pottery clay was especially favored by Midwestern Mississippians, thus making Fort Ancient look "Mississippian-related" to archaeologists, while beans were not being grown by Midwestern Mississippians (until Oneota), a surprising contrast to Fort Ancient. Beans thus link Fort Ancient eastward to Iroquoians. Historic Iroquois claimed their military forces drove the Algonkian-speaking Shawnee from the central Ohio Valley, which suggests Fort Ancient represents Late Prehistoric Shawnee, neither "Mississippian" nor Iroquois.

At a large Ohio Fort Ancient village, graves alongside a central plaza had an interesting contrast, men on one side buried with arrows and pipes, men on the opposite site buried with small sets of objects likely to have constituted healers' or diviners' amulets. A pipe buried with a man at a West Virginia Fort Ancient site was carved as a raptor bird holding a human head in its claws. Conch shell masks, better termed "faces" because many could not have been worn as masks, have been found in Fort Ancient as well as other Interior South (Mid-South) sites, not to mention along the Missouri and even in north-central Montana. With little round mouths, the "faces" resemble the simplest versions of Iroquois False Faces, spirits who come whistling from the forest. Since elaborately grimacing masks were a nineteenth-century development among the Iroquois, the earliest preserved masks being simple, the late Mississippian/ Late Woodland shell masks may represent such spirits sent by the Face at the Western Rim of the World to help humans.

In the protohistoric sixteenth century, Fort Ancient people were in trading contact with Mississippians to the south who passed on Spanish objects, and with Iroquoians to the northeast who passed on, among other items, iron kettle lugs from Basque fishermen using the Gulf of St Lawrence shores to dry fish and render whale oil. Such precisely identified artifacts prove relationships – trading, possibly tribute or looting in certain cases – that override political and ethnic territoriality. With both continuities and discontinuities in the material culture of upstate New York and the St Lawrence Valley, historic Iroquois homeland, over the Late Woodland centuries, and different boundaries between "Mississippian" and "Northeast" depending on what trait is selected to define them – shell-tempered pottery? beans? – the only clear conclusion is that archaeologists are not going to find the final answer to the debate on Iroquois origins.

Iroquois towns are recognized by really long longhouses, curved-roof multifamily dwellings shaped like quonset huts, built of poles covered with slabs of elm bark. About six meters (twenty feet) wide, a longhouse could extend over one hundred meters (four hundred feet). Divided into family compartments, cooking hearths along the

center, longhouses sheltered generations of related women consti-
tuting a matrilineal clan. Clanswomen worked together in the fields,
shared childcare and domestic responsibilities, and selected representatives from their brothers and sons to sit on village and national
councils. It wasn't a matriarchy because women did not alone rule,
rather it was (and is) a representative democracy where women's
rights and opinions were guarded by customary law. Women's soli-
darity in their clans facilitated Iroquois men traveling on extended
hunts or trading journeys, knowing their wives and children had
the assistance of clanswomen. This social structure was behind the
military force of the Iroquois, especially the Five Nations allied in
the Haudenosaunee, and may have supported an Iroquois expansion
as early as the eleventh century.

Around the Iroquoians holding prime farmlands in the Northeast
were Algonkian-speaking nations. Early seventeenth-century observers
characterized Northeast Algonkians as less formally organized, living
in smaller communities of smaller houses, than the Iroquois. There's
an ecological angle here, Algonkians occupying rocky coasts, estuaries, and hills of New England, the Maritimes, and Canadian Shield
forests. Unlike the broad, fertile valleys of the Mohawk, St Lawrence,
and eastern Great Lakes, these lands cannot support large agricultural populations. Their inhabitants adapted by dispersing seasonally into family bands to hunt, fish with weirs on tidal flats or during
spawning runs, and collect berries and other wild or semi-cultivated
plants, maintaining maize-bean-squash fields in suitable valley locations. Houses, oval or comparatively short "longhouses," sheltered
nuclear or extended families.

Archaeologists working in New England find that some settlements in coastal estuaries have remains of indigenous nuts and fruits
(cherries, raspberries, and grapes), wild rice, chenopods, and sunflower seeds, but none of maize, although the sunflowers, and possibly chenopods, were likely cultivated. Sites on the lake-dotted rolling
uplands similarly may lack evidence of maize, their inhabitants
focusing on lake and swamp animals and plants. Upland sites could
have been seasonal camps for people from agricultural villages in
the major river valleys such as that of the Connecticut. Only in these
wide, warmer valleys are there large permanent villages; the coastal
estuary zones may have supported comparable populations but in
dispersed neighborhoods. Where coastal residents wanted to raise
maize, beans, and squashes, they had to deal with limited and less
fertile arable land than river-valley people had. The historically
reported practice of burying a fish for fertilizer in each corn hill

may have been an idea introduced not only to the Pilgrims at Plymouth but also to the Indians by "Squanto" (Tisquantum), who had been taken to Europe in 1614 and sold as a slave. Tisquantum would have observed use of animal-product fertilizers in Europe, perhaps specifically fish in France or the Canadian Maritimes where he landed after his escape from Europe.

Aristocratic lineages among the Algonkians trained their children to assume leadership over a group of villages. With modest resource bases and populations, these sachems neither lived nor were buried ostentatiously; at best, some Late Woodland sites in Algonkian territory show a house or a few graves larger or with a few more grave goods than those adjacent. Still, this contrasts with the strong clan communalism of the Iroquois, whose longhouses and graves did not differentiate aristocratic from commoner lineages. The Huron, a northern Iroquoian nation, went so far as to disinter village dead about once every decade, gathering hundreds of skeletons from a region and deliberately mixing the bones in one large grave pit, dramatically symbolizing the common humanity of all Huron.

Negotiations between European colonists and New England Indian communities in the seventeenth century provide us several close observations of these First Nations, albeit not before Canadian Maritimes trade and epidemics from European landings had affected the New Englanders. William Wood, a Massachusetts Bay Colony immigrant probably in 1628, recorded that the Ninnimissinuok sachem at present Salem, Massachusetts:

> hath no kingly robes to make him glorious in the view of his subjects, nor daily guards to secure his person, or court-like attendance, nor sumptuous palaces, yet do they yield all submissive subjection to him, accounting him their sovereign, going at his command and coming at his beck, not so much as expostulating the cause though it be in matters thwarting their wills, he being accounted a disloyal subject that will not effect what his prince commands.[2]

Sachems, reciprocally, concerned themselves with the welfare of their subjects. Daniel Gookin, an immigrant arriving in Boston sixteen years later than Wood, noted that dissatisfied Nipmuck could move to another sachem's territory,

> so that their princes endeavour to carry it obligingly and lovingly unto their people, lest they should desert them, and

thereby their strength, power, and tribute would be diminished.[3]

Most tellingly, Sachem Massasoit, whose territory included Plymouth, found Tisquantum had been acting deviously against Massasoit's interest and ordered him executed, sending a knife to the Pilgrim colony to perform the sentence on "Squanto." He died of a sudden illness in 1622 before his hosts might do so. It may be that in Gookin's time, after thousands of immigrants had taken over much of Massachusetts Bay, sachems' "strength, power, and tribute" was more fragile than prior to the European invasion.

Middle Atlantic Region

New York City and Long Island mark the boundary between heavily glaciated New England with its granite outcrops, and the more generous coastal plain and river valleys to the south. The zone was predominantly Algonkian-speaking as far south as North Carolina, and bordered by Siouan languages to the west, Iroquoians to the northwest. Patterns of settlement, house structures, agriculture and collecting described above for New England Algonkians apply to the more southern Coastal Plain Algonkians, too. The custom of exhuming skeletons to rebury them with dozens or even more than a hundred others in regional community ossuary pits was common but not the exclusive mode of grave for Late Woodland Middle Atlantic Algonkians.

A major question challenging archaeologists in the Middle Atlantic region is that of the antiquity of the kingdoms encountered by European colonists in the beginning of the seventeenth century. The fourteenth century here, as in the South, southern New England, and Midwest, saw more intensive maize–beans–squash agriculture, larger villages, and fortifications. Organization into small kingdoms exacting tribute from villages in a region may have begun at that time. From the chronicle of De Soto's 1540 journey through the South, tribute presented to the rulers of these small kingdoms were "maize, dogs, tanned skins, blankets, venison, salt, corncakes, turkeys, persimmon bread, fish, woven mantles, and nut oil."[4] Little of this would be preserved, nor would any be readily distinguishable, archaeologically, from a community's own harvests – one would need to see piles of tribute goods placed in the plaza or before the ruler's house, or ceremoniously presented. There are hints, from the patterns of structure posts visible as stains in sites, that in this final prehistoric period above-ground granaries and storage sheds were supplementing the older lined pit storage, suggesting greater quantities of goods to be stored, but these, too, could have been a village's own products rather than tribute or goods gathered preparatory to rendering tribute.

Because major rivers in the Northeast and Middle Atlantic regions flow southeastward, building good farmland along their lower reaches before turning into estuaries, the interior coastal plain attracted the largest population in the Late Woodland period. The same physical feature of southeastward-flowing major rivers channeled wars of conquest for those farmlands. From the mid-fifteenth century, the uplands above the fall line in the Potomac and Chesapeake region seem to lose small villages, while settlements in the agriculturally favorable interior coastal plain valleys increase and many are fortified. Historically, the Susquehanna River in particular was a "war road" for Iroquois out of the eastern Great Lakes-Mohawk Valley, and parallel rivers served the same purpose. "War roads" explain the late depopulation of the small upland villages, vulnerable to attack from the rivers they depended upon for resources, and the congregation of principal towns just below the fall line where war parties journeying downstream were hindered by rough terrain. Forests above the fall line became buffer zones, utilized mainly for hunting – since hunters are armed! Smaller and more dispersed communities could continue in the coastal zone, protected from the big war expeditions by the towns at the base of the fall line.

Late Woodland and Mississippian

By and large, "Mississippian" refers to agricultural towns with platform mounds, and "Late Woodland" to camps and villages without monumental architecture. "Mississippian" characteristically is in areas favorable for maize agriculture, "Late Woodland" in the north and in uplands where a shorter growing season or poor soils threaten maize. Regional styles of pottery are classed as "Mississippian" or "Late Woodland" according to attributes such as crushed shell (generally, Mississippian) versus crushed rock temper, smoothed (Mississippian) versus fabric-impressed surface, or "castellated" rims (thickened, high rims with raised sections, supposedly resembling castle walls) typical of Iroquoians and their neighbors. As more surveys and excavations are conducted, mandated today before most construction

KING ALFRED'S COLLEGE
LIBRARY

projects, larger pictures can be drawn, and these often indicate that "Late Woodland" small sites in the hinterlands of Mississippian towns were hamlets or seasonal gathering locales, outliers of the agricultural societies of the towns.

Common throughout the Eastern Woodland and prairies were the shift to reliance on maize, around the tenth century, and then in the late fourteenth century to aggregated villages, often fortified. These shifts are related, in that reliance on maize as a staple food created demand for good farmland, which forced communities with it to defend against others desiring the resource. Whether the shift to more intensive agriculture and its consequent need to defend territory represented efforts to cope with population increase that had been accruing for centuries, or was a choice to follow a more prestigious lifestyle, cannot be told from the archaeology, and indeed both factors could be valid. Once the grandiose mounds and plazas, processions and ceremonies, of Cahokia were set before them at the riverine hub of eastern North America, Americans had to live with unprecedented political and economic forces. Climate, soils, mineral resources all acquired greater and more critical value. So, too, did human labor. What European invaders saw was a country where ecological differences loomed large, underlying cultural differences. These ecological features affected European colonizations, too.

Research Puzzles

"Late Woodland" has been a "default" category, those Late Prehistoric Eastern Woodlands sites and associated artifacts that don't show Mississippian characteristics. Partly as a result of cultural resource management (CRM) surveys carried out after 1960s federal and state laws mandated precautions against destroying patrimony, many sites have been recorded away from arable river valleys. No longer is there a simple contrast between Mississippian towns and camps of less sophisticated hunter-gatherers in the hills; villages in the uplands and small stream valleys may be frontier posts, or bases for exploiting resources integrated in diversified economies or, perhaps sometimes, summer residences for town dwellers. Relating Late Woodland sites to Mississippian towns a day's walk away is a research puzzle promising a more realistic picture of both Mississippian politics and economies, and communities that chose to retain, or produce, more traditional Woodland technologies and foods.

Another type of research puzzle for archaeologists working with Late Woodland sites is identifying settlements visited by early European explorers. This is not an esoteric exercise, because a number of First Nations have claimed treaty rights or uncompensated land cessions, and must demonstrate in court that their forebears are documented to have resided in the claimed territory. More than one First Nation may lay claim to the same land, occupied by a succession of displaced nations or as a common for fishing, quarrying, or trading. One would think that if, for example, Jean Nicolet writes of voyaging to what must be Green Bay, Wisconsin, and seeing the Ho-Chunk main village, known as Red Banks, an archaeologist could locate the settlement. It turns out that there are several substantial Late Prehistoric village sites in the Green Bay vicinity, and none shows the distinctive red banks below the site. Adding to the puzzle, the Ho-Chunk seem to have relocated their main village more than once, always calling it Red Banks (like York, Pennsylvania, or Mount Vernon, Iowa, similarly named after other, admired places). Potawatomi and Menominee are documented in Green Bay, too, but only one Late Woodland site, on a small island near Green Bay, has artifacts and a location fitting a late seventeenth-century Potawatomi village – and preceding it was a stockaded village of Huron refugees from the 1649 Iroquois conquest of their homeland far to the east on Lake Huron. Exact fits between seventeenth- and eighteenth-century explorers' itineraries and archaeological sites are more often debated than confirmed.

Bibliographical Notes

Lynn M. Alex's *Iowa's Archaeological Past* (Iowa City, IA, 2000) is an exceptionally well-written survey of the prehistory of a Midwestern region; Alex never loses sight of the human beings who created the archaeological record. Thomas Vennum Jr's *Wild Rice and the Ojibway People* (St Paul, MN, 1988) does not focus on the prehistoric period but richly describes the way of life, and its historic vicissitudes, of these northern Minnesota people. Bruce G. Trigger's *The Children of Aataentsic: A History of the Huron People* (Montreal, 1987) covers that northern Iroquoian nation from archaeological remains to their disastrous defeat by the Five Nations Iroquois in 1649. Kathleen J. Bragdon accessibly surveys *Native Peoples of Southern New England, 1500–1650* (Norman, OK, 1996).

Notes

1. The complex of maize, beans, and squash includes nitrogen-fixing bacteria on bean plant roots and fungi on maize roots that improve the plants' absorption of minerals such as phosphorus. All three species of food plants grow better when planted together.

2. Quoted in Kathleen Bragdon, *Native People of Southern New England, 1500–1650* (Norman, OK, 1996), p. 147.

3. Quoted in ibid.

4. David Dye, quoted in Adam King and Jennifer A. Freer, "The Mississippian Southeast: A World-Systems Perspective," in Michael S. Nassaney and Kenneth E. Sassaman (eds), *Native American Interactions: Multiscalar Analyses and Interpretations in the Eastern Woodlands* (Knoxville, TN, 1995), p. 271. See also David Dye's "Feasting with the Enemy: Mississippian Warfare and Prestige-Goods Circulation" in the same volume.

References

Alex, Lynn M. (2000), *Iowa's Archaeological Past.* Iowa City, IA: University of Iowa Press.

Birmingham, Robert A., Carol I. Mason and James B. Stoltman (eds) (1997), *Wisconsin Archaeology.* Wisconsin Archeologist 78(1/2) (Special Issue).

Bragdon, Kathleen J. (1996), *Native People of Southern New England, 1500–1650.* Norman, OK: University of Oklahoma Press.

Crawford, Gary W. and David G. Smith (1996), "Migration in Prehistory: Princess Point and the Northern Iroquoian Case," *American Antiquity* 61(4): 782–90.

Dent, Richard J., Jr (1995), *Chesapeake Prehistory: Old Traditions, New Directions.* New York: Plenum.

Emerson, Thomas E., Dale L. McElrath and Andrew C. Fortier (eds) (2000), *Late Woodland Societies: Tradition and Transformation across the Midcontinent.* Lincoln, NE: University of Nebraska Press.

Funk, Robert E. (1983), "The Northeastern United States," in Jesse D. Jennings (ed.), *Ancient North Americans.* San Francisco, CA: W. H. Freeman, pp. 303–71.

Haviland, William A. and Marjory W. Power (1994), *The Original Vermonters: Native Inhabitants, Past and Present.* Hanover, NA: University Press of New England.

Nassaney, Michael S. and Kenneth E. Sassaman (eds) (1995), *Native American Interactions: Multiscalar Analyses and Interpretations in the Eastern Woodlands.* Knoxville, TN: University of Tennessee Press.

Overstreet, David F. (2000), "Cultural Dynamics of the Late Prehistoric Period in Southern Wisconsin," in Steven R. Ahler (ed.), *Mounds, Modoc, and Mesoamerica: Papers in Honor of Melvin L. Fowler.* Springfield, IL: Illinois State Museum Scientific Papers, vol. XXVIII, pp. 405–38.

Rice, James D. (2000), "Of Piscataways and Beltways," paper presented October 19, 2000, at annual meeting, American Society for Ethnohistory, London, Ontario.

Schlesier, Karl H. (ed.) (1994), *Plains Indians, AD 500–1500*. Norman, OK: University of Oklahoma Press.

Snow, Dean R. (1995), "Migration in Prehistory: The Northern Iroquoian Case," *American Antiquity* 60(1): 59–79.

Vennum, Thomas, Jr (1988), *Wild Rice and the Ojibway People*. St Paul, MN: Minnesota Historical Society Press.

Williamson, Ronald F. and Christopher M. Watts (eds) (1999), *Taming the Taxonomy: Toward a New Understanding of Great Lakes Archaeology*. Toronto: Eastendbooks.

**From Walter McClintock, *The Old North Trail*,
pp. 422–3, 434–6**

My father was the leader of the clan of Grease Melters. Later, when he was chosen head chief of the Blackfeet, he was known by the name of Iron Shirt, because he wore a buckskin shirt decorated with pieces of shining metal. He was a large, muscular man, with a wonderful memory and a great knowledge of our customs. He could tell a horse's age by its whinny, and a man's by the sound of his voice. He kept "winter counts" on buffalo hides, marking the principal events in the history of the tribe. He recorded our tribal camps, the battles, the names of our leaders, when the great chiefs died, the years of sickness [scourge of smallpox], the summers of droughts and the hard winters, when game was scarce and snows lay deep.

Sixty-nine winters have passed, since we had our first "Great Sickness" [smallpox, 1836]. Fifty winters, since eight Indian tribes assembled together in a big camp on the Yellowstone River, when Little Dog, Big Snake and Lame Bull were the head chiefs [1855]. Thirty-one winters since the coming of the Mounted Police [1874], and twenty-nine since the severe winter, when many of our horses were frozen [1876]. One year later, there was a big camp in the north, when Big Crow Foot was head chief [1877].

Other important events that my father marked in his "winter counts" were: the winter, when many of our people died from the "Cough Sickness."

The winter, when the children broke through the ice.
The winter, when the moose came into camp.
The winter, when our horses had the mange.
The winter, when it was necessary to eat dogs to keep from
  starving.
The winter, when the antelopes broke through the ice.
The winter, when buffalo were scarce.
The winter, when we caught antelope in the deep snow.
The winter, when a treaty was made with the white men.

I was born in the year, when white men were seen for the first time in our country, and in the spring, during the moon, when the grass is green. Grass, as you know, is the head chief of

From Walter McClintock, The Old North Trail, *pp. 422–3, 434–6*
(continued)

everything. The animals depend upon the grass for food, and without the animals our chidren could not live.

There is a well-known trail we call the Old North Trail. It runs north and south along the Rocky Mountains. No one knows how long it has been used by the Indians. My father told me it originated in the migration of a great tribe of Indians from the distant north to the south, and all the tribes have, ever since, continued to follow in their tracks.... In many places the white man's roads and towns have obliterated the Old Trail. It forked where the city of Calgary now stands. The right fork ran north into the Barren Lands as far as people live. The main trail ran south along the eastern side of the Rockies, at a uniform distance from the mountains, keeping clear of the forest, and outside of the foothills. It ran close to where the city of Helena now stands, and extended south into the country, inhabited by a people with dark skins, and long hair falling over their faces [Mexico]. My father once told me of an expedition from the Blackfeet, that went south by the Old Trail, to visit the people with dark skins. Elk Tongue and his wife, Natoya, were of this expedition, also Arrow Top and Pemmican, who was a boy of twelve at that time. He died only a few years ago at the age of ninety-five. They were absent four years. It took them twelve moons of steady travelling to reach the country of the dark-skinned people, and eighteen moons to come north again. They returned by a longer route through the "High Trees" or Bitter Root Country, where they could travel without danger of being seen. They feared going along the north Trail because it was frequented by their enemies, the Crows, Sioux, and Cheyennes. Elk Tongue brought back the Dancing Pipe. He bought it nearly one hundred years ago and it was then very old. The South Man, who gave it to him, warned him to use it only upon important occasions, for the fulfilment of a vow, or the recovery of the sick. Whenever anyone was starting on a war, or hunting expedition, a safe return could be secured by vowing to give a feast to the Dancing Pipe.

Told by Brings-Down-the-Sun, Natosin Nepeë, elderly leader of the North Piegan Blackfoot, to Walter McClintock, 1905.

From Walter McClintock, The Old North Trail, pp. 422–3, 434–6 (continued)

McClintock renders conversations into formal English, and seldom notes whether the speaker used English or required a translator.

McClintock, Walter (1910), *The Old North Trail: Life, Legends and Religion of the Blackfeet Indians*. Lincoln, NE: University of Nebraska Press facsimile reprint, 1968.

12

OVERVIEW:
THE UNITED STATES, 1600

A perspective on the United States at 1600 should recognize that historically documented European discoveries of American First Nations began more than a century before 1600 and continued well into the nineteenth century. At 1600, indigenous nations in Florida had already suffered De Soto's rapacious army sixty years previous and the Spanish colony at St Augustine for thirty-five years. West of the Appalachians, from two to ten or more generations would live independent of alien imperialism.

An American perspective should not view the continent from its eastern periphery on the Atlantic. Major population centers lay inland, in western New York, the Midwest, South, Southwest, and California. Only De Soto traversing the South in 1539–42 saw Indian nations virtually unaffected by European incursions and epidemics. Marching with an army of knights, infantry, servants, artisans, porters, plus horses, attack dogs, and a herd of pigs, De Soto's chroniclers were in no position to record native daily life or nuances of social structure. One could say that books on the First Nations were closed before they could be written.

Overall, American nations differed from Europeans in several ways that misled assessments by invading explorers, colonists, and later statesmen. European economies depended on breaking the soil with animal-drawn plows, sowing it with small-seeded grains ground into flour at commercially operated mills, and supplementing grain with meat and milk from domesticated livestock. Agriculture was labor-intensive, demanding daily care of the livestock in addition to seasonal work in the fields. Because plows are clumsy to turn, fields are optimally long rectangles, and because plowshares are ruined by hitting stones or trees, much labor went into removing these obstacles, leaving nothing but the sown grain or hay in the field. American agriculture, in contrast, developed on variations of raised beds built and maintained by human labor. Long parallel planting ridges superficially resemble plowed furrows, but tall, well-spaced maize stalks are quite unlike thickly growing grasses such as wheat. American agriculture interplanted nitrogen-fixing beans as well as squashes with maize, whereas European grainfields were mono-cropped. The combination of hand labor, lacking draft animals with plows, and multi-cropped fields looked to Europeans like gardening, not business-like agriculture.

American economic animals were not wholly dependent upon human care, unlike European livestock. Deer, in the woodlands, and bison on the plains benefited from Indians burning off range to prevent tree encroachment and stimulate growth of tender new grass. Deer and bison, and rabbits in the West, were driven into corrals or rings of nets for slaughter. These activities were occasional in contrast to the unceasing attention required to keep domesticated stock. Turkeys and parrots were kept primarily for their feathers (turkey feathers were sewn on to fabric for light, warm cloaks), not in large numbers. In America, only dogs were genetically affected by selective breeding. European observers in the Eastern Woodlands saw that deer were fostered by Indians maintaining maximum browse near settlements, like European aristocrats' hunting preserves, so they considered First Nations' hunting to be sport rather than an alternative form of stock keeping.

Around 1600, no nations in the United States were building the massive structures that had been theaters of power in the eleventh and twelfth centuries, at Cahokia and Chaco. Southeastern nations kept up smaller mounds in the towns that superseded the Cahokian state, and Pueblos constructed multi-storey housing blocks, but neither region on the earlier scale that would awe visitors. European observers who saw the ruins of Cahokia and Chaco assumed they had been the work of a vanished race, possibly Mexican, possibly Eurasian. Contemporary Indian nations, at 1600, were analogous to Europe after the collapse of the Roman empire, smaller kingdoms or independent towns in volatile relations with neighboring polities. Europeans recognized small kingdoms like their own in the sixteenth century, but thought United States Indians had never created large states.

A century before 1600, professional scribes of the Maya kingdoms were fully literate, using phonetic syllabaries to write screenfold books. Targeted for wholesale destruction by Spanish missionaries, thousands were burned, leaving only a tiny remnant as curiosities in European colonial archives. More documents survive from the Aztecs and Mixtecs in central Mexico because they recorded land-holdings, but their notations use ideographs, not full texts. Indian nations of the United States had systems of conventional signs, different by region and purpose. Iroquois ritual leaders and Midé priests in the Great Lakes area learned a number of symbols to guide them through lengthy recitations. Algonkian-speaking Abenaki leaders in the Northeast signed treaties, in the seventeenth century, with symbols of their names similar to the syllabics. European observers in the United States considered symbols and syllabics on birchbark scrolls, wooden staffs, or worked out in wampum beads on belts, to be crude signs rather than evidence of limited literacy. Lack of fully alphabetic writing was adduced as evidence of savagery among American First Nations.

Another aspect of First Nations cultures contrasting with European custom was a habit of dressing lightly. Much of the United States suffers summers more hot and humid than usual in Europe, and indigenous people sensibly dealt with this by wearing few clothes, a breechcloth for men and skirt for women. Of course in winter, more would be worn, but European observers writing reports traveled mostly in the summer. Mesoamerican noblemen could be resplendent in bejeweled belts over elaborately tied breechcloths with bustles of flamboyant feathers, exquisite feather cloaks around their shoulders and dramatic headdresses crowning the lord; ladies wore long skirts and blouses of finely woven fabrics, plenty of jewelry, and their own impressively ornamented headdresses. United States leaders, lacking the variety of brilliant tropical birds to be found in Mesoamerica, were likely to wear cloaks of turkey feathers, decorated velvety-tanned deerskins, or woven strips of rabbitskin. Along the Pacific, men might not bother even with breechcloths, but Northwest Coast noblemen would put on costly sea-otter fur cloaks to receive foreign visitors. Throughout America, copper was often valued above other elements, even gold, incredible as that seemed to Europeans. Americans' unconcern with totally covering the body, their prizing beautiful feathers over fur, their preference for a more common metal, copper, over scarcer gold, led Europeans to suppose Americans were unsophisticated children of nature.

These differences in values and style provoked disrespect and misunderstanding on both sides. Compounding biases, European nations attempted to justify, or at least technically legitimate, territorial conquests by claiming moral superiority. Sixteenth-century

Spaniards read out, by order of their government, these uncompromising statements to indigenous communities they met:

> On behalf of the king...and the queen...subjugators of barbarous peoples, we, their servants, notify and make known to you...that God, Our Lord, living and eternal, created the heavens and the earth...and great numbers of people.....Of all these people God, Our Lord, chose one...who was to be superior to all the other people of the world, whom all should obey...called the Pope.....We beseech and demand that you...accept the Church and Superior Organization of the whole world and recognize the Supreme Pontiff, called the Pope, and that in his name, you acknowledge the King and Queen...as the lords and superior authorities of these islands and mainlands.[1]

Came the Reformation rejecting the authority of that Supreme Pontiff called the Pope, and Protestant conquerors needed to substitute some other universalizing formula. Colonists could settle on land that looked unoccupied, disregarding First Nations' designation of it as hunting preserve or long-fallow arable (agricultural fields left to second-growth vegetation for several years to restore fertility). They might barter with the indigenous community, giving goods in exchange for what the native group understood, according to common American practice, to be limited usufruct but the Europeans claimed to constitute permanent alienation of the land. Or seventeenth-century Protestants, like sixteenth-century Spaniards, could declare the indigenous people inferior by act of God, placed before invading Europeans to be Christianized and civilized for the sake of their own benighted souls. With the rational Enlightenment on the horizon by the close of the seventeenth century, Englishman John Locke penned treatises on human nature and on government that argued the improvement of personal property through labor to be most praiseworthy. Locke, who served as executive secretary to the British Board of Trade, ingenuously declared written title to land and exchange of such titles for money (not bartered goods) to be the marks of civilized government. American principles of landholding could be disregarded by Locke's civilized compatriots.[2]

Overall, callous ignorance and evangelical fervor, lust for power and wealth and desperate hope for a decent living, alike wreaked destruction on American First Nations, forcing their people to adapt to radically changed population ratios, alien technology and economic practices, and powerful attacks upon their autonomy. Four centuries after 1600, we view the landscapes of that era through veils of stereotypes born sometimes of confusion, sometimes of deceit, sometimes of political rhetoric.

The Eastern Seaboard in 1600

English colonists were late among Europeans coming to America. Norse had been taking American resources of timber, furs, and walruses since AD 1000, Basque probably from the fifteenth century, Portuguese and other fishermen in the north from 1500, and Spanish expanding their Mexican empire from 1513. England had sponsored Cabot's explorations of the American coast in 1497 and 1498, the venture lost when Cabot failed to return. French efforts to colonize America began with Cartier in 1534. The entire century after Columbus was a time of regular European exploitation of American coastal resources.

The Atlantic is not as impassable a barrier between continents as most contemporary Americans assume. Columbus' pilot, in 1492, already knew steady winds and current that would carry boats westward from North Africa to the Caribbean, and then the Gulf Stream circling north and eastward to take them home to Europe. People trying to win fame in the Guinness Book of Records have crossed the Atlantic, usually by these natural routes, in an amazing variety of things that float, the smallest a sailboard 5 foot 4 inches long that in 1993 carried its sailor – who was taller than the board was long – from Newfoundland to England in 106 days. It is quite possible that Phoenicians and related Carthaginians explored the Atlantic before their rivals, the Roman empire, finally crushed them in 146 BCE, deliberately obliterating their history. Some Romans, or more likely North Africans within the Roman empire, may have reached Mexico, if so without creating any interest from their government or historians; bits of evidence include use of a Roman type of cement for low domed roofs on a couple of buildings in the Veracruz prehistoric city of Tajín, the head of a small broken Roman clay figurine buried in a Toluca Valley Aztec-period tomb (possibly an heirloom preserved for eleven centuries, possibly a relic traded by one of Columbus' men that rapidly passed inland, preceding Cortés), the unusual use of fired bricks with makers' stamps at the Gulf of Mexico Maya site of Comalcalco, and the odd coincidence that a few Nahuatl words, notably *teo* "deity," closely resemble Latin.[3]

The Norse era may have begun with Irish monks seeking hermitages far from madding crowds. Irish histories telling of St Brendan, sixth century, voyaging in a leather-covered curragh were pooh-poohed until experimenter Tim Severin constructed a large curragh according to the legend description and sailed it from Ireland to America, taking two summers and overwintering in Iceland where Irish monks are known to have preceded Norse colonization. Norse themselves pushed rapidly from Iceland to Greenland to Canada in the late tenth century. Their settlement at the tip of Newfoundland, L'Anse aux Meadows, apparently didn't last long, but American timber used for their buildings in Greenland prove they continued to cross Davis Strait for centuries. A large stone found in 1898 near Kensington in Minnesota is inscribed with Norse runic letters, telling of ten men of a 1362 exploring party ambushed and killed. Authenticity of this inscription has been hotly debated, but in 2000 the stone was examined under high magnification in a geophysics laboratory and the runes appear weathered as would be expected were they chiseled in 1362. Presumably, the Norse traveled up the St Lawrence and through the Great Lakes to Minnesota seeking new sources of fine furs, spurred by the German Hanseatic League's 1360 takeover of Norse trade in Russian furs.

Furs were important components of established trade along the Eastern Seaboard centuries before the 1670 chartering of the Hudson's Bay Company by Britain. Greenland Norse traded American furs, including the highly prized sable (marten), to the home kingdom of Norway, whether principally through their own trapping in Baffinland and adjacent northeastern Canada, or by trading with Inuit, Innu, and other indigenous trappers cannot be determined. French entrepreneurs found Algonkian-speaking groups in Canada, too far north to reliably grow maize, came down to Iroquoian-speaking Huron towns in what is now southern Ontario to trade furs for tobacco and maize. By the mid-seventeenth century, contests between Huron and New York Iroquois, between French and British and Dutch, and smaller nations such as the Mahican of the Hudson River Valley over the fur trade came to be called the Beaver Wars, beaver being a prime item to make European luxury felt hats. The alliance of five New York Iroquois nations, Seneca, Cayuga, Onondaga, Oneida, and Mohawk, into the Haudenosaunee League is said to have occurred in the late sixteenth century (the date is debated), which may reflect Beaver Wars already being fought at this time, perhaps over access to Gulf of St Lawrence trade with Europeans.

South of the cold latitudes where desired furbearers flourish, deerhides were the principal indigenous product for trade. Indian women worked hard to tan the hides to a remarkable velvety softness. Tanning being an unpleasant task, demand for well-tanned hides fostered keeping slaves to do the task. Thus slaves captured in ambushes and wars, and it may be children of slaves – whether Southeastern nations kept slaves' offspring in bondage is unclear – were also marketed. The Carolinas were the center for shipping fine deerhides, while Indian slaves were bought, or free persons (like Tisquantum in Massachusetts) seized, all along the Seaboard. The background to the well-established active trade in hides, slaves, and items not coveted by Europeans, such as copper and conch shells, is the consolidation of populations in agricultural towns on the inner coastal plain below the fall line, and in major river valleys of the interior South.

Spanish, French, and English accounts of Southeastern nations describe those in the favorable agricultural lands as small kingdoms ruled by aristocratic families. Royals were carried in litters, rugs were placed on the ground where they alighted, attendants fanned them, brought them food and drink, colorful cloaks and pearl necklaces. Agricultural products, dried meat, and manufactured objects were rendered as tribute to the rulers, either carried to their principal town or given when they traveled in state to visit subordinate villages. This political economy benefited European explorers and colonists who relied for their own food on surpluses stored in First Nations granaries. These nations, in turn, readily adopted European foods imported for colonists' farms, so that by the eighteenth century, peaches, wheat, pigs, cattle and horses were common. The Cherokee, Chickasaw, Choctaw, Creek, and Seminole came to be called the Five Civilized Tribes, many of their leading families running cotton and tobacco plantations from brick European-style houses, wearing suits and dresses, dining from imported china, and relying on the labor of black slaves they purchased. Notwithstanding, in 1823 Chief Justice John Marshall, defending United States title to First Nations' lands, officially declared that

> the tribes of Indians inhabiting this country were fierce
> savages...whose subsistence was drawn chiefly from the
> forest.[4]

The Midwest

Sixty years before 1600, the Midwest had been visited by two Spanish expeditions, De Soto marching northwest from Florida and Coronado marching east from New Mexico. Coronado had stopped short, in Kansas, of the Midwest's population centers, angrily believing he had been lied to by his Wichita guide The Turk. De Soto confronted hundreds of indigenous communities during his three-year trek, meeting many aristocratic leaders and their entourages, pillaging towns and enslaving people. His death – timely, one would say, from the point of view of the pillaged settlements – and those of the majority of his literate troop, with the long journey of the few survivors back to Mexico, deprives us of immediate firsthand accounts. Most of the chroniclers' descriptions of De Soto's adventures pertain to the Southeast and its western zone, the Lower Mississippi Valley.

The Central Mississippi Valley including Missouri, Arkansas, and western Tennessee belonged to the persisting Mississippian tradition. Communities lived from their maize fields, as indicated by analysis of human bones. Women worked hard in the fields, again indicated by stress features on their bones; men apparently engaged in war, if a peak in male mortality in the early 30s can be interpreted as the result of warfare. De Soto's chroniclers noted that women and children captured in war raids frequently labored in the cornfields. So much cooked corn in the daily diet produced many cavities and loss of teeth. A number of villages resembled earlier Mississippian towns in that they incorporated what look like platform mounds, but investigation has revealed that at least some of these were natural river levees, modified and used as cemeteries. Drudgery of daily life was relieved by an exuberant ceramics art, ranging from elegant long-necked bottles to realistic effigy pots probably meant to portray trophy heads taken in battle. Forms include open bowls with handles shaped like snarling big cats or simple ducks, or frogs or fish molded on the body, and polished beakers with incised designs of rattlesnakes and spirals. Most striking are effigy pots shaped as seated men. The pots' ears with multiple piercings link with burials wearing spool-shaped earrings of wood covered with thin beaten copper, and strings of beads including glass ones obtained from the Spanish, possibly De Soto's party. Spanish-manufactured small brass bells further evidence sixteenth-century trade reaching these Late Mississippian communities.

Facilitating that trade was widespread use of a pidgin language, Mobilian Jargon. Derived from a simplified Muskogean, it served as lingua franca throughout the region of Mississippian cultures, from southern Illinois to the Gulf, eastern Texas to Florida. Spanish, French, and English traders learned it to carry on their business.

The lingua franca seems to have been in place before the European intrusions, probably serving communication needs – political, economic, and religious – among post-Cahokia Mississippian kingdoms. Communication did not necessarily promote peace; De Soto's troops were several times invited to join an indigenous army attacking a rival town. Insults might be yelled in Mobilian Jargon at the enemy. One observation recorded by De Soto's chroniclers is that the Central Mississippi Valley armies, several thousand men strong, traveled by preference in large canoes, their paddlers singing to keep stroke. The chroniclers record also naval engagements between fleets of big but highly maneuverable war canoes, bowmen standing in a row between paddlers bent behind shields. Archaeology has verified the chroniclers' pictures of Mississippian towns defended by stout log palisades with bastions and arrow slits and encircling wide moats on which war canoes could be moored, but no archaeological excavation project has been so extensive as to uncover all the several hundred houses in any of these principal towns.[5]

To the north, around 1600, Oneota culture had spread widely over the Midwest, as far south as Missouri and Arkansas where it met the persisting Lower Mississippi societies. This protohistoric expansion of an Upper Midwest culture seems to fit the legendary histories of the principal Midwest Siouans, the Chiwere speakers – Ho-Chunk (Winnebago), Ioway, Oto, and Missouri – and the Dhegiha speakers – Omaha, Ponca, Osage, Kansa, and Quapaw. These nations agree that Chiwere migrated west and south from ancestral homelands in eastern Wisconsin and Dhegiha from homelands in the Ohio Valley, eventually residing along major rivers from Wisconsin and southern Minnesota through Iowa, Nebraska, Kansas, into Arkansas. Oneota culture was also practised by Midwest Algonkian speakers such as the Potawatomi and Mesquakie. European encounters with Oneota peoples began in the mid-seventeenth century, recording large villages with extensive maize fields near lake shores and in river valleys. Contrasting with the pomp of the small kingdoms in the South, Oneota communities appeared relatively egalitarian, but the French who met their various nations in the 1600s usually mentioned strong territorial claims defended, or aggressed against, with military force. Because oral histories recounted to the French in the late seventeenth century describe severe population losses due to illnesses, and archaeology finds apparent abandonment of many sites in this century of early European intrusions, it appears that epidemics spreading out from the colonial frontiers drastically affected the Midwest as they did the South and East.

Southwest

Spain sent explorers to conquer the Southwest beginning with Coronado in 1540, and authorized a colony under the governorship of Juan de Oñate in 1598. The Pueblos at that time were aggregated into a series of independent villages along the Río Grande Valley, with Pecos an eastern outlier trading center at the edge of the Southern Plains and a few towns on mesas to the west – Hopi, Zuni, Acoma and Laguna. The southern desert region was home to the scattered ranchería hamlets of the 'O'odham, Uto-Aztecan-speaking nations related to those in northwestern Mexico. Around and beyond the Pueblos were Diné, Apacheans who had moved into the region from the north only a few centuries earlier, farming where they could find enough water to raise crops for a few families and supplementing that with hunting, wild plants, and raids on the storehouses of the permanent towns. With many of the Río Grande pueblos having been refugee settlements from the abandonment of Colorado Plateau Anasazi sites about the time Diné appeared in the Southwest, the region would have been volatile even if no Spanish had intruded.

Basically, the Southwest is marginal land for agriculture. Heavy investment in water distribution systems makes it possible to support population clusters; these are vulnerable to political as well as environmental changes, because they depend on labor commitment. Paquimé's near demise in the mid-fifteenth century indicates that political factors could override sustainable environmental adaptation, for farming continued in the valley after the town's trade dominance ended. Pecos' importance in the protohistoric and early historic period lay in its access to both Southwestern and Southern Plains travel routes. This is underlined in Coronado's adventures: first stopping at Zuni in Arizona, he was persuaded to go to Pecos rather than the more northern pueblos and to engage Southern Plains men for guides to march northeastward toward their homeland. Some historians see this as a cunning plot by Pueblos to deflect the rapacious Spaniards from their own people, but it is equally credible that The Turk and his friend "Mustaches" (Bigotes), as the Spaniards nicknamed them, were honest insisting that the wealthiest nations lay to the east. Coronado grew exasperated on the endless march across the arid plains and too readily gave up at the simple Wichita villages in Kansas. The Turk and Mustaches knew, probably firsthand, the kingdoms of the Central and Lower Mississippi Valley. The intervening Southern Plains were rich in bison, for those familiar with the herds' habitats, and hides and dried meat were commodities in Pueblo markets such as that at Pecos – shields made of tough bison hide were in constant demand, which tells us something about the political climate as well as the economics of the protohistoric Pueblos.

One clue to the indigenous point of view are the number of plain cooking pots made in Pueblo style but of local clays in Southern Plains protohistoric sites. Pots of Southern Plains styles occur in the same sites. Archaeology alone can't tell us whether the Pueblo-style pots represent Pueblo families living with Plains bands, perhaps to amass hides and dried meat to bring back to home villages, or Pueblo women married or enslaved to Plains men.[6] Later European observers throughout the Plains commented on how common it was for individuals and families from other nations to be living in a Plains band, how many people spoke two or three languages; nearly all these observations came after the terrible disruptions from smallpox epidemics, but the occurrences of the two distinct styles of cooking pots in the protohistoric Southern Plains suggest the entire southern United States from the Mississippi Valley to California was a macro-region familiar to entrepreneurs such as The Turk and "Mustaches." Densely inhabited agricultural pueblos, dispersed 'O'odham and Diné hamlets with their limited fields, and Southern Plains highly mobile bison hunters, some of them also Diné (Apache), inter-digitated with a degree of freedom strange to European eyes.

Interior West and Northern Plains

Farthest from the oceans, the Northern Plains and intermontane Basin were the last regions of the United States to experience European invasions. (It should be noted that European intrusions were even later in interior northern Canada, which signed treaties with some small subarctic nations as late as 1930.) At 1600, each region seems to have been fairly stable, the Numa speakers spread throughout the Basin after their expansion a few centuries earlier. It would be another century until their eastern bands, the Shoshone and Comanche, acquired horses from their distant relations the Utes along the Spanish New Mexican border, giving these bands power, for a generation or so, to press against Plains nations east of the Rockies.

Northern Plains at 1600 were home to Blackfoot, Kutenai, Gros Ventres, Sutai Cheyenne (later to merge with the eastern Cheyenne who farmed in southwestern Minnesota, adjacent to the Arapaho), and the agriculturalists in the larger river valleys, Mandan, Hidatsa, Arikara, and Pawnee. These town-dwellers hunted bison as well as purchased meat and hides in exchange for maize. Eventually, western Hidatsa would split from the main settlements in central North Dakota and would remain in Montana as the Crow. Western Lakota hunted through the Dakotas, although at 1600 they were based in agricultural villages along the Minnesota–North Dakota border. Whether the Dhegiha and Chiwere Sioux regularly went on long bison hunts far into the Plains before they acquired horses, in the eighteenth century, is unclear; some may have journeyed on religious pilgrimages to the Rockies even if most of their nations remained closer to their farmlands. The Kiowa lived in south-central Montana in the eighteenth century but, since their language is related to that of Jemez and other Río Grande Pueblos, they may have removed to Montana to escape Spanish domination in the seventeenth century.

Trade linked Northern Plains nations at 1600. Ornaments made from Pacific shells as well as the finest stone for tools, obsidian from Yellowstone and the Plateau and Knife River flint from North Dakota, and catlinite pipestone from southwestern Minnesota betoken the extensive procurement systems of the time. Without horses to cover overland distances more rapidly, travelers may have kept to the major rivers not only for boat use but also to be assured of drinking water. Settlements in the protohistoric period were usually on river terraces or along valley bluffs, often placed with an eye to defense, containing a thousand or more residents in substantial sod-block lodges. Fully nomadic nations such as the Blackfoot lived in hide tipis in bands of about one hundred people, camping near springs and beaver-dammed streams adjacent to rimrocks and bluffs where they could build corrals to run bison herds into. How often a band might visit an agricultural town, we cannot tell, since the exotic materials that evidence trade could have been transported by enterprising individuals or by bands including a stopover in their seasonal round. Life was comfortable enough that when a Hudson's Bay Company outreach in 1690 made its first contact with Blackfoot, band leaders said they saw no reason to journey to the foreigners' post.

Out in the Basin and the Plateau, there were no agricultural towns. Bands did plan on congregating at pine nut harvests in the foothills, at fish runs at lakes and, on the Plateau, rivers, and to carry out antelope drives into corrals. Through these gatherings of several hundred people, trade as well as marriage arrangements and religious worship took place, creating widely shared cultural patterns in spite of the low population density. Europeans did not push into the "Great American Desert" and Plateau until the beginning of the nineteenth century; when they did, they disdained the simple brush wickiups and lack of clothing through which Numa adapted to summer heat, and did not recognize that thick stands of seed-bearing grasses in valley bottoms had been sown by Numa. Nor did those commercial beaver trappers and commissioned explorers appreciate the women's impressive achievements in the art of basketry. At 1600, each stream valley, marsh, and lake basin had its core band and the relations and acquaintances joining them for a season or more, managing plant and animal resources in a sustainable, deceptively simple-looking regime. Utes along the southern border of the Great Basin had just seen the first of the alien invaders from Mexico. It would be another two centuries before commercial exploitation and agricultural colonization destroyed the indigenous economy.

Pacific Region

First Nations living along the Pacific and the rivers emptying into it had seen Spaniards in 1539 and Spain's enemy Francis Drake in 1579. Again Spanish ships would coast California in 1602. None of these sightings a generation apart affected the indigenous nations maintaining their territories of valley and hill lands. Like so many other western American nations, they cultivated native plants including, here, groves of oaks bearing nutritious acorns, directed by generations of older people trained in botanical, zoological, and ecological knowledge. Their villages of semi-subterranean earth-roofed winter houses and camps of brush structures seemed part of the landscape, itself much modified through selective burns. With routes linking San Francisco Bay to the Central Valley and beyond to the Southwest, Californians on the coast manufactured quantities of shell beads and pendants that are the imperishable relics of trade that included bright feathers, fancy baskets, fine deerhides and, from the Southwest, woven cotton mantles. Obsidian was common for sharp-edged tools and entered the trade from several sources.

Physically, the Sierra Nevada and Cascade ranges, and farther north the Rockies, separate the Pacific coastal regions from interior North America. Practically, the mountains channeled people through their passes. At 1600, east–west traffic moved along the major passes, and foothills and upland meadows were utilized by communities with regular series of camps keyed to seasonal resource harvests. Nations on the coast itself used boats to hunt sea mammals, fish, and travel. Because considerable sections of the Pacific coast are rocky, with few harbors (compared to the Atlantic coast), marine-orientated nations settled in estuary bays or where offshore islands broke the force of the ocean, for example in the Channel Islands section of southern California and the Inland Passage zone of British Columbia–southern Alaska. Such rich but delimited areas had high population densities – relative population densities prehistorically roughly match comparative densities today, since geographical characteristics underlie settlement choices.

San Francisco Bay demarcates the southern half of California tenuously linked to the Southwest and West Mexico, from northern California and Oregon orientated toward Northwest Coast cultural patterns. From the California–Oregon border northward, observers at 1600 would see houses built of wooden planks. On the northern tip of the United States, the Olympic Peninsula of Washington, they might catch the excitement of Makahs' whale hunting, the solemn rituals consecrating the crews and the festive joking of villagers hacking at the huge carcass days later. Their basket-woven hats, flat for commoners and knob-topped for aristocrats, rain capes of shredded cedar bark, big plank houses in a row at the back of the beach, piles of ropes, fishnets, fishhooks, harpoons and clubs, long canoes lined up on the shingle, elderly people and kids gathering shellfish from the rocks and crabs from the sand, all would make a picture typical of Northwest Coast life.

Southeastern Alaska is the other, northern end of the Northwest Coast pattern. Continuing along the Pacific past the Tlingit villages and then the rather similar ones of the Yupik, observers at 1600 would meet the Iñupiaq of the Bering Sea and Arctic coasts. Clusters of round sod-covered, sunken-floored houses, one larger than the rest to serve as men's workshop and community party room, sheltered people from the harsh climate. Two types of boats, sleek fast decked-over kayaks for hunting and big open umiaks for transporting families and goods, showed how the absence of trees suitable for canoes was compensated for by covering lashed frames with sewn hides. Groups of sled dogs lounged by the tunnel-shaped doors of the houses. On high racks or in storerooms by the houses, hunting equipment, hides, and caches of food preserved for winter were kept out of the dogs' reach. If the community appeared egalitarian to the observers, they had failed to notice that, although everyone worked, a few men and women led task groups and rituals. Inland, in the vast forests and tundra of interior Alaska, small bands of Dené needed to be more mobile than the Iñupiaq beside the rich marine life of the ocean. Only a few pithouses made up a winter settlement, and people out hunting and checking traps survived the nights in lean-tos of conifer branches fronted by a good fire. In the summer, Iñupiaq and Dené alike could be seen in hide tents, carried in canoes to prime fishing locations. Necessity demanded tanning and tailoring skill to prepare adequate clothing, but an observer in 1600 would have been impressed with the artistic decoration women appliquéed onto parkas and waterproof coats of fishskin or whale intestine (improbable as it sounds, these silky-textured coats are beautiful). Metal knives, some of native copper but many of iron ultimately imported from Asia, attested the trade systems as operative here as in southern regions. It would be a century and a half before Europeans documented these coasts, but what for Europeans was an end of the earth was for northern Asians the eastern side of the Pacific Rim.

Summary

A history of the United States that follows the convention of viewing its beginning to be the 1607 founding of Jamestown skews the picture of the continent at 1600. Tidewater Virginia, where Jamestown was situated, was quite literally a backwater. Its local king, the Powhatan, had his capital upriver at a better location. His nation, the Pamunkey, was effectively organized to defend its territory and care for its citizens by maintaining public granaries and supporting local exchange and long-distance trade in higher-cost goods. Unlike the builders of Cahokia in the Midwest five centuries earlier, or the Hopewell in Ohio fifteen hundred years before, the Pamunkey did not construct awesome monuments – exorbitant expenditure of labor did not interest them. Still, the Jamestown colonists recognized social classes and court etiquette, politics, and policy decisions. These were no children of nature, nor did they live in a wilderness.

It is important to realize that at the time, neither 1492 nor 1607 would have impressed the world as a watershed year. Since around 1000, Norse had been using northeastern America as the western sector of their extraordinary trading system stretching in the other direction east and south to what is now Turkey. Columbus was part of a competition between Portugal, Spain, and England to find Atlantic routes to Asian riches blocked from overland caravans by the establishment of the Ottoman Turk empire in 1453. Portuguese sailed around Africa and out from northwestern Africa to islands in the mid-Atlantic, from which in the 1520s it brought Azores peasants to Newfoundland to colonize, unsuccessfully. England funded Cabot, who failed to return from his second voyage for that nation. Meanwhile, Columbus's series of voyages encouraged Spaniards to invade Mexico, allying with the enemies of the Aztec state. Assisted by devastating epidemics of smallpox and other terrible diseases, Spanish overcame their allies as well as the Aztecs and reached out across the Gulf of Mexico, attempting Florida nearly a century before Jamestown would be set up.

On the other side of the continent, China from the late fourteenth to mid-seventeenth centuries was ruled by the Ming dynasty, uninterested in trade beyond Asia. There was certainly trade along the North Pacific Rim, carried by private enterprise on a scale small enough that it did not attract the attention of the Chinese or Korean bureaucracies. The Pacific is considerably wider than the Atlantic and the distance from the temperate-latitude cities of Asia to America greater than from northwestern Europe to eastern America. Visits and exchanges between Siberians, Aleuts along the Aleutian Islands chain across the northernmost Pacific, Bering Sea Iñupiaq, Yupik and Northwest Coast nations lay beyond the pale of written documentation. Spain was reaching westward far past Mexico only twenty years after Cortés landed on Mexico's east coast, and colonizing the Southwest sixty years later. Activity in the Pacific coastal regions snaked far inland up the principal rivers and through mountain passes, touching in the Plains and Midwest the trade coming up from the Gulf of Mexico and from the Appalachians.

At 1600, something of the order of ten million people populated the United States, the bulk of them east of the Plains or west of the Sierra but every region inhabited. None of the nations in the United States were then building impressive monumental architecture like the forebears of some had a few centuries previous, but there were no trackless wildernesses: everywhere in the United States, the landscapes reflected human technology, if one knew the signs. The significant difference between Europeans and American Indians at 1600 was invisible, microscopic; at 1600, Europe had been winnowed by smallpox, typhus, cholera, and other plagues and its population was rebounding, but the Americans had no immunity yet. America's First Nations were on the edge of decimation by invading forces no one could see. Their populations would not rebound until the twentieth century.

Notes

1. Quoted in Jerald T. Milanich, *Florida Indians and the Invasion from Europe* (Gainesville, FL, 1995), pp. 100–1.

2. Robert A. Williams Jr's *The American Indian in Western Legal Thought* (New York, 1990) is an excellent discussion of this subject. Williams is a Lumbee Indian as well as legal scholar.

3. Stephen C. Jett's "Precolumbian Transoceanic Contacts," in Jesse D. Jennings (ed.), *Ancient North Americans* (San Francisco, CA, 1983) demonstrates the probabilities of transoceanic pre-Columbian contacts with America.

4. Quoted in Williams, *The American Indian* p. 323, n. 133.

5. Michael P. Hoffman believes there is sufficient archaeological data to identify De Soto's named political territories: from north to south along the Mississippi in Arkansas, Pacaha, Casqui, Quizquiz and Aquixo (allies), Quiguate, and Anilco on the Arkansas River close to its confluence with the Mississippi ("Ethnic Identities and Cultural Change in the Protohistoric Period of Eastern Arkansas," in Patricia B. Kwachka (ed.), *Perspectives on the Southeast* [Athens, GA, 1994], pp. 61–70). Geoffrey Kimball, in the same volume (p. 77) suggests that Casqui is the Muskogean word for "warrior," *kaskí* in Koasati, possibly mistaken by De Soto for a town name when perhaps his informant was only telling him many soldiers lived in the town.

6. Judith A. Habicht-Mauche, "Pottery, Food, Hides, and Women: Labor, Production, and Exchange Across the Protohistoric Plains-Pueblo Frontier," in Michelle Hegmon (ed.), *The Archaeology of Regional Interaction* (Boulder, CO, 2000), pp. 209–31.

References

Hegmon, Michelle (ed.) (2000), *The Archaeology of Regional Interaction: Religion, Warfare, and Exchange Across the American Southwest and Beyond*. Boulder, CO: University Press of Colorado.

Jett, Stephen C. (1983), "Precolumbian Transoceanic Contacts," in Jesse D. Jennings (ed.), *Ancient North Americans*. San Francisco, CA: W. H. Freeman, pp. 557–613.

Kwachka, Patricia B. (ed.) (1994), *Perspectives on the Southeast: Linguistics, Archaeology, and Ethnohistory*, Southern Anthropological Society Proceedings, no. 27. Athens, GA: University of Georgia Press.

Milanich, Jerald T. (1995), *Florida Indians and the Invasion from Europe*. Gainesville, PL: University Press of Florida.

O'Brien, Michael J. and W. Raymond Wood (1998), *The Prehistory of Missouri*. Columbia, MO: University of Missouri Press.

Overstreet, David F. (1997), "Oneota Prehistory and History," in Robert A. Birmingham, Carol I. Mason and James B. Stoltman (eds), *Wisconsin Archaeology*, vol. 78, no. 1/2 of *The Wisconsin Archeologist*, pp. 250–96.

Williams, Robert A., Jr (1990), *The American Indian in Western Legal Thought*. New York: Oxford University Press.

Captain John Smith of Jamestown Colony, Virginia

The forme of their Common wealth is a monarchicall government. One as Emperour ruleth over many kings or governours. Their chiefe ruler is called Powhatan. Some countries he hath, which have been his ancestors and came unto him by inheritance. All the rest of his Territories they report have beene his severall conquests.

Arriving at Weramocomoco, their Emperor proudly lying uppon a Bedstead a foote high, upon tenne or twelve Mattes, richly hung with manie Chaynes of great Pearles about his necke, and covered with a great Covering of Rahaughcums [raccoons]. At his heade sat a woman, at his feete another; on each side sitting uppon a Matte upon the ground, were raunged his chiefe men on each side the fire, tenne in a ranke, and behinde them as many yong woman, each with a great Chaine of white Beades over their shoulders, their heades painted in redde: and powhatan with such a grave and Majesticall contenance, as drave me into admiration to see such a state in a naked Salvage. When he dineth or suppeth, one of his women, before and after meat, bringeth him water in a wooden platter to wash his hands. Another waiteth with a bunch of feathers to wipe them instead of a Towell, and the feathers when he hath wiped are dryed againe.

William Strachey, of Virginia

The great king Powhatan hath devided his Country into many provinces, or Shiers (as yt were) and over every one placed a severall absolute Commaunder, or Weroance to him contributory, to governe the people there to inhabite, and his petty Weroances in all, may be in number, about three or fower and thirty, all which have their precincts, and bowndes, proper, and commodiously appointed out, that no one intrude upon the other, of sevrall forces, and for the grownd wherein each one soweth his corne, plants his Apoke [tobacco], and gardeyn fruicts, he tythes to the great king of all the Commodityes growing in the same, or of what ells his shiere brings forth apperteyning to the Land of Rivers, Corne, beasts, pearle, Fowle, Fish, Hides, furrs, copper, beads, by what means soever obteyned, a peremptory rate sett down.

Every Weroance knowes his owne Meeres and lymitts to fish fowle or hunt in, but they hold all of their great Weroance Powhatan, unto whome they paie 8, parts of 10, tribute of all the commodities which their Countrey yeildeth, as of wheat [maize], peaze, beans, 8, measures of 10, (and these measured out in little Cades or Basketts which the great king appooints) of the dyeing roots 8, measures of ten; of all sorts of skyns and furrs 8, of tenne, and so he robbes the poore ineffect of all they have even to the deares Skyn wherewith they cover them from Cold, in so much as they dare not dresse yt and put yt on untill he hath seene yt and refused yt; for what he Commandeth they dare not disobey in the least thing.

Henry Spelman, of Virginia

If any of ye Kings wives have once a child by him, he (never lieth with hir more) keeps hir no longer but puts hir from him giving hir sufficient Copper and beads to maytayne hir and the child while it is younge and then it is taken from hir and maytayned by ye King, it now beinge lawfull for hir beinge thus put away to marry with any other. The king Poetan [Powhatan] having many wives when he goeth a Huntinge or to visitt another Kinge under him (for he goeth not out of his owne country) He leaveth them with tow ould men who have the charge on them till his returne.

Strachey

Twelve [wives] in whose company he takes more delight then in the rest, being for the most parte very young women, and these Commonly remove with him from howse to howse, either in his tyme of hunting, or visitation of his severall howses.

Quotes by historian E. Randolph Turner (pp. 196–202), from three English observers of the kingdom into which the Jamestown colonists moved.

Turner, E. Randolph (1985), "Socio-Political Organization within the Powhatan Chiefdom and the effects of European Contact, AD 1607–1646," in William W. Fitzhugh (ed.), *Cultures in Contact: The Impact of European Contacts on Native American Cultural Institutions AD 1000–1800.* Washington DC: Smithsonian Institution Press, pp. 193–224.

13

ISSUES AND PUZZLES

A history of America can be constructed from the data of prehistory. It should be prepared, to do justice to America's First Nations and to present the circumstances at the inauguration of United States history. The project – like any history – is neither straightforward nor satisfying to all interested parties. Among the problems and issues are dates, which in American archaeology are nearly all not actually dates but estimates of time elapsed before present; related to the time resolution challenge, apparent discontinuities between Late Prehistoric and the first historically documented nations; regionally orientated studies and particular ethnic traditions that disregard a broader picture; and controversies over whose account should be privileged over competing accounts. Should the more "scientific" archaeologist, looking for general patterns of adaptation, tell the story of America's past, or the humanist archaeologist endeavoring to discern clues to religions, social behavior, and long-term ethnic roots? Sometimes the choices seem to pit non-Indian archaeologists over First Nations' legendary histories, a stereotyped conflict belied by the number of respected professional archaeologists who are members in good standing of First Nations, and the increasing number of archaeological projects ordered by First Nations.

Why doesn't the direct historic approach work well?

Once it was generally accepted – after 1920s discoveries of Paleoindian weapon points in skeletons of extinct bison and mammoth – that American prehistory had considerable time depth, archaeologists figured that by excavating in a historically documented site down through a stratigraphic sequence of earlier occupation layers, they could chronicle the histories of known First Nations, hopefully far back into the past. A model project was carried out in the 1930s in central Nebraska, the territory of the Pawnee. Half a century later, as many more sites were investigated and radiocarbon determinations amassed, a gap in time appeared between the protohistoric Pawnee occupations and earlier ones. The gap is only a century or so, but if real, it cuts short the archaeological record that can be attributed to the Pawnee and leaves the ethnicity of earlier Nebraskans unknown.

More and more, fine-tuning chronologies and expanding archaeological data sets point to gaps in sequences of occupations and several contenders for contact-era named settlements. Perhaps nowhere is this more contentious than regarding De Soto's route. We have four accounts, written years later from notes and interviews with the few survivors. Every few years, an archaeologist finds bits of Spanish chain mail in a Southern site and postulates it identifies one of De Soto's camps, only to have other scholars argue that their reconstruction of the entrada route does not take the army to that point, therefore the chain mail remnant should represent a curiosity traded by Indians who might never have seen Spaniards. How in the world could an army of hundreds of men, their baggage, horses, and a sizable herd of pigs stomp their way across the landscape without leaving any obvious traces (other than the pigs, whose descendants are the razorback hogs of Arkansas)?

Another example of what would seem to be identifiable is the ancestral main town of the Ho-Chunk (Winnebago) of Wisconsin. Their oral histories describe a sizable village they call Red Banks. Their first contact with Europeans was in northeastern Wisconsin, 1634. Archaeologists have searched for a protohistoric site with substantial habitation on a stream or lake that has reddish banks; red clay soil is common in the lower Fox River valley of northeastern Wisconsin. The more one delves into the possibilities, the more uncertainties appear. To start, the 1634 meeting between Jean Nicolet and five thousand Indians who feasted him is described not directly by Nicolet but by a Jesuit nine years later. Second, not only the Ho-Chunk but also the Menominee lived in the area, around Green Bay; the Menominee live there still, but archaeologists have no more been able to pinpoint which site was their principal town of 1634 than to locate Red Banks. There are protohistoric settlements with a few European trade items, and there are Late Prehistoric settlements with only Indian manufactures, but any of these might be Menominee or Ho-Chunk, or for that matter, Potawatomi who were also in the pleasant reaches of Green Bay in the seventeenth century. The matter is not merely scholastic, because Potawatomi have been to court in a complicated land claim case. Some anthropologists who have talked at length with Ho-Chunk consider the possibility that "Red Banks" refers to any locality where they had, for a time, their principal town. Others hypothesize that Aztalan, the Mississippian palisaded town in southeastern Wisconsin, was Red Banks – and that the people who built it were Chiwere Siouans not yet separated into Ho-Chunk, Iowa, Oto, and Missouri. Maybe the platform mound at Aztalan was plastered with red, or red-painted, clay? None of these uncertainties deterred the good citizens of Green Bay from erecting a bronze statue of Nicolet (of whom no portrait exists), challenging a monument in the neighboring city of Menasha with a plaque that reads,

NEAR THIS SPOT LANDED, 1634, FIRST WHITE MAN IN
WISCONSIN, JEAN NICOLET – MET THE WINNEBAGO TRIBE –
HELD EARLIEST WHITE COUNCIL WITH 5,000 SAVAGES – ERECTED
BY WOMEN'S CLUBS OF MENASHA, 1906.[1]

The direct historic approach assumed the early historic documents specified locations as precisely as maps today, an impossibility before the national grid of township and range was constructed. Without precise coordinates, a phrase such as "at the mouth of the Fox River" covers many acres, and there are likely to have been settlements through time that overlap. One group can abandon a settlement, another take it over a generation later, without the break being visible if soil accumulation is slow; this is particularly misleading in the early historic period when epidemics depopulated many nations, leaving husbanded land disencumbered. Material culture may reflect fashions of the time more than ethnic distinctions. Sixteenth- and seventeenth-century European observers depended on interpreters to name and explain the various nations they visited, often recording names that were only derogatory put-downs, for example "Stinkers." Trying to match that to the proper name used by a nation for itself is slippery.

Decades of combing through explorers' records, some of them blatantly self-serving, others manifestly confused, have taught archaeologists that a great deal of interpretation and evaluation is usually required before identifications can be proposed. There are now archaeologists who specialize in this work, researchers more often found sitting at microfilm readers than in excavations. Their data are crucial not only in land claim cases brought, or contested by, contemporary First Nations, but also in cultural resource management, employing a significant proportion of archaeologists and historians today.

Who owns the past?

Britain and then the United States signed treaties with First Nations, respecting their sovereignty. Plenty of chicanery compromised those treaties, culminating in Chief Justice Marshall's 1831 invention of the unheard-of status of "domestic dependent nation." In the 1840s, agitation to make vastly more land open for homesteading and the businesses that could profit from it, created the notion that it was the United States' "Manifest Destiny" to overcome and dispossess both First Nations and Mexico. The two World Wars of the twentieth century, in each of which American Indians enlisted readily and earned honors, shifted American attitudes toward First Nations. After the First World War, in 1924, American Indians were acknowledged US citizens (they had not been previously unless they gave up tribal membership), and after the Second World War, in 1946, an Indian Claims Commission was named to encourage First Nations to seek redress for irregular deprivation of their lands. The Claims Commission worked until 1974, amassing millions of pages of documents on territorial locations. Many Indian nations did recover land, others were offered money settlements that in some cases, for example the Lakota claim to the Black Hills, has been rejected because the nation cares more for the land than for cash. Land claims research greatly expanded documentary and oral-history data available to scholars.

Partly as the result of legal confirmation of treaty stipulations, partly because the American Indian population has been growing[2] and increasingly obtaining education and off-reservation employment, First Nations' sovereignty under treaty relations is increasingly acknowledged. This means that a nation can withhold permission for archaeological work on its land, or demand control of data relevant to its history. Lawyers and courts are pursuing more sensitive definitions of "intellectual property." Instead of "informants" paid by the hour to give data, First Nations people increasingly are collaborators in scholarly enterprises. Archaeologists and historians confront tribal knowledge seemingly at odds with "Western" information.

On a growing number of reservations, the tribal government itself employs archaeologists and historians. The tribe directs the questions to be investigated, expecting discussion to bring together the perspectives of Ph.D. and custodians of First Nations knowledge. Both are concerned with cultural resource management, that which is mandated by federal regulations and that answering the nation's own values. A non-Indian archaeologist or historian accepting employment from a tribal government obviously has, or will soon develop, respect for that nation's heritage.

1990 saw a landmark bill pass the Congress, the Native American Graves Protection and Repatriation Act (NAGPRA). Designed to answer grievances about museums and universities holding skeletons and holy objects looted from Indian communities, NAGPRA required any institution receiving federal funds to identify American Indian human remains and objects in its collections and inform Indian tribes of their patrimony in its custody. A tribe could ask for return of remains and artifacts, or permit the institution to continue its curation. The happiest outcomes have been cases in which, as at Zuni, suitable conservation facilities are built for the repatriated material, or with the Omaha, its "Sacred Pole" (Umon'hon'ti, "Venerable Man," personification of the Omaha nation) curated off-reservation while available to the nation for its ceremonies.[3] Under the law, a tribe must prove its affiliation to the remains or objects. If this stipulation were scrupulously observed, only a limited number of remains and objects would be repatriated. Unfortunately, NAGPRA has been viewed as pacification, with popular pressure to give 'em all back to the poor, mystically spiritual Indians, rather than rectification of clearly unauthorized seizures. The red-flag case has been Kennewick Man, an astonishingly complete skeleton 9,500 years old by radiocarbon dating. Found eroding out of a Columbia River bank, the skeleton does not closely resemble contemporary Plateau Indians, and the only artifact with it is a stone weapon point embedded in its pelvis. The Umatilla Tribe, on the reservation nearest the find spot, claimed the skeleton under NAGPRA, demanding it be immediately given for respectful reburial. When the US Army Corps of Engineers, holding the skeleton because the riverbank was in its jurisdiction, announced it would honor the Umatilla demand, outraged biological anthropologists from several major research laboratories filed suit for an injunction: no way could the Umatilla *prove* Kennewick Man had been Umatilla, indeed the obvious physical differences between Kennewick and Umatilla make it unlikely Umatilla are direct descendants – and there are approximately four hundred generations between Kennewick and today's Umatilla. Without strict enforcement of its rules, NAGPRA becomes a political tool.[4]

The issue is sovereignty: a sovereign nation controls its territory, makes and enforces laws, determines who is a citizen, promulgates policies for the public weal. Can a nation consider itself sovereign if another nation exercises its domain over the same territory? Umatilla say they were taught that Umatilla always lived along that section of the Columbia, from the beginning of time. By what right could the Smithsonian in Washington DC, take the bones of a man who in all likelihood spent his life in the territory that was recognized as Umatilla in 1860 when that nation signed its treaty with the United States? On what grounds can the United States claim domain over a man who lived nine thousand years before the United States, by its own documentation, came into existence?

Kennewick Man brought to a head the question of who owns the past, the data by which it can be known and the interpretations of those data. The question is by no means limited to prehistoric relics. Contemporary historians challenge governmental restriction of classified material kept from public scrutiny. Medical and educational records may be closed even to families of the people they describe. Individuals and private institutions normally limit access to their files. A historian's interpretation of the significance of an event, even of its actual happening, is often rejected – consider, for example, the arguments over whether slaves were generally reasonably happy or mostly miserable. What information and ideas are made available to general audiences through publication or Internet posting depends upon editors' opinions and their choice of how to use the pages or sites they control. An American First Nation not only can logically argue its right to that which lay in its treaty-recognized territory, it can argue that its versions of history are as, or more, legitimate as those constructed by outsiders ignorant of its language and knowledge.

What constitutes a history?

Literate people, especially highly educated ones, depend upon writing things down (or into electronic databases) to remember them. Non-literate societies train individuals to recall correctly. Certain persons may be formally trained for years to memorize genealogies and chronicles, ordinary children will be encouraged to learn songs and rhymes and play actions that encode useful knowledge (like, "Thirty days hath September . . ."). Where a trained oral historian's information can be checked against written documents, as in some areas of Africa and Asia, it has often proved surprisingly accurate. Conversely, written histories may be biased, omitting unsavory or unsuccessful events and lower-class or minority people. Standard histories of archaeology, for example, credit Sir John Lubbock, baronet, president of a London bank, close associate of Charles Darwin, with creating a scientific prehistoric archaeology, whereas Lubbock actually only put together a book, upon the suggestion of a publisher, modeled on one published, and quickly sold out, three years earlier by Daniel Wilson, a Scottish tradesman's son earning his living teaching in a raw new college in Toronto, Canada. Wilson himself complained of the injustice in letters to his Scottish compatriot and friend the noted geologist Charles Lyell. Wilson is now remembered in Canada as the first president of the University of Toronto, politically a much more significant achievement than working out a method and principles for a science of prehistory! Whether considering such instances of social status influencing what is presented as history, or the instances of non-literate people's well-exercised memories such as Baffin Land Inuit describing miles and miles of named landmarks in correct order, learned as chants when young, we cannot assume written histories are accurate nor dismiss oral histories.

First Nations histories preserved as oral accounts or mnemonic symbols, sometimes phonemic syllables, learned in association with complex recountings must be taken seriously. Contrary to popular lore, American Indians do not live in a mystical cycle of nature; their nations care about their histories and take pains that they should not be forgotten. Plains communities designated a responsible person to keep a hide, rather like a parchment, on which each year a symbol of the year's most memorable event was painted. The keeper used the symbol to remind himself of the event and others of the year, and trained a successor. Some of these "winter counts" can be correlated with literate observers' notes and demonstrate the value of the records. From studying winter count hides, one realizes that each band had its own particular history; putting together several such histories, an ethnohistorian can see some of the dynamics of pre-conquest nineteenth-century Plains life.

Many First Nations histories have been misunderstood as myths by non-Indian observers. The Omahas' Venerable Man is now a wooden pole, so the story of how he led the people to their homeland has been dismissed as pure myth, until a respected anthropologist listened closely to Omaha friends and was able to understand that Umon'hon'ti is the Father of his Country, not simple fantasy but a George Washington figure around whom inspiring stories accrue. Pueblos and other nations have long accounts of how this clan and then that clan and that next clan, or bands, joined the nation after journeying. The journeys can in many cases be traced along native-named landmarks – a Hopi filmmaker has videos showing this – and probably do describe historical movements of segments of what became a larger community. Not all named places are one and one only geographic spot, Red Banks may well be a series of Ho-Chunk principal villages rather than one specific site in Green Bay, but that does not mean all the geographies of histories should be derided. When a team of informed and respected members of a First Nation, academic historians and geographers, and archaeologists listen to one another, seek to perceive each others' way of referring to the landscape and its beings, a history can be written that melds these complementary data. Excluding any of these fields is, basically, political maneuvering to preach a narrow advocacy.

How should an archaeologist construct a history?

The United States highly values science and, particularly during the Cold War from the 1950s to 1980s, funneled millions and millions of dollars to scientific research. Partly because such considerable funds have been granted to scientists for research costs and sometimes salaries, partly because "pure science" is alluringly noble – never mind the crass competition for grant money – many archaeologists profess their work to be objective science. After all, archaeologists work with hard data: stone tools and hard-fired potsherds. They collaborate with geologists, soil scientists, geographic-positioning-systems specialists, chemists in material science, and physicists who operate radiocarbon-dating labs and magnetometers. Insofar as archaeologists normally work only with the physical residue of past human behaviour, they are comfortable with the scientific mode of collecting, analyzing, and comparing these actual bits from the past as if they were fossils. The conclusion of an archaeological report may be presented as a model organizing these data to suggest cause and effect or systems of relation. An extreme of archaeology-as-science is the notion that the researcher *begins* with a model already constructed and looks for data to confirm, or disconfirm, the appropriateness of that model.

Real science is a back-and-forth exercise between gathering data and testing them against what seems a coherent explanation or model. Ethnographic observations of science labs have revealed that the focused, logical scientific publication cloaks the reality of experiments fouled up or fizzing out, people wondering "what if?" and trying something seat-of-the-pants without clear justification, ambitious lab directors insisting expensive equipment must be used, and eureka! moments lit by a chance remark from someone on their way to the water cooler or coffee machine.[5]

Coming down to archaeology, real practice is usually troweling to slowly uncover a fragmentary artifact or stain in the soil, eyeing the context to see what the item seems to be associated with, noting a reasonable identification based on one's prior experience, then going through it all again months later in the lab, weighing what seem to be contradictory possibilities. Archaeologists have a pretty good idea of what they're likely to find, based on reading existing publications on the region and on the archaeologist's own earlier fieldwork and analyses. The same background tells them what their peers expect from the site or artifacts. They know of interpretations that have been denounced as foolish; like everyone, they seek the approbation of their peers. Research funds and job security rest on approval from senior professionals. These considerations affect archaeologists' decisions on where and how to work, their recognition of significant data, and their publications.

There are archaeologists who think testing a hypothesis is a straightforward procedure, and that is science. When you ask such persons where they get their hypotheses to test, they're nonplussed: out of books, of course. For European prehistory, this might be less of a problem than for American prehistory, since the practice of academic archaeology is part of the European cultural tradition. America's First Nations come from other cultural traditions, so "the way a society works" may be quite different for them – a simple example would be Iroquois government based on representatives from matrilineal clans, instead of the European custom of patrilineal, patriarchal households. This suggests the collaboration of First Nations members who grew up in their nations' culture can be productive of hypotheses and models that might not occur to a Western-trained archaeologist lacking the experience of living in a non-European culture. The dispersed pattern of houses in much of the Midwest Late Prehistoric fits the settlement practice of Midwest Siouans in the historic period, and preference today, of farm homesteads "close enough to yell for help, but far apart enough that you don't hear the family arguing," a Lakota once told me. Interpretation of the archaeological data could be enhanced by familiarity with descendants' way of life on a contemporary reservation.

Trying to be "scientific," some archaeologists want to restrict their study to things that can be measured and quantified, interpreting prehistoric life as so many mininum-number-of-deer butchered, kilograms of chert knapping chips, numbers of post holes, and decorative motifs on pot rims. It is astonishing that one can find monographs on archaeology conducted at Cahokia arguing that it wasn't a state because the material collected by archaeologists predominantly comes from a radius of about seventy miles around the city. No discussion of what material would not be preserved for the archaeologist to study – feather cloaks, woven fabrics, fine tanned hides, wooden artifacts, foodstuffs, in fact most of the major classes of tribute goods paid to the Aztec state by its vassals. No discussion of the implication of Monks Mound, the stupendous man-made mountain looming above the grand plaza, a theater of power on a scale seen only in states.

Roger Kennedy, Director of the Smithsonian's National Museum of American History, was amazed late in his career to realize, as he put it, "only a few specialists seem to be informed about" Cahokia:

> Why was that knowledge not...made a necessary prelude to American history? The antiquities of Mexico or of Egypt are far better known than those of Indiana, Illinois, or Ohio, and not because they are larger or more ambitious intellectually. As I have learned, there is as much to say about Euroamerican lack of understanding of Indian history as there is to say about the Indians themselves.[6]

His answer refers to the conviction and propaganda in the United States, beginning in the 1840s, that it is Euro-Americans' "Manifest Destiny" to exterminate Indian societies – kill or assimilate, whichever. Ruthless conquest is justified by the savage condition of the natives. Evidence that the First Nations built cities on a par with those of the same time in Europe had to be ignored. American archaeologists went to the same schools as their fellow citizens, reading about First Nations only in a few pages at the beginning of some history textbooks. Indians were described as unlettered nomad hunters or simple farmers living in bark wigwams or mud pueblos. Sixteen or more years of formal schooling that consistently downgrades Indians, if it mentions them at all, leave a deep impression. Americans are unprepared to recognize alternative civilizations in the United States.

Pushed by the economic structure of research support to look like scientists, measuring and quantifying the things other scientists measure and quantify – stone, bones, pollen, seeds, isotopes – and conditioned by education from kindergarten through graduate courses to believe American First Nations were unsophisticated barbarians, American archaeologists have, by and large, found it difficult to challenge the picture of primitives. Senior scholars' review of applications for research grants, of manuscripts submitted to journals and scholarly publishers, and of junior academics tends to protect conservative views. Rejecting Manifest Destiny still makes Americans uncomfortable, uneasy; we pride ourselves on being fair, being just, and that pride crumbles when we realize the terrible injustices suffered by First Nations. It is humbling to perceive we too are flawed, and humiliating to sense how naively most of us accepted the propaganda of Progress.

The ground has been shifting, as another millennium begins for Western societies, toward more humanistic interpretations of archaeological data. For one thing, with the Cold War ended, the United States turned to winning the hearts and minds of allies and subjects instead of building an overpowering arsenal. National Endowment for the Humanities funding increased, archaeologists followed suit by seeking means to identify values, ideology, and decision-makers in the remains of past societies. Meticulous excavation and recording and extensive laboratory analyses involving other sciences remain fundamental to American archaeology; efforts to link contemporary First Nations knowledge to archaeological material, and develop research questions from their perspective as well as conventional Western standpoints, increasingly find approval in the profession.

Research Questions

Several major questions persist as we endeavour to wrest First Nations' history out of archaeological data. Among these are the issues of population size, of societal structures, of relationships between sites, or beyond, and of the meaning of enigmatic constructions. These questions may never be firmly determined, nor are they by any

means unique to American prehistory. Archaeology is always challenging because the more we know, the more we know we don't
know. Documented history is no different.

Population size

The overall population of America at 1492 has been variously
estimated by adding up reports on village or tribal populations by
early visitors. This yielded estimates of one or two million altogether.
Then, in the 1960s, an ethnohistorian picked up the fact that European disease epidemics usually preceded the reports. He figured
from accounts of the epidemics that populations were often literally
decimated, reduced by 10 per cent or more. Therefore, he multi-
plied the report numbers by a constant factor, e.g., a village reported
to have one hundred inhabitants would have had perhaps a thousand
before disease decimation – the multiplication factor would be
determined from the few accounts actually documenting a particular population. A most generous estimate, figuring that only one in
twenty Indians survived epidemics, gave an overall American population of eighteen million, including Canada but not Mexico. A
survival rate of one-third rather than one in twenty would probably
be more reasonable. One careful study evaluating the conflicting
claims arrived at an estimate of five million people in the (48)
United States at 1492.[7]

Estimates for regions vary as widely as for the continent. Two
locales where the question relates to societal structure are Cahokia
and Chaco. In each case, both the population residing in the impressive structures and that in the small communities or farmsteads
in surrounding country are debated. If the residents of the urban
core were fed only from the immediate countryside, fewer could
have been sustained; if they were supplied by tribute-payers from
subordinated smaller nations, more could have lived in the core.
Cahokia lies on a major waterway along which bulk products could
have been rafted, so its lords, priests, and craftsworkers could have
been supplied from farmlands in America's breadbasket, the valleys
of the Mississippi, Illinois, Missouri, and Ohio rivers. Chaco, in the
semi-arid Southwest, is on only a small stream, necessitating carrying
products by human porters overland. Bulk food would have been
much more costly to bring to Chaco; on the other hand, Chaco in
its canyon is much smaller than Cahokia in the great floodplain of
the confluence of the Missouri and Mississippi. Population estimates
for Cahokia and its environs in the American Bottom floodplain

range from eight thousand to forty thousand, for Chaco Canyon about five thousand.[8]

Societal structure

Debates over the population numbers appropriate for Cahokia and Chaco overlie debates over the character of their societies. Each case represents a cluster of buildings monumental in appearance, entailing countless hours of directed human labor. Was it slave labor? corvée? a civic or religious duty? paid workers? Did they labor for the glory of their state, their lord, their God? Why were the monumental structures abandoned?

Conservative archaeologists mindful of sticking close to data they can hold, measure, quantify insist both Cahokia and Chaco could have been built by the part-time or seasonal labor of local farmers. Pointing to the Gothic cathedrals of Europe, they remind us that donated labor can accomplish great buildings. Monumental structures in Cahokia and Chaco, like those cathedrals, required experienced architect-engineers to direct the labor, but these, too, could have been citizens motivated by religious enthusiasm. Conservatives compare Cahokia and Chaco to the huge stone-faced pyramids and palaces of prehistoric Latin America, emphasizing that Cahokia's mounds are built of earth and its largest residences or temples were wooden halls, while the stone masonry at Chaco used only roughly dressed slabs and (so far as is preserved) simple or no ornamentation. Compared to the Latin American empires, these were only "chiefdoms," conservatives insist.

That term, "chiefdom," and its affiliate term "tribe" turn out to be minefields. They have been used to refer to frontier nations conquered by aggressive larger states. The Romans, for example, called the Germanic nations at the frontiers of empire "tribes." "Tribe" implies barbarians, uncouth unsettled people contrasting with the disciplined, literate, law-abiding citizens within state boundaries. "Tribal nations" must differ from nation-states. A "chiefdom" must be less than a kingdom, since chiefs are only local leaders. Critiques of anthropological usage of these terms, "tribe" and "chiefdom," reveal they were applied to states and kingdoms overcome, sometimes after many decades of fighting, by Western empires. Africa had empires ruling over a million people, kings living in pomp and wealth but, after nineteenth-century competition with European industrial powers, the African states were generally called tribes and their rulers, chiefs. In Polynesia, Western imperialists preferred to use the terms chiefdom and chief for the native kingdoms. "Tribe" and "chiefdom" are not neutral scientific terms; they are politically loaded.

Spanish invaders picked up the Caribbean Taino word *cacique* (*cacica* for women) for ruler and used it later in the American Southeast, in addition to Southeastern indigenous terms for ruler such as *holata* and *utina* (Timacua), and *mico* (Muskokee). These rulers ruled:

> [The Timacua of Florida] have their natural lords among them.....These govern their republics as head with the assistance of counselors, who are such by birth and inheritance. [The lord] determines and reaches decisions on everything that is appropriate for the village and the common good with their accord and counsels, except in the matters of favor. That the cacique alone is free and absolute master of these, and he acts accordingly; thus, he creates and places other particular lords, who obey and recognize the one who created and gave them the status and command that they hold.[9]

Sometimes Spaniards used their word for king, *rey*, for a native lord. Englishmen such as John Smith at Jamestown readily applied the words "king" and "lord" to indigenous rulers they met. We must keep in mind that at 1500, and into the nineteenth century in Germany and Italy, many European kingdoms were no larger than the realms of these American lords. Britain's several kingdoms battling each other and within competing noble families would be most comparable to Southeastern kingdoms of the same late medieval period. Spaniards at 1500 easily understood the systems of lords and vassals familiar at home and encountered in Latin America and the Southeast.

Northwestern Mexico had already been devastated by epidemics by the time literate Europeans took note of its nations, then living in hamlets rather than the cities discovered by archaeologists. On the frontier in New Mexico, governance of the Pueblos appeared to be in the hands of an elected official who answered to a council of clan heads and priests. Considering that not only had Chaco disintegrated three centuries earlier, but a century or two later large areas of the northern Southwest were abandoned by Pueblo communities that moved into the Río Grande Valley, extrapolation of historic Puebloan societal structure to Chaco may be unjustified.[10] Possibly Chaco was constructed by an ambitious Napoleon who, like the

Corsican, initially professed to be a republican leader. Chaco's domination can be reconciled with oligarchic governance different from the personalized power seen in the Southeast and Mexico.

A societal structure and culture really unfamiliar to us seems to be revealed by Ohio Hopewell. No other society, anywhere, constructed so many immense earthen perfect geometric figures. Open space inside – at Newark, Ohio, one circle encloses an eighteen-hole golf course – seems to have been maintained clean. Although wooden buildings and log chamber tombs then covered with a mound occupied some of the space, the geometric embankments did not wall in villages. Societies where most people lived in dispersed hamlets of very modest pole and thatch homes, cultivating indigenous plants well adapted to the environment, yet gathered periodically for rituals at huge linear configurations that make the landscape resemble pages out of Euclid's textbooks – coupling wholly unpretentious simple farming with extraordinary intellectual abstractions is unique to Ohio Hopewell. It does seem from the tombs that, aside from the geometries, Hopewell societies were not so very different from successors in the eastern Midwest and Mid-South, ruled by lords boasting of war prowess and wealth in objects brought to them at great expense. Sacrificed retainers in the tombs indicate that, as in contact-period Florida, "the cacique alone is free and absolute master of these" serving his lordship. Hopewell, too, may have been structured as commoners, vassals, and lords, their subsistence coming from a greater diversity of foods mostly native to the Midwest but sustaining traders and craftsworkers contributing pomp to the overlords' ceremonies.

Relationships between and beyond sites

Questions about societal structure involve whether communities were politically linked. Years ago, archaeologists followed cultural anthropologists in seeking to identify "kinship," said to be the system organizing "primitive societies" in contrast to our own "civilized society" said to be organized on contractual relationships. Somehow, no one noticed that our "civilized society" requires each resident to pay income taxes determined in part on kinship factors: married or single, dependents' kin relationship specified. Cities may zone neighborhoods to forbid more than two adults who are not kin living together. Conversely, as evolutionary biologists learned more about the actual course of evolutionary changes and rejected the nineteenth-century conviction that evolution equated with "progress" from simple to complex, cultural anthropologists came to perceive "simple" societies to be alternate evolutionary adaptation trajectories, often quite complex in certain features. "Anomalies" of small societies valuing contractual relations such as trading partners or sharecropping, or rationally affiliating young couples to the landholding group offering the best economic opportunities, piled up to the point of overwhelming older (and racist) axioms about "primitives."[11] Archaeologists can no longer assume what appears to have been a hamlet of subsistence cultivators was organized according to family relationships.

Cultural resource management archaeology created practical problems paralleling the shift in anthropological assumptions. Surveying and testing an area defined by development plans rather than by a research question, archaeologists had to explore the extent of cultural remains, and not infrequently could not easily map limits. Artifacts are often scattered over large fields, more here, fewer there. Do the rough clusters each represent a site? a household? a hamlet? Where farmsteads are dispersed, to what distance would a community extend? When an entire landscape shows human utilization and modification, shouldn't it all be considered a site? Federal and state agencies protecting cultural heritage are compelled to make rulings that may leave field archaeologists dissatisfied.

Between more ethnographic and ethnohistoric data on varieties of social organization, a realization that conventional anthropology harbored racist assumptions, and the ambiguities experienced in fieldwork, archaeologists are becoming less confident of orthodox models. Going by the chronicles of the Spanish entradas, Southeast sites should be linked as principal towns and their tributaries. French and British officials recorded many alliances between economically independent groups in the East and Midwest; how are these reflected in archaeological data? How far back in the past can historic ethnic identities be traced? by what signs? By what data might we distinguish trade (between political equals) from tribute (taxed or extorted from subordinates)?

Beyond the problems of defining the boundaries of a site and of political alliances, kingdoms and, in the case of Cahokia, a state, lie the questions of cultural influence. Was agriculture independently invented by Eastern Woodland nations cultivating indigenous chenopods and other small grains and a native squash, or had they taken over the idea from Mexicans? The earlier maize is found in United States sites, the more likely it is that agriculture was basically invented in Mexico and spread north, where in the temperate Woodlands people applied the concept to indigenous grains; the longer the time gap between cultivation of indigenous plants and maize, the more likely agriculture was independently invented. Hence the critical debates over whether five-thousand-year-old squash in the Ozarks was a native species or feral (gone wild from a cultivated import), and over the antiquity of maize in the Midwest, with the puzzle (to us) of centuries of raising a little maize as a secondary rather than major crop. Regardless, it is inescapable that maize originated in Mexico and came to the United States through human contacts. The practice of planting in raised beds, whether labor-intensive ridge and furrow or corn hills, is so widespread in the Americas it, too, ultimately must have come to United States farmers via human contacts.

Do Chaco and Cahokia show Mexican influence? Chaco's masonry resembles some styles in West Mexican cities, and of course its macaws incontrovertibly prove direct human transport from eastern Mexican tropics. A few porters transferring the cages to a new set of porters every few hundred miles? Or a caravan whose merchants lived in Mexican cities for months or years, and sold the macaws as part of a package of religious ideas? Apartment-block pueblos with dozens or hundreds of attached rooms are distinctive of the Southwest, but are they adaptations of urban concepts in Mexico? Cahokia with its great pyramid mounds and rectangular plazas, and its residential zones of households of small buildings around little courtyards, looks Mesoamerican: then why no stone masonry? And a chorus of American archaeologists shouts, "Why no Mexican goods?" No macaw bones! Well, what about dependence on full-scale maize agriculture? There's also the curious correlation in time between Chaco and Cahokia, both constructed in the same century and both apparently collapsing two centuries later. Their dates correlate, too, with the Toltec period in central Mexico. Did the Toltecs aggressively expand their trading empire northward, stimulating responses from perhaps an oligarchy in New Mexico and a native lord on the Mississippi? The correlations are tantalizing, the residual nature of the archaeological record frustrating.

Meaning of enigmatic constructions.

Rock art above all defies unequivocal interpretations. Most of it is highly stylized, realistic animal outlines, simplified anthropomorphs (human-looking figures), and geometric figures. Narrative scenes are relatively rare, other than what look like hunts. Some of it may be only graffiti, marking a visit to an exciting cave or lookout. Some are surely territorial signs, for example on Writing-on-Stone rimrock at the edge of Blackfoot territory on the Montana–Alberta border, where certain panels record historic events. "Thunderbirds" and serpents on outcrops at river and lake narrows might mark territorial boundaries, or might be manifestations of the patron spirits of the locale, or could be both, the patron spirits of the local nation. A bighorn sheep on a Nevada rock might record a hunt, or represent a plea to the spirit leaders of the bighorns to let their animal-people sustain Indian people, or, according to one interpretation, would mark where a priest believed he could reach holy beings who would vouchsafe rain. Maybe large number of bighorn sheep images just tell us that indigenous people admired the species and made pictures for the pleasure of it. Most likely, one explanation does not fit all occurrences; furthermore, as generations pass and new ethnic groups may move in, the original artist's intention is forgotten and the image interpreted anew.

Effigy mounds, those in southern Wisconsin and others such as the apparent large bird mound at Poverty Point in Louisiana or the Mississippian Serpent Mound in Ohio, are equally enigmatic. Birds as symbols of heaven, large carnivores (bears, tigers, jaguars) as symbols of earthly power, and serpents as symbols of the underworld are obvious and widespread around the world. We know that a number of Eastern Woodlands First Nations, such as the Cheyenne, Ojibwe, and Iroquois, divided communities into moieties (halves) called Sky and Earth, or clans such as Bear, Wolf, and Turtle, or a combination in which several clans belonged to one moiety and others to the opposite moiety. Compounding ambiguity, a bird-shaped mound might glorify a lord known as, let us say, Hawk Chief – around the northern Rockies, Swan Chief was the title given to the most respected leader, he who was said to be most powerful, go farthest and see farthest ahead, like wild swans. Europeans are familiar with this kind of imagery, used in heraldry and royal insignia (lions, German and Russian eagles). Wisconsin effigy mounds tend to have "panthers" (underwater serpent-tailed creatures, consort of the land and vegetation deity Grandmother-Who-Never-Dies in historic traditions) built as if moving up from adjacent water, birds on the higher ground, and bears between, but exceptions abound and many mounds in effigy clusters are geometric straight-line or conical shapes.[12]

Enough has been said of the Ohio Hopewell geometric embankments. Archaeoastronomy can demonstrate some alignments with sun, moon, and star movements, especially popularly observed summer and winter solstice points, without being able to tell us the meaning stellar movements held for these Indian people two thousand years ago. Early Woodland-period Moose Mountain "medicine wheel" on the Canadian prairie north of western North Dakota is a construction of boulder lines and cairns pointing to horizon points for summer solstice and associated risings of the bright stars Sirius, Aldebaran, Capella, and Fomalhaut. The builders must have been bison hunters, not agriculturists, so the probable explanation of so much effort put into a permanent calendrical device must be that they used it to ensure scattered bands could rendezvous at a fixed time, regardless of whether spring weather speeded up or held back vegetation growth signs.[13] Hopewell figures have fewer astronomical alignments than this prairie monument, communication between villages in the stream valleys of Ohio should have been quicker and easier than out on the wide Canadian prairies, so calendar-keeping doesn't seem sufficient explanation for Hopewell constructions.

A really cautious archaeologist can hold back on what most of us see as obvious. Could be, that the gargantuan mounds and plazas at Cahokia and the lavish wastage of human lives in the sacrificial pits at its Mound 72 don't mean an aggressive state ruled by a Hawk Lord whose afterlife would be attended by more than fifty maidens, their bodyguards, other nobles, and nearly a hundred servants, one bearing the Lord on his back. Could be, a fanatic religious cult; could be, mound-building was a regular religious duty expected of every adult in the American Bottom floodplain. Calculations say that Monks Mound equals 621,921 cubic meters, and the known measured mounds at Cahokia altogether total 1,177,701 cubic meters. Calculating the amount of earth a person could carry working five hours a day (not counting breaks), with the borrow pit where the earth was dug about 150 meters distant from the mound, 1,201,000 person/work-days would have been required to build the mounds.[14] Now let us say there were eight thousand people living in the American Bottom – the same cautious estimator's maximum figure – of which one in five was an able-bodied adult liable for community duty. If each worked ten days a year, the mounds could be constructed in seventy-five years. No doubt similar calculations could render mundane the Egyptian pyramids at Gizeh, the Taj Mahal in India, the Colosseum in Rome, the Parthenon in Greece.

Conclusion

America has a history thousands of years long. America's First Nations were and are populated by people as fully evolved, as fully human, feeling and intelligent as people anywhere on earth. These nations have been struggling for five hundred years against invaders coming from Europe, men driven by blighted opportunities there to strive for better lives in America. Wishing to believe themselves moral, invaders and their descendants pictured First Nations citizens as damned heathens, bloodthirsty savages, childlike gatherers of nature's bounty, or benighted creatures on the margin of the world. However stereotyped, First Nations Americans had no histories before Columbus discovered them: "In the beginning, all the World was *America*," said John Locke,[15] which reverses to "America represents the beginning of time."

Flowing from this politically charged misrepresentation of America, conventional anthropologists saw First Nations as molded by geography rather than history. Analyses of their cultures in the context of their geographies would reveal these forces of nature masked in Eurasia by "civilized" technologies. America was a stand-in for prehistoric Eurasians, one end of a yardstick stretching millennia to educated well-to-do urban Europeans. Looking at American Indians was rending asunder the veils of time. America was a laboratory, its indigenous peoples so many strains of genetically – in this case, geographically – engineered mice. Archaeologists could be scientists studying the variables.[16]

Against this convenient laboratory, some anthropologists insisted America has history. Franz Boas, the liberal German immigrant to the United States in 1887, tirelessly campaigned to collect data on First Nations histories, including adaptations to geography in worldwide perspective. Vilified by anti-Semitic "patriots," Boas did inspire generations of anthropologists. The opposition also persisted, continuing to write up archaeological data as if they had formed in small closed systems, like gas in a chemist's retort. Radiocarbon dating nibbled at this position, forcing archaeologists to realize how very long First Nations had lived on this continent. A few finds, such as tropical macaw remains in Southwestern Pueblos, undermined the closed-systems models. Overall, reluctance to look for extraneous contacts, to focus on recognizing historical factors, remained the conventional mode through the twentieth century.

NAGPRA catalyzed American archaeology. Its passage reflected, as well as contributed to, a shift in American attitudes toward First Nations. Perhaps the mere fact that no one now alive had been in the wars of conquest permitted a more generous attitude. Perhaps fighting two world wars for democracy and human rights against imperialism and terrible racism brought Americans to notice their own backyards. Certainly the outstanding participation of First Nations men and women in our armed forces earned much respect, and gave these men and women determination to assert their rights. Pride in their histories was one outgrowth.

The histories of the First Nations of America are substantial components of American history. These histories do not suddenly stop short in 1492 or 1607; they are strands in the fabric of United States (and Canada and Latin America) history. Indigenous nations literally shaped the land and resources taken over by European invaders and their descendants. Their labor and production constituted significant components of the United States economy, generally left out or underestimated in economists' tabulations of the gross national product (GNP) and waged labor.[17] The resilience of First Nations after the holocaust of epidemics and conquerors' policies of marginalization and neglect proved they were, and are, neither inferior nor simple. Their exponentially growing populations and increasingly sophisticated legal expertise pressure the dominant Anglo classes to tolerate alternative values and concede the stipulations of treaties. United States history must be inclusive of its First Nations, not because that is generous but because their histories are absolutely integral to the larger history.

Notes

1. Robert L. Hall, "Red Banks, Oneota, and the Winnebago: Views from a Distant Rock," *Wisconsin Archeologist* 74 (1–4) (1993): 10–79.

2. The 1890 federal census counted 228,000 Indians. One century later, the 1990 census counted 1,959,234. These figures do not include Indians in tribes that for one reason or another are not listed as federally recognized, nor the several million persons of mixed heritage who choose not to identify "American Indian" as their racial classification on the census form.

3. Robin Ridington and Dennis Hastings, *Blessing for a Long Time: The Sacred Pole of the Omaha Tribe* (Lincoln, NE, 1997), a moving account of the venerated national symbol that conveys Omaha history and contemporary revitalization.

4. David Hurst Thomas, *Skull Wars* (New York, 2000), covers Kennewick and the underlying issues of racism and sovereignty in a very balanced and readable manner. Thomas is a respected archaeologist.

5. Classic studies of this reality are Bruno Latour and Steve Woolgar, *Laboratory Life: The Social Construction of Scientific Facts* (Beverly Hills, CA, 1979), and Karen Knorr-Cetina, *The Manufacture of Knowledge* (Oxford, 1981).

6. Roger G. Kennedy, *Hidden Cities: The Discovery and Loss of Ancient North American Civilization* (New York, 1994), p. 2.

7. Russell Thornton, *American Indian Holocaust and Survival: A Population History Since 1492* (Norman, OK, 1987), p. 32.

8. Jill E. Neitzel, "Examining Societal Organization in the Southwest: An Application of Multiscalar Analysis," in Jill E. Neitzel (ed.), *Great Towns and Regional Polities in the Prehistoric American Southwest and Southeast* (Albuquerque, NM, 1999), p. 198.

9. Quoted from the early seventeenth-century missionary Father Francisco Alonso de Jesus, in Jerald T. Milanich, "The Timacua Indians of Northern Florida and Southern Georgia," in Bonnie G. McEwan (ed.), *Indians of the Greater Southeast: Historical Archaeology and Ethnohistory* (Gainesville, FL, 2000), pp. 6–7.

10. John A. Ware and Eric Blinman, "Cultural Collapse and Reorganization: The Origin and Spread of Pueblo Ritual Sodalities," in Michelle Hegmon (ed.), *The Archaeology of Regional Interaction: Religion, Warfare, and Exchange Across the American Southwest and Beyond* (Boulder, CO, 2000), pp. 381–409.

11. British anthropologist Adam Kuper describes this change in anthropological understanding, *The Invention of Primitive Society* (London, 1988).

12. Robert A. Birmingham and Leslie E. Eisenberg, *Indian Mounds of Wisconsin* (Madison, WI, 2000), pp. 115–25.

13. Alice B. Kehoe and Thomas F. Kehoe, *Solstice-Aligned Boulder Configurations in Saskatchewan* (Ottawa, 1979).

14. George R. Milner, *The Cahokia Chiefdom: The Archaeology of a Mississippian Society* (Washington DC, 1998), pp. 144–50; population estimate, p. 123.

15. John Locke, *Second Treatise on Government* (London, 1690).

16. Distinguished archaeologist Don D. Fowler develops this perspective in *A Laboratory for Anthropology: Science and Romanticism in the American Southwest, 1846–1930* (Albuquerque, NM, 2000).

17. Alice Littlefield and Martha C. Knack (eds), *Native Americans and Wage Labor: Ethnohistorical Perspectives* (Norman, OK, 1996), especially the chapters by the editors and by John H. Moore.

References

Birmingham, Robert A. and Leslie E. Eisenberg (2000), *Indian Mounds of Wisconsin*. Madison, WI: University of Wisconsin Press.

Fowler, Don D. (2000), *A Laboratory for Anthropology: Science and Romanticism in the American Southwest, 1846–1930*. Albuquerque, NM: University of New Mexico Press.

Hall, Robert L. (1993), "Red Banks, Oneota, and the Winnebago: Views from a Distant Rock," *Wisconsin Archeologist* 74 (1–4): 10–79.

Kehoe, Alice B. and Thomas F. Kehoe (1979), *Solstice-Aligned Boulder Configurations in Saskatchewan.* Ottawa: Canadian Ethnology Service Paper no. 48, Mercury Series, National Museum of Man.

Kennedy, Roger G. (1994), *Hidden Cities: The Discovery and Loss of Ancient North American Civilization.* New York: Free Press. Penguin edition 1996.

Knorr-Cetina, Karen (1981), *The Manufacture of Knowledge.* Oxford: Pergamon.

Kuper, Adam (1988), *The Invention of Primitive Society: Transformations of an Illusion.* London: Routledge.

Latour, Bruno, and Steve Woolgar (1979), *Laboratory Life: The Social Construction of Scientific Facts.* Beverly Hills CA: Sage.

Littlefield, Alice and Martha C. Knack (eds) (1996), *Native Americans and Wage Labor: Ethnohistorical Perspectives.* Norman, OK: University of Oklahoma Press.

Milanich, Jerald T. (2000), "The Timacua Indians of Northern Florida and Southern Georgia," in Bonnie G. McEwan (ed.), *Indians of the Greater Southeast: Historical Archaeology and Ethnohistory.* Gainesville, PL: University Press of Florida, pp. 1–25.

Milner, George R. (1998), *The Cahokia Chiefdom: The Archaeology of a Mississippian Society.* Washington, DC: Smithsonian Institution Press.

Neitzel, Jill E. (1999), "Examining Societal Organization in the Southwest: An Application of Multiscalar Analysis," in Jill E. Neitzel (ed.), *Great Towns and Regional Polities in the Prehistoric American Southwest and Southeast.* Albuquerque: University of New Mexico Press, pp. 183–213.

Ridington, Robin, and Dennis Hastings (1997), *Blessing for a Long Time: The Sacred Pole of the Omaha Tribe.* Lincoln, NE: University of Nebraska Press.

Thomas, David Hurst (2000), *Skull Wars.* New York: Basic Books.

Thornton, Russell (1987), *American Indian Holocaust and Survival: A Population History Since 1492.* Norman, OK: University of Oklahoma Press.

Ware, John A. and Eric Blinman (2000), "Cultural Collapse and Reorganization: The Origin and Spread of Pueblo Ritual Sodalities," in Michelle Hegmon (ed.), *The Archaeology of Regional Interaction: Religion, Warfare, and Exchange Across the American Southwest and Beyond.* Boulder, CO: University Press of Colorado, pp. 381–409.

INDEX